THE GREAT TRIALS
OF THE TWENTIES

The
GREAT TRIALS
of the
TWENTIES

The Watershed Decade in America's Courtrooms

By ROBERT GRANT
and JOSEPH KATZ

SARPEDON
Rockville Centre, NY

Published by
SARPEDON
49 Front Street
Rockville Centre, NY 11570

ISBN 1-885119-52-6

Cataloging-in-publication data is available from the
Library of Congress.

10 9 8 7 6 5 4 3 2 1

MANUFACTURED IN THE UNITED STATES OF AMERICA

Contents

Introduction

The drama of the courtroom has served many a writer from Shakespeare to Kafka to Grisham. It is a staple in our literature because it can reveal character and motivation even as it illuminates opposing ideas and points of view. In real life also, courtroom dramas can be fascinating. Adversaries confront one another, and their moves and countermoves resemble a chess game played under the rules of law. Unlike the game of chess, however, courtroom drama has flesh-and-blood players whose actions develop out of weakness or strength, cupidity or generosity, brilliant analysis or bumbling stupidity, and a whole range of human emotions.

In great trials there is more to stimulate interest, however, than mere curiosity. Trials can constitute a stage that allows examination of society's stresses and strains and of the political, social, and cultural conflicts with which society contends. The Salem witchcraft trials in the seventeenth century, for example, exposed the grave troubles of that Puritan community of early America. The trial of Alger Hiss in the late 1940s manifested public concern about the threat of Communism that Senator Joseph McCarthy was to exploit a few years later. In the 1960s the trial of the Chicago Eight brought into focus not only the political but cultural tensions of that decade. More recently, the O.J. Simpson trial and the legal pursuit of President Bill Clinton in his second term have doubtless informed future historians of something profound about the character of America in the 1990s, although at this writing, speculation on exactly what these latest events have revealed may be premature.

1

This book contains the stories of ten great trials of the 1920s, chosen because they reflect one or more of the social issues of the day. The trial itself, or the person accused, or some other major figure in the legal proceedings had a significant impact on society and its institutions or on the law. These trials do not, however, fit neatly within the third decade of the century. Just as the Sixties have been described in cultural terms as spanning the period from John F. Kennedy's assassination to Richard Nixon's resignation, the Twenties are better thought of as beginning with the Red Scare in 1919 and ending with the Great Crash of 1929. Although the trials of Al Capone and Samuel Insull described in this volume did not take place until the early years of the 1930s, the careers of the two men climaxed earlier and the substance of their trials well reflect the character of the 1920s.

The volume begins with a brief account of the great changes in American life in that watershed decade. It is an account that explores urban–rural conflict at a time of cityward migration, nativist hostility during a period of immigration restriction, and intellectual and emotional turmoil caused by Americans' confrontation with many new and unsettling ideas. The book is an account also of self-indulgence and corruption in the worlds of entertainment, politics, and business.

Chapter 1 tells the story of a shoemaker and a fish peddler, Nicola Sacco and Bartolomeo Vanzetti. Foreign-born anarchists, they were caught up in a maelstrom of xenophobic hostility and sent to the gallows, and to this day the argument over their guilt or innocence persists. Chapters 2 and 3 deal with scandals in the world of sports and entertainment. The way a nation amuses itself reveals much about its character and aspirations. The country seemed to stagger in disbelief when it learned that its national pastime was tainted by corruption— that baseball's 1919 World Series may have been fixed by gamblers. Someone would have to shoulder the blame. Chapter 2 tells the story of the Chicago "Black Sox." In Chapter 3 the peccadillos of the Hollywood fast set are laid bare in the rape-murder trial of Roscoe "Fatty" Arbuckle. To preserve themselves from possible federal regulation both the baseball and movie industries took vigorous steps to create a system of self-regulation by installing a commissioner of baseball and an overseer of morality for the silver screen. Self-regulation in all of industry became a major theme in the late 1920s.

The book moves from wild and woolly Hollywood to wild and

woolly Chicago and the shocking and notorious career of Al Capone. One part of the conflict between an emergent and vigorous urban America and a rural America of declining power and influence was fought out in Chicago. The bloody struggle over Prohibition pitted Wets against Drys and corrupted that great midwestern metropolis; but Capone was vulnerable to no more than a federal charge of income tax evasion. The story is told in Chapter 4.

Corruption in Chicago and Illinois was rivaled by the corruption in Indianapolis and Indiana, the center of a revived and clamorous Ku Klux Klan. The KKK of the 1920s clung to the tradition of supremacy by white, Protestant, Anglo-Saxon Americans and found much of its support among rural migrants transplanted to the city. So powerful did the Klan become that Indiana leader D.C. Stephenson could proclaim at one stage in his career, "I am the law in the state of Indiana." The story of Stephenson's conviction for rape and murder is told in Chapter 5.

Dayton, Tennessee, some 300 miles south of Indianapolis, is a town of the rural South where another struggle between "old" and "new" America was carried out. The issue was the teaching of evolution in the state's schools. John Scopes, a high school biology teacher, violated the laws of Tennessee when he taught his students about the ideas of Charles Darwin. At his trial, described in Chapter 6, Scopes was defended by Clarence Darrow, whose confrontation with William Jennings Bryan, three-time candidate for U.S. president (1896, 1900, and 1908), underlined the sharpness of divergent views about science and religion and posed clearly the still-unresolved question of who should determine what our children are taught.

In the decade of the Twenties, human psychology became a major focus of scientific emphasis. All who claimed to be up-to-date could at least talk about Sigmund Freud. Newstands carried numbers of magazines that popularized the "new psychology." The mental state of two young killers, Nathan Leopold and Richard Loeb, was at the center of the defense in their trial for the brutal murder of little Bobby Franks. The story of that trial and a further look at the skill of America's foremost defense attorney, Clarence Darrow, is told in Chapter 7.

Politics in the Twenties was rife with a degree of thievery unseen since Ulysses S. Grant's administration. The most famous episode is described in Chapter 8. Teapot Dome was the name given to a region of oil-bearing land in Wyoming, set aside for use by the U.S. Navy. High public officials subverted the public interest for their own enrichment and were caught with their hands in the till. The scandal wrecked the lives of several of the perpetrators and threatened to ruin the Republican Party.

Self-aggrandizement and self-enrichment were also the motivations of Samuel P. Insull. The story of Insull's rise to leadership of the electric light industry and of his fall is also a story of speculative frenzy and a mania for bigness that characterized the late 1920s. Insull's successful defense against a charge of mail fraud is the subject of Chapter 9.

The volume ends with the court-martial of General "Billy" Mitchell, a transitional figure whose military experience in World War I and during the following decade enabled him to foresee the rise of air power to a level of importance that other military leaders could not envision. He sacrificed his career to follow his star, and his predictions were borne out during World War II. It is fitting to end the book with Mitchell's case. The insight he had during the first war matured during the Twenties and led to his clash with traditional military thinking as America and the world moved toward the horrors of the second.

Prologue

THE SETTING

The decade that came to known as the "Roaring Twenties" opened with a binge of emotion. There was growing fear among the American public of the presence of radicals, revolutionaries, and Reds. Although the Red Scare was short, it cast its shadow over the entire decade. It revealed that the nation was in a mood to punish dissent, to enshrine nativism with restrictive immigration laws, and to tolerate such organizations—once again—as the Ku Klux Klan. For almost two years after the Bolshevik coup in Russia, the delirium of the Red Scare led millions of Americans to believe that their own country, too, was on the verge of revolution. How can this anxiety be explained? The Red Scare was neither planned nor provoked by any individual or group. Rather, it came about as a result of a number of severe social and economic dislocations.

The First World War and American participation in it, 1917–18, were enormously disruptive. The physical movement of the population cityward from rural America played havoc with settled patterns of life. Four million men served in the armed forces, in many cases after leaving small communities for the first time. Thousands of women left home, too, to work in war industries. Black Americans departed the South by the tens of thousands for jobs in the Northeast and Midwest—a migration that often led to violent conflict in major cities. The "Red Summer" of 1919 saw terrible race riots in Washington, D.C., and in Chicago.

Changes in the national economy also brought dislocation, and a steady rise in the cost of living caused uneasiness among the public.

Wartime controls notwithstanding, prices almost doubled between 1914 and 1920. Woodrow Wilson's League of Nations was far less important to most people, however, than the price of beef or a pair of shoes. Attempting to act against inflation, in early 1920 the Federal Reserve Board raised the rediscount rate, curtailing credit and discouraging expansion. A sharp depression followed.

In addition, labor unrest in 1919 disconcerted the American people. Strikes broke out in many locations throughout the country. There was not much general support for labor in the 1920s and even less tolerance for strikes, as high government officials blamed the rash of them on radicals. J. Edgar Hoover claimed that Communist agents were the instigators, and the bloody upheaval in faraway Russia suddenly did indeed seem close. In 1919, American Communists formed two political parties, and no fewer than ninety percent of their members had been born in eastern Europe. Anarchist groups, too, captured the attention of the American people with their literature and their bombs. The anarchists were almost all Italian, Spanish, and Slavic aliens. In the public mind, the new immigrants, those from eastern and southern Europe, posed a foreign threat. This perception of threat led to an upsurge of nativism that was both deep and widespread.

In 1920 Nicola Sacco and Bartolomeo Vanzetti were convicted of killing two men in a payroll robbery. Both men closely fit the stereotype that nativists held of foreigners; for many Americans, the two seemed to embody all that threatened the American way of life. For many Americans, though, Sacco and Vanzetti became martyrs to social prejudice, persecuted because of who they were and what they believed rather than because of what they had done.

But irrational and atavistic hostility in America was generated not only against foreigners. White society outside the South had now come into contact with black Americans in large numbers for the first time as the black populations of New York, Chicago, Cleveland, and Detroit increased sharply. The neighborhoods in which black migrants settled soon expanded into contiguous white residential areas, and when recently demobilized soldiers competed for jobs with recent black migrants, passions flared. Moreover, because blacks were barred from labor unions, little was left for them except to work as scabs during some of the major strikes—notably the great steel strike of 1919. Violence against blacks and hostility toward aliens were the ugly offspring of the unrest, anxiety, and dislocation that plagued the United States in the immediate postwar years. These were the elements that laid the basis for the Red Scare.

The public demanded action. Attorney General A. Mitchell Palmer, hoping that the national tide of fear and paranoia would carry him into the White House, moved quickly. In the first week of January 1920, in a series of coast-to-coast raids on Communist and Communist Labor Party organizations, Palmer's agents arrested more than ten thousand, many not members of either party, and other egregious violations of civil liberties took place. Aliens were detained for varying lengths of time without legal process, for the Department of Justice was more concerned with preserving the anonymity of its informers than with protecting the rights of aliens. Expecting to uncover huge caches of arms and other contraband, the raiders netted a grand total of three pistols.

In addition to raids on alleged radical centers, almost 500 men and women who were not citizens were summarily deported; most of them had no criminal record and had committed no criminal offense. Aside from the federal level, not only did almost 30 states enact sedition laws, but citizens in many communities went after the "subversive" and "radical" books in their public libraries as well as the "radical" professors in universities. In city after city, private vigilante groups acted on their own.

By the end of 1920, the Red Scare had spent itself, but the cast of mind that it evinced persisted throughout the decade. It revealed itself in the popularity of the Ku Klux Klan and in the movement to restrict immigration. The scare came to an end, however, because the social and economic difficulties which had helped create it had receded by the end of 1920. First, there was growing realization that the United States had really been in no imminent danger of a Bolshevik takeover. Second, inflation, which had appeared so menacing in the rising prices of food and clothing, began to abate. In addition, the strikes and labor unrest that had seemed so insoluble simply vanished. Public attention now turned to more exciting and pleasurable matters of amusement and diversion. Further, new inventions and the increasing availability of the automobile gave Americans additional sources of recreation and entertainment, and movies and sports occupied more and more of the public's time and interest.

After recovery from the economic downturn that opened the decade, the remainder of the 1920s was marked by high prosperity, even though its benefits were unevenly distributed. In part, the prosperity was motored by new technology, but it was spurred even more by the increasing availability of a variety of goods already in existence. Mass production had made its first fruits available in large numbers of cars, radios, refrigerators, and countless other items. Industry and consumer purchasing power grew hand in hand and Americans bought for the sheer joy of buying. Much of the growth in consumerism can be attributed to the growth of the advertising industry and some of the newer techniques it had created. Advertising became an extraordinary engine of American affluence.

The development of a national communications system was also a product of the decade. Without such new vehicles of communication as the automobile, the movies, radio, and new developments in newspapers and magazines, the messages of the advertisers could not have reached national audiences so speedily. Newspapers used wire services, developed syndicates, and created chains that provided national circulation for columns, features, and comic strips. *Time* and *Reader's Digest* became familiar magazines throughout the United States and the number of such nationally distributed magazines grew.

Among the infant industries at the beginning of the 1920s was motion pictures. By the end of the decade, the movie industry had become a two-billion-dollar business, providing some of the important heroes and heroines of the decade and serving as a unifying cultural force. The message that the movies conveyed, according to at least one critic, was that of "conventional and banal middle class values and stable middle class lifestyles." Radio now became an even more popular means of entertainment. By the end of the decade, the number of families owning radios was more than 15 million, and radio stations numbered more than five hundred. Americans could listen to broadcasts of the election returns as these were reported. They could follow the progress of Charles Lindbergh's historic transatlantic flight. And although none of these tools of communication intentionally challenged traditional American values and assumptions, millions were exposed to a wide range of new ideas and new standards. As a consequence, significant changes were launched in American tastes, morals, and behavior.

The automobile in particular had an enormous impact on American life, engulfing the landscape, chewing it up, and blighting it. The auto made Americans an even more mobile and restless people. By 1929 almost five million cars were produced each year, and the astonishing expansion of the automobile industry brought concomitant growth in rubber, steel, road building, glass, and the refining of gasoline. The result of such expansion made the industry the linchpin of the nation's economy. A half-century later, the country's motor transport industry would account for more spending than did Americans' food, educational, health, and library expenses combined. In 1923 the basic Ford touring car cost $295 and the average working man could buy one with three month's earnings. Everyone wanted a car.

The automobile had a profound influence on town and city life. Cities such as Los Angeles experienced rapid, almost explosive growth as workers achieved a mobility they had never had before. They could get to their jobs by motorbus or car and were free to live farther from the vicinity of their workplace. Socially, the automobile influenced a revolution in the behavior of the young, making possible an escape, if only temporarily, from the supervision of parents and the older generation. A short drive brought young people beyond the reach of the watchful eyes of neighbors, to a dance or a roadhouse and to freedom from supervision. The closed car was a mobile bedroom, making possible clandestine sexual activity. It could even be, and sometimes was, a brothel on wheels.

It was the automobile, along with the Thompson machine gun, that allowed successful gangsters to extend their control over entire cities and states. During Prohibition, rum runners and bootleggers needed fast, roomy cars that were capable of carrying 25 to 40 cases of liquor. They used every kind available but preferred Cadillacs, Packards, and Pierce-Arrows. They were imaginative and ingenious in outfitting their cars for maximum capacity. They learned to use cars with reinforced springs; they concealed liquor behind or under the seats, in tool boxes and in spare tires. They created space with false floors through which lengthened pedals were placed, and they devised false gas tanks that were divided so that one part carried gasoline and the other liquor. They learned the best routes to travel and came to know and exploit the personal weaknesses of border patrol guards.

During this period movies, enormously popular, became a big industry. While often wallowing in banality, motion pictures could also subvert genteel tradition, mirroring a nation that was experimenting and seeking new experiences—asserting its right to live its own life. James Barrie's play *The Admirable Crichton* became, on screen, *Male and Female*. Advertising for the film described it as the intimate adventures of a lady and her butler on a desert island, and revealed the power of the sexual drive over traditional class barriers. (It even seemed to condone marital infidelity.) Public attitudes were changing. Cecil B. DeMille, whose films markedly depicted the new perspectives, once quipped: "The ruined woman is about as stylish as the Victorian who used to faint." From the silver screen soon came a message often repeated: that of the joy of uninhibited sex. Film stars such as Clara Bow—the "It" girl—showed how far a young woman could go with "It," and no one needed to ask what "It" meant. The public idolized the most popular of the silent screen's romantic leads—Mary Pickford, Clara Bow, Theda Bara, Douglas Fairbanks, and Rudolph Valentino. When Valentino died suddenly in 1926, his funeral procession contained a line of weeping women eleven blocks long. Meanwhile, the popularity of sports matched the growing popularity of the movies. Indeed, the 1920s was a golden age for both. The public devotedly followed the feats of Babe Ruth in baseball, the "Galloping Ghost" Red Grange, in football, "Big Bill" Tilden in tennis, and Bobby Jones in golf.

Increasing technology, growing prosperity, burgeoning consumerism, and a faithful attention to the doings of leaders in the world of entertainment all took place against a background of growing cultural conflict between the values of a new urban, urbane, and modern civilization and those of small-town America—a conflict which lay just below the surface of American life. It influenced the struggle to restrict immigration, the battle over Prohibition, the crusade for religious fundamentalism, the growing strength of the Ku Klux Klan, and even the election of 1928. Contention over the Klan of the 1920s is sometimes seen as nothing more than a rural–urban issue. In fact, however, the matter is more complex, for the idea that the heterogeneity of the city fostered tolerance and acceptance was simplistic.

The cities of America were indeed growing and becoming more heterogeneous. The census of 1920 listed 68 cities of 100,000 or more inhabitants, each of which was the center of a much larger suburban population. A decade later 96 metropolitan centers contained 44.6 percent of the population of the entire United States. The city did more than eclipse the countryside in population. It became an important agent of social change, a dynamic force that caused a reorientation of the traditional structure of behavior and thought. The city became "the imaginative center of American life," the "archetype of the good life." Here were to be found books, magazines and newspapers, theater and movies, radio and jazz, saloons and liquor. Here were the ideas that seemingly brought on an uncontrolled change that was so repugnant to many citizens of provincial America.

The nation's cities had also become enclaves of immigrants and, since about 1900, these came primarily from southern and eastern Europe. It was in the cities that newcomers—the Poles, the Italians, the eastern European Jews—met the new arrivals from the small towns and rural villages, Americans who were a part of an internal migration from the countryside to urban centers. By the second decade of the twentieth century, only in some cities did the American-born outnumber the immigrants; in Boston, Chicago, New York, Philadelphia, and many others, the immigrants actually outnumbered the natives. From the point of view of rural America, urban life—with its crowding, poverty, crime, corruption, impersonality, and ethnic chaos—presented not merely a new way of life, but a dangerously subversive countercurrent, even a threat to civilization itself.

What it lost in numbers, rural and small-town America retained in political power that permitted over-representation in Congress and in state legislatures. Power lay, too, in the cast of mind that held sway over the thinking of much of America, that of its towns and villages and of its transplanted villagers in the nation's cities. In its role in national policy making, this mindset was committed to arresting change and restoring the simpler values and verities that had been sacrificed to industrialization, urbanization, and explosive immigration. It wanted to purge national life of "foreign" religions and ideologies. It was the populations of small towns and small cities that opposed America's participation in the League of Nations. As one example, they worried about the Roman Catholic, "wet," Tammany background of presidential candidate Alfred E. Smith of New York. It was largely in metropolitan areas that Smith gained the bulk of his support in 1928, for he lost even in southern states that had not voted Republican since the end of Reconstruction. Smith's Catholicism may not have been the most responsible factor in his defeat, but it was hardly insignificant. Methodist Bishop James Cannon wrote in *The Nation* in 1928: "It is a fact that attacks in Congress upon the prohibition law are made chiefly by men who are themselves Roman Catholics or who represent constituencies with large Roman Catholic populations. Certainly it is likely that Governor Alfred E. Smith is influenced by the views of the Pope and the cardinals on the subject of prohibition." Such foreign influences were, to many citizens, a clear threat to the well-being of American standards.

Foreign influences in the lifeblood of America could only be stopped, it was alleged, by cutting off the evil at its source. The distinction was not simply whether one had come from Europe, but from where in Europe one had come. Some 800,000 immigrants lived in Chicago in 1920, and more than half of them had come from southern or eastern Europe. In that year there were more Poles living in Chicago than there were people in any other city in Illinois. The Russians in Chicago, mostly Jews, were almost as numerous as the total population of Des Moines, Iowa. The answer, for those who feared foreign influences, was immigration restriction. The National Origins Act of 1924 imposed a quota system, brought to a virtual halt immigration from the least-favored areas, and choked off the least-favored peoples: Catholics from Italy and Poland, Jews from Poland and Russia, Slavs from Russia and the Balkan states.

Part of the campaign of those favoring restriction was to call upon pseudo-scientific racism in order to alert America to the dangers of aliens and to propagate specific ethnic stereotypes. The Jew was treated as a double negative, a greedy and exploitive capitalist and a menacing radical. As Representative Tincher of Kansas asserted in the debate on the immigration bill, "On the one side is beer, bolshevism, unassimilating settlements and perhaps many flags—on the other side is constitutional government [and] one flag, stars and stripes. . . ."

For many Americans nothing symbolized urban corruption more than the liquor problem. The strongest support for national Prohibition came from areas where the population was Protestant, rural, and nativist. Voting and ethnic statistics show a high correlation between prohibition sentiment and native rural Protestantism. The core of such anti-liquor militancy lay in the South and the Midwest, not in the East. The Anti-Saloon League, as its name indicates, singled out for attack not alcohol alone but a chiefly urban institution widely identified with a different culture. And the problem, as the rural mind saw it, was not confined to the largest cities, New York and Chicago. It was present in smaller cities like Quincy, Illinois, where it was reported that a judge had to disqualify nine of 24 prospective jurors in a Prohibition trial because they admitted hostility toward the Volstead Act.

The rural–urban cleavage can be seen clearly in the vote in the House of Representatives over the Eighteenth Amendment in 1918. Some supporters of the amendment were motivated by patriotism: they identified beer with the Kaiser, for the names of the leading American brewers were German. Others supported the measure for medical reasons. Still others saw Prohibition as a way of conserving grain necessary to support the war effort. But the prohibitionists, in their eagerness to win ratification, exploited this country's fear of alien nations—it was the immigrant and his drinking habits, his "alcoholization," that was bringing America toward destruction. An alliance between rural and urban advocates of Prohibition was forged—but its existence was short-lived, and in rural-dominated state legislatures urban allies were not needed.

Did Prohibition—the era's "noble experiment"—do what its advocates had promised? If the saloon was eradicated as the source of evil, it was soon replaced all over America by the equally evil speakeasy. If the Eighteenth Amendment ended the legitimate distribution of beer, wine, and spirits, a bootlegging industry with its attendant syndicated crime rose up in its place. Criminal gangs existed before Prohibition, but Prohibition greatly expanded the consumer audience for smuggled goods. Al Capone and the gang warfare of the 1920s became subjects of daily conversation and bootlegging became big business. Did Prohibition change American's drinking behavior? The image created by the flapper, bathtub gin, and illicit sex among the young suggests an increase in drinking. Nevertheless, despite that stereotype it is probable that Prohibition caused a sharp reduction in the rate of alcohol consumption in the United States, perhaps by as much as one-half.

Among the strongest supporters of Prohibition in the 1920s was the Ku Klux Klan. Although the Klan figured in the rural–urban conflict, it was never a rural movement to the same degree that Prohibition was; instead, it had an important urban dimension. In such a rural state as Iowa, for instance, the center of Klan strength lay in the capital and largest city, Des Moines. Although the Klan of the Twenties had taken the same name as the Reconstruction Klan of the American South, it cast a wider net than had its predecessor. Where the first Klan directed its animosity against the newly freed black man, the KKK in the 1920s opposed the Catholic Church, immigrants— particularly the "new immigrants"—cities, and modernity in general. It fought to restore the values of an earlier America, and it could be violent, using terror and torture, especially in the South and Southwest. The Klan proclaimed its opposition to "Jew, Jug and Jesuit," and where it was strongest the Klan assumed the role of censor and policeman of local morality.

From the Klan's point of view, according to Hiram Wesley Evans, the Imperial Wizard and Emperor of the Klan, the problem of "colored people" was not simply an American problem, it was a world problem. "The White Race must be supreme, not only in America, but in the World," he wrote. The Klan regarded the black American as a special problem toward which the Nordics had a particular obligation. Since a black person's limitations of mental capacity and culture were taken as axiomatic, "we will not permit him to gain sufficient power to control our civilization. Neither will we delude him with promises of social equality." The Klan looked forward to the day "when every state [would] enforce laws making any sex relations between a white and colored person a crime."

So far as Jews were concerned, the issue was more complex, or so Evans stated. The Jew from western Europe posed no problem: "His abilities are great, he contributes much to any country where he lives." But this was not so of the Jews from eastern Europe, who were "not true Jews, but only Judaized Mongols. . . ." Despite the distinction, Evans somewhat contradictorily stated that the "melting pot" was a ghastly failure because Jews simply refused to melt.

To the Klan, real Americans were Nordic Americans, descended from the English, Dutch, German, Huguenot, Irish, and Scots—forebears of the early days of America—endowed with a distinctive racial understanding of such principles as democracy, fair dealing, impartial justice, equal opportunity, religious liberty, and nation and race before all else but God. These principles were fundamental, according to Evans, and although foreigners might use the words, few were able to understand the principles.

The Klan sought to protect American society and get things back to the way they had been earlier. It was conservative, not revolutionary. Nationally, the Klan worked for immigration restriction and it won its greatest victory with the National Origins Act of 1924. Further, the Klan opposed membership in the League of Nations and in the World Court; it supported federal aid to education in order to counter the attraction of parochial schools; it supported Bible reading in public schools; and it called for compulsory education for all children between the ages of eight and sixteen.

Religious fundamentalism, the Ku Klux Klan, and the struggle over Prohibition constituted the three great cultural controversies of the decade of the Twenties. Not all "drys" were fundamentalists and not all fundamentalists belonged to the Klan. Alignments were not so consistent. William Jennings Bryan, for example, the best known of the fundamentalists, strongly condemned the saloon as "the festering source of political and moral corruption." He was, however, in no hurry to eliminate it, and he had nothing to do with the Klan. Bryan was a strong supporter of Louis D. Brandeis, the first Jew to rise to a seat on the Supreme Court, and he had been a longtime friend of the Catholic Church and a defender of its right to maintain its own schools. One must be cautious about seeing religious fundamentalism as a simple rural–urban conflict. There were even some fundamentalists who opposed the Tennessee anti-evolution law on the ground that it violated academic freedom and democratic ideals. The *Monticello Express*, for example, a rural Iowa newspaper that was strongly nativist, held the fundamentalists up to public ridicule for their attempts to enact laws forbidding the teaching of evolution. In one issue the paper noted that the fundamentalists were the same kind of people who persecuted Galileo.

Religious fundamentalism did not appear unheralded at the end of the First World War. Scientific advances of the nineteenth century, particularly the ideas associated with Charles Darwin, had wrought changes in American religious practices and beliefs. At first, the conflict over Darwin's ideas was largely confined to the educated clergy and the academic world. By the 1920s, however, Darwinism had been widely disseminated and most of the leading ministers in the United States believed that the conflict between science and theology was over. It was after World War I that ordinary churchgoers learned that the eternal truths of an earlier time were apparently no longer immutable. In Muncie, Indiana, according to Robert and Helen Lynd in their famous study, *Middletown,* most people continued to attend church regularly and to affirm a belief in God, but fewer seemed to believe in hell and increasing numbers were becoming doubters. Orthodox Protestantism was facing a formidable enemy in modernism.

The publication in 1916 of Professor James Henry Leuba's *The Belief in God and Immortality* had a significant impact on the controversy over fundamentalism. A statistical study, the book revealed a clear loss of faith among college students after a four-year exposure to modern science. Leuba found that of 1,000 respondents from nine top colleges, only 15 percent of freshmen reported a loss of faith, but 40 to 45 percent of graduating males had been so affected. According to friends of William Jennings Bryan, it was Leuba's survey that brought Bryan actively into the fundamentalist controversy and to the defense of the Tennessee anti-evolution law.

Fear of change marked the sensitivities of fundamentalists as it did members of the Ku Klux Klan. It was a fear that the world they knew was passing and they were not at all happy with the new world they saw emerging. Fundamentalists longed for certainty—the certainty that a literal interpretation of the Bible provided. Higher education was of limited value, for too much schooling was likely to lead to atheism and immorality. Bryan said that "only 2 percent of the population were college graduates and that there was [sic] 98 percent who still had souls."

Fundamentalists were also concerned about the insidious effects of Nietzschean philosophy. They frequently asserted that Friedrich Nietzsche and his disciples were the intellectual products of Darwin's philosophy of the survival of the fittest and that Nietzsche's teachings "condemned democracy . . . denounced Christianity . . . denied the existence of God, overturned all standards of morality, eulogized war . . . praised hatred . . . and endeavored to substitute the worship of the Superman for the worship of Jehovah."

A year after the Scopes anti-evolution trial in Tennessee, Bryan's antagonist, Clarence Darrow, was defending Richard Loeb and Nathan Leopold. The trial of Loeb and Leopold reveals what became almost a national mania over psychology and, more specifically, Freudianism. Words such as "fixation," "complex," "libido" and "subconscious" became part of everyday speech. In addition to Freud, advocates of the "new psychology" focused popular attention on the motives of the human animal and on the role of glands in affecting behavior. Advocates of Freudianism and glandism were as committed to their secular ideas as the fundamentalists were to their religion.

Politically, the decade was marked by the repudiation of Wilsonian idealism and the restoration of what President Harding called "normalcy." Instead of a government committed to attacking social injustice and curbing corporate power, the Republican administrations of Harding, Coolidge, and Hoover seemed to have become the agents of private industry, enthusiastic advocates of the business community.

Ohioan Warren G. Harding was elected by a landslide vote in 1920 after having been selected by party leaders to break a deadlocked Republican convention. It was a staggering landslide: Harding won with 404 electoral votes out of 531. At the same time, no Democratic congressmen were elected in 24 states; the Republicans sent 307 representatives to the House to sit with only 127 Democrats. By his own admission, however, Harding was not qualified to hold the nation's highest office. He had told friends, in honest recognition of his own unfitness, "I am a man of limited talents from a small town." The spokesmen for financial and industrial interests knew what they wanted from government and were looking for someone whom they could manipulate easily. But Harding's nomination was not the result of a conspiracy. He embodied the kind of conservatism the delegates wanted. He was handsome. He had charm. He was an extrovert, affable, and was a "nice guy" who looked like a president.

Recognizing his own limitations, Harding realized the importance of capable subordinates in key posts and three of his appointments were first rate: Charles Evans Hughes as Secretary of State, Herbert Hoover in Commerce, and Andrew Mellon as Secretary of the Treasury. Henry Wallace as Secretary of Agriculture was a capable spokesman for the interests of the farmer. But the remainder of his appointments, with few exceptions, were hacks and card-playing buddies. They gave his administration the reputation of being among the worst in American history.

The corrupt "Ohio Gang" consisted of Harding's old cronies from his earlier days in local politics and in the United States Senate. The President appointed Harry Daugherty, an Ohio party boss, to the Attorney General's post. Daugherty and his pal Jess Smith lived high off the hog by selling immunity from prosecution. Pardons and appointments were also bought and sold, as were permits to withdraw liquor from bonded government warehouses, introductions to the "right people," and government surplus that was not altogether unwanted. When news of these goings-on reached the President's ears, Smith was fired; he committed suicide shortly after. Harry Daugherty was eventually dismissed by President Coolidge. But by far the most spectacular scandal involved what has come to be called Teapot Dome. Warren Harding's untimely death on August 2, 1923, preceded the revelation of the full extent of the corruption of his administration.

Under Coolidge, the Harding cabinet remained intact until pressure from Congress and from the public forced some dismissals. As for Harding's pro-business policies, Coolidge's support was immediate. He furthered the high tariff policy and supported broad tax reduction. To come was further immigration restriction, opposition to a veterans' bonus, no recognition of the Soviet Union, and vigorous enforcement of the Volstead Act. At the urging of Secretary of Commerce Herbert Hoover there was to be greater cooperation between government and business, encouragement for trade associations, and a concomitant relaxation of the anti-trust laws.

By the end of 1922 a business setback which had begun the previous year had run its course. For this return of prosperity Republican politicians took credit, claiming that the party's businessman's program was responsible. Not all Americans participated in this return of prosperity. American farmers and workers failed to get a full share in it, although workers did enjoy some of its benefits. Their standard of living rose, but at the same time their wage increases were proportionally far below the growth in corporate profits, and they worked in an atmosphere that was increasingly hostile to unionization.

The income of farmers, on the other hand, declined during the decade. Farming in the 1920s was, like industry, becoming increasingly mechanized. The number of tractors increased fourfold during the decade and opened up millions of new acres to cultivation. However, the increase in farm production drove down agricultural prices. Moreover, European markets, which had been wide open during the war, had contracted once the war ended. A change in American dietary habits and in clothing styles also contributed to a declining domestic food market. The market for starches, particularly wheat, slipped as machinery lessened the need for heavy manual labor. Americans started to eat more fruits and vegetables. Cotton farmers suffered as Americans turned away from cotton goods to fabrics such as rayon. The result of these changes was a drastic decline in agricultural prices and a severe drop in farm income. In 1919 farmers enjoyed 16 percent of the national income; by 1929 this had shrunk to 9 percent. In the latter year the average income for Americans engaged in nonagricultural work was $870; for farmers it was $223. Neither Coolidge nor Harding made much effort or showed much concern for the plight of America's farmers.

No Democrat could have defeated Herbert Hoover in the 1928 presidential race. Despite the unhappy situation of the farmers, the Republicans were riding the high tide of prosperity. Hoover, the most prominent member of both the Harding and Coolidge cabinets, had been untouched by scandal. He'd been a first-rate administrator at the Department of Commerce, devoting his energies to promoting American business. In Hoover the nation's dominant business and industrial interests had found their ideal candidate. Further, he was a vigorous advocate of trade associations: national organizations of businessmen in particular industries who wanted to establish agreement on common production techniques and to promote efficiency in production and marketing. If businessmen shared information and worked toward limited cooperation, Hoover believed, competition would be less destructive. Any concern for social and economic justice was left to the decade's small Progressive Party. During the three Republican administrations of the 1920s, the federal government became an adjunct of American business.

By the end of the decade, not only was it true that "the business of America is business," as President Coolidge had announced, but business came to be regarded as the *summum bonum* of American life. Businessmen enjoyed respect and a reputation for perception and sagacity that went well beyond the boardroom and the production line. "We in America today," Herbert Hoover announced just before his election, "are nearer to the final triumph over poverty than ever before in the history of any land. The poorhouse is vanishing from among us."

Very soon, these words came back to haunt both their author and the American people. The homage paid to business—so marked in the 1920s—became an object of ridicule. After the Great Crash came the Great Depression. There is no simple explanation for the cause of the speculative binge that began in 1928 and came crashing down in October of 1929. Some economists insist that the crash was due to the monetary errors of the Federal Reserve Bank and its easy-money policy. Easy money meant low bank interest rates and low bank interest rates meant, for example, inexpensive "call money." Borrowers could obtain a call-or-demand loan, usually for a twenty-four-hour period but renewable by both parties at varying rates each business day. Speculators preferred this kind of loan since they were interested in quick and easy in-and-out transactions. They took advantage of low rates to purchase stocks that might otherwise have been beyond their reach, for call money was often available at less than 20 percent collateral. Banks liked call loans because they could call in their funds in a matter of hours should the market fall and because they could gain interest on extremely short-term advances and thus use their resources to the maximum.

Popular myth has it that the stock market crash was the beginning and even the cause of the Great Depression. It was neither. But the crash was the crucial link in the chain of events that led to the breakdown of the U.S. economy. When thousands of investors lost their savings, they were faced with the grim necessity of buying less. As a result storekeepers sold less. Factories consequently produced less or closed completely, and the spiral continued downward. There is no better example to illustrate the speculative opportunities of the 1920s than that of the famed empire of Samuel Insull in electric utilities. From the ashes of the Insull empire rose such important New Deal creations as the Securities and Exchange Commission, the Tennessee Valley Authority, and holding company legislation.

By the time Harding took office in 1921, the League of Nations had been rejected by the United States Senate, but attempts to find ways of avoiding future wars did not cease. An effort to limit armaments, especially naval armaments, received close attention. There was a strong desire to check the costly race in capital ship construction. For Secretary of State Charles Evans Hughes, the only way to disarm was to disarm substantially, and he looked forward to the scrapping of nearly two million tons of existing capital ships. From the Washington Conference of 1922 emerged a Five Power Treaty signed by the United States, Great Britain, Japan, France, and Italy. The treaty imposed rigid limitations on capital ship tonnage. In thirty-five minutes, as a British observer put it, the Secretary of State "sank more ships than all the admirals in the world have sunk in centuries."

There were discussions and agreement on aircraft carriers as well. Still experimental, the potential of the carriers had not been fully realized. During the summer of 1921, Brigadier General William "Billy" Mitchell conducted a series of highly publicized and controversial bombing tests a hundred miles off the Virginia coast. Contention over Mitchell's ideas regarding air power took place in the context of a major political debate over disarmament, military budgets, and misgivings about the nature of future conflicts and the vulnerability of traditional naval fleets. World War II attested to the accuracy of his prophecies.

The decade of the 1920s was a time of great changes and of stresses so severe as to test national coherence. Violations of the law were in a sense rends in the fabric of society. The trials described in this volume reveal the efforts of the American system of justice to repair these rends, as well as the efforts of the American nation to deal with the stresses that caused them.

1

SACCO AND VANZETTI

On April 15, 1920, a robbery and two murders shattered the peace at a factory in South Braintree, Massachusetts. Frederick Parmenter, the paymaster, and Alessandro Berardelli, a guard, were carrying the payroll of the Slater and Morrill Shoe Company into the factory when two gunmen opened fire, left them for dead, and stole the money. The robbers sped away in a car with several accomplices. Three weeks later, Nicola Sacco and Bartolomeo Vanzetti were arrested.

In 1977, Massachusetts Governor Michael Dukakis proclaimed August 23 as Nicola Sacco and Bartolomeo Vanzetti Memorial Day. "The Commonwealth of Massachusetts," he said, declares that "any stigma and disgrace shall be forever removed from their names." The governor, without offering an opinion as to their guilt or innocence, noted that the trial and appeals process had gone on for seven years and had been "permeated by prejudice against foreigners and hostility toward unorthodox political views." This poisoned atmosphere and the conduct of many of the officials involved in the case "shed serious doubt on their willingness and ability to conduct the prosecution and trial . . . fairly and impartially." The governor hoped his proclamation would finally conclude the most widely discussed and written-about trial in American history.

In 1927 Felix Frankfurter, at that time a professor of law at Harvard University, wrote a lengthy article for the *Atlantic Monthly* in which he took strong exception to the way the case had been handled. Since that time the character of the crime, the nature of the evidence, the conduct of the courts, the ideology of the anarchist movement, and the eloquence of Vanzetti have been written about in Italian, German, Spanish, French, and Russian, as well as in English. Despite the 1977 Massachusetts proclamation, the flow of words continued.

When Sacco and Vanzetti were arrested on May 5, 1920, they were bristling with firepower. Sacco carried, underneath his vest, a fully loaded ten-shot .32 Colt automatic tucked into the waistband of his trousers. His pocket held 23 loose shells. Vanzetti had a five-shot .38 Harrington & Richardson revolver. It too was loaded, and although he was carrying no extra cartridges for it, police found in his pocket four twelve-gauge shotgun shells. The two suspects were Italian immigrants, foreign radicals, and they were heavily armed. Their plight was made worse by the hostility of Red Scare nativism then raging through the nation.

Both men told lies. Vanzetti said he had bought his gun several years earlier for $18 in Boston's North End. Later he changed his story, claiming that he had purchased it from a friend just a few months before. He lied also when he said that he had known Sacco for only about a year and a half before his arrest. And Sacco lied as well—about where he had gotten his gun and about his whereabouts on April 15, the day of the crime.

At the time of their arrest, Sacco and Vanzetti were not charged with murder; nor were they charged with robbery. They were given no intimation that they were murder suspects. So far as they were informed, they believed they had been arrested because they were suspicious characters. When asked directly at the trial what they thought at the time of their arrest, Sacco replied, "I understand they arrested me for a political matter."

Q. Why did you feel you were being detained for political opinions?
A. Because I was asked if I was a Socialist. I said, "Well."

Why did Sacco and Vanzetti lie when they were arrested? Both men were anarchists; they belonged to a circle of associates led by Luigi Galleani, who had come to the United States in 1901 and founded the anarchist periodical *Cronaca Suvversiva*. In 1917 Galleani opposed American entrance into World War I and pointed out that alien anarchists who did not register for the draft probably had nothing to fear. The Justice Department's Bureau of Investigation came to regard Galleani as the leading anarchist in the United States and the *Cronaca* as the nation's largest and most dangerous anarchist newspaper. From its pages came a stream of articles advocating the destruction of all political, economic, and religious authority. Galleani glorified acts of terror and provided useful information for his readers on how to manufacture bombs.

On June 2, 1919, bombs went off in several American cities, including explosions in Washington, Boston, and Newtonville, Massachusetts. The federal government suspected the Galleani group of perpetrating these bombings and the Bureau of Investigation began a probe of Galleani, the *Cronaca*, and its subscribers— among them Sacco and Vanzetti. The two men lied about their activities on the night of their arrest, but on that evening they had been on their way to get a car in order to carry away incriminating anarchist literature to a place of safekeeping. Their lies, they said, were meant to protect friends, relatives, and political associates in the anarchist movement.

Sacco and Vanzetti had somewhat credible (though far from persuasive) reasons for being armed. They testified that on the morning of their arrest they had planned to hunt in some nearby woods. On deciding instead to go for the car, they forgot to leave their weapons at home. Both men were accustomed to guns. Sacco began carrying a pistol when he was a night watchman. As his employer testified: "Night watchmen protecting property do have guns." He concealed the gun in his belt because he had no permit, and not, as some claimed, so he could make a quick draw. For his part, Vanzetti said he needed a gun because "it was a very bad time, and I liked to have a revolver for self-defense when I went to Boston for fish. I can carry eighty, one hundred dollars, one hundred and twenty-five dollars."

Nicola Sacco and Bartolomeo Vanzetti were dedicated revolutionaries. They belonged to a wing of the anarchist movement that believed in using violence to force political change and they may even have been involved in some of the 1919 bombings attributed to anarchists. But robbery and murder are something else. There exists no evidence of banditry ever having been committed by Italian-American anarchists. No evidence, however, does not eliminate the possibility that the wish to obtain bail money for comrades caught up in the dragnet of the Red Scare may have pushed some anarchists to act in unaccustomed ways.

Although an anarchist revolutionary, Sacco was in some ways a model of respectability. One of seventeen children born to a prosperous family in southern Italy, he came to the United States in 1908 with an older brother when he was seventeen. Here he worked at a number of different jobs before becoming a shoe edger—a craft at which he grew highly skilled. He earned as much as $80 a week at the 3-K Shoe Factory in Stoughton, Massachusetts, and had managed to save the very substantial sum of almost $1500 by the time of his arrest. His employer saw him as an excellent worker and a devoted family man: "A man who is in his garden at four o'clock in the morning and at the factory at seven o'clock, and in his garden again after supper and until nine and ten at night, carrying water and raising vegetables, and beyond his own needs which he would bring to me to give to the poor, that man is not a 'hold-up man.'" All the same, Sacco was often busy demonstrating on behalf of strikers, raising money for labor and radical causes, and distributing left-wing anarchist literature among Italian-born workers.

When the United States entered the Great War in 1917, Sacco, a pacifist, refused to participate or even buy Liberty Bonds. Following Luigi Galleani's advice, he and about a hundred other anarchists, including Vanzetti, fled to Mexico rather than register for the draft. They may have been fearful that if they remained in the United States they would be forcibly restrained from leaving for Europe, where the revolution that had burst out in Russia in February promised to spread over the continent. Sacco, however, returned from Mexico before the end of the war because, he said, "I could not stay no more. I leave my wife here and my boy. I could not stay no more far away from them."

Of the two defendants, Bartolomeo Vanzetti was the more romantic figure. His admirers came to see him as a hero, a man of warmth and intelligence—philosophical, articulate, even eloquent. On hearing the verdict that convicted him, Vanzetti again denied his guilt before the court in a statement has been quoted many times.

Now, I should say that I am not only innocent of all these

things, not only have I never committed a real crime in my life . . . I struggled all my life to eliminate crimes [including] the exploitation and the oppression of man by man, and if there is reason why you in a few minutes can doom me, it is this reason and nothing else . . . I would not wish to a dog or to snake, to the most low and misfortunate creature of the earth—I would not wish to any of them what I have had to suffer for things that I am not guilty of. I am suffering because I am a radical and indeed I am a radical; I have suffered because I was an Italian, and indeed I am an Italian; I have suffered more for my family and beloved than for myself; but I am so convinced to be right that if you could execute me two times, and if I could be reborn two other times, I would live again to do what I have done already.

Vanzetti was a drifter, a somewhat shiftless wanderer. Born in a small village in northern Italy in 1888 to a sober, pious, and well-established family, his passion for reading began early, so that by his teen years he had read Dante, St. Augustine, and eighteenth-century playwright Carlo Goldoni. In these same years he learned to respond with his fists to those who taunted him for his traditional piety.

A few months after his mother died in 1908, Vanzetti came to the United States. He never married. From the time he first arrived he held a number of jobs, often menial, in various towns and cities in New England. He was a dishwasher, a worker in brick furnaces and stone pits, a common laborer, and a pastry cook. From 1918 until his arrest, he peddled fish from time to time among Italian families in Plymouth, Massachusetts. It can be surmised that Vanzetti wanted freedom from responsibility. Preferring outdoor work, he drifted from job to job. At the same time, he continued his reading, and between 1908 and 1920 he explored Marx, Ernest Renan, Darwin, Tolstoy, Hugo, Zola, and many others.

Sacco and Vanzetti were passionate radicals. "Both Nick and I are anarchists," Vanzetti once declared, "the radical of the radical— the black cats, the terrors of many, of all the bigots, exploiters, charlatans, fakers, and oppressors." Because today anarchists are a disappearing fringe in most countries it may be difficult to recall that prior to World War I and into the 1920s there were many anarchists among the radical left in both Europe and the United States. An-archism came to be equated with terrorism, for the movement was responsible for the assassinations of monarchs in Italy and Austria-Hungary (Empress Elisabeth), heads of government in France and Spain, and President William McKinley of the United States. In 1886 seven policemen were killed by an explosion in Haymarket Square, Chicago, during a labor disturbance. Eight anarchists were convict-ed, six of them immigrants, and thereafter the image of bomb-carry-ing anarchists stirred the kind of fear that Communism would evoke in later generations. Beside anarchism developed the image of all immigrants, particularly those from southern Europe, as inclined toward violence and disorder.

The anarchism of Sacco and Vanzetti had as its millennial dream a communal society in which the trinity of Old World evils—the state, the church, and private property—would be abolished. According to Luigi Galleani, this achievement could come about only by revolutionary action. Galleani glorified the "propaganda of the deed," which endorsed the use of the dagger, the gun, and dyna-mite to awaken revolutionary fervor. Terrorism, sabotage, and assas-sination were considered legitimate ways to stir the masses. Sacco and Vanzetti believed this. Nevertheless, on May 3, 1927, Vanzetti petitioned the governor of Massachusetts as he waited under sen-tence of death, reiterating his innocence and that of Sacco, and deny-ing that either of them had ever committed acts of violence. He argued that anarchists only resorted to terror when "they were impelled by persecution and self-defense . . . provoked by violence, oppression, and intolerance on the part of the persons in power . . . [and] moved by sincere intentions caused by their deep sympathy [for] . . . human suffering. . . ."

Did Sacco and Vanzetti commit the crime for which they were executed? There is no reliable evidence they committed violent acts before the payroll robbery and murder. Vanzetti said that most of his political activity consisted of writing articles and letters and talking on street corners to "scorning men." But both men were close fol-lowers of the Galleani philosophy. They were not just "a good shoe-maker and a poor fish peddler," not just the harmless dreamers often pictured in the vast literature on the case.

* * *

The trial of Nicola Sacco and Bartolomeo Vanzetti in Dedham, Massachusetts, began on May 31, 1921, the day following Memorial Day, when the nation mourned those who had died in America's wars. Less than three years had passed since the most recent war, during which the defendants left the country to avoid the draft. The point was not permitted to escape notice.

In an ordinary criminal trial, jury selection may often be a more or less perfunctory matter. The 14 to 16 members who made up the Massachusetts jury of the 1920s, including two to four alternates who served until the jurors began deliberations, were usually drawn from a panel made up of 75 to 100 veniremen. At the Sacco-Vanzetti trial the process involved 653, the largest number of prospective jurors ever required in a Norfolk County trial. Judge Webster Thayer personally examined each one and permitted both the state and the defense to enter challenges. Nearly 200 of them were challenged peremptorily while the others were rejected for cause, some because they had previous knowledge of the case and some because they had strong feelings against capital punishment. The names of 153 talesmen have been preserved in the record. There appear to have been no "Boston brahmins," few who had "foreign-sounding" names, and not one name that looked Italian.

It took five days to empanel a jury of two dealers in real estate, an ex-policeman, a photographer, a farmer, a grocer, a salesman, a stockkeeper, and four industrial workers. It appeared to be a good jury, representative of the community, but given the climate of opinion in the United States at the time, it is hard to imagine that a jury could have been selected in Massachusetts or in any state completely free from fear, prejudice, or hatred toward defendants like Sacco and Vanzetti. New England, as well as other regions, was rife with hostility toward foreigners. The Immigration Restriction League counted some of the leaders of the Boston business and intellectual communities among its members. Both aliens and citizens suspected of radicalism were subject to arrest without warrant or process of law. Homes were entered and property seized. Men and women were jailed and held without recourse to friends or counsel. And there was hostility toward those who had avoided military service during the war. Many on the officially issued "slacker's list" were probably foreigners not eligible for the draft, but the public rarely made such a distinction. During the trial, remarks by both the judge and the prosecuting attorney called attention to the defendants' avoidance of military service, even to the point of browbeating Sacco during cross-examination.

Q. Did you say yesterday you love a free country?
A. Yes, sir.
Q. Did you love this country in the month of May, 1917?
A. I did not say—and I don't want to say I did not love this country.
Q. Did you love this country in the month of May of 1917?
A. I can't answer in one word.
Q. You can't say whether you loved the United States of America . . .
A. That is pretty hard for me to say in one word, Mr. Katzmann [the district attorney].
Q. There are two words you can use, Mr. Sacco, yes or no. Which one is it?
A. Yes.
Q. And in order to show your love for this United States of America when she was about to call upon you to become a soldier you ran away to Mexico?
Defense counsel: Wait.
The Court: Did you?
Q. Did you run away to Mexico?
The Court. He has not said he ran away to Mexico. Did you go?
Q. Did you go to Mexico to avoid being a soldier for this country that you loved?
A. Yes.
Q. Was it for the reason that you desired to avoid service that when you came back in four months you went to Cambridge instead of to Milford?
A. For the reason for not to get in the army.
Q. So as to avoid getting in the army.
A. Another reason why, I did not want no chance to get arrested and one year in prison.
Q. Did you love your country when you came back from

Mexico?

A. I don't think I could change my opinion in three months.

Q. You still loved America, did you?

A. I should say yes.

Q. And that is your idea of showing your love for this country?

A. (Witness hesitates) . . . I don't believe in war.

Q. You don't believe in war?

A. No, sir.

Q. Do you think it is a cowardly thing to do that you did?

A. No, sir.

Q. Do you think it is a brave thing to do what you did?

A. Yes, sir.

Q. Do you think it would be a brave thing to go away from your wife?

A. No.

Q. When she needed you?

A. No.

A committee for the defense of Sacco and Vanzetti had been organized in 1920 following their arrest. George Vahey was retained, a criminal lawyer of conservative bent. Vanzetti soon grew dissatisfied with Vahey's defense. He thought he lacked energy and enthusiasm for the case, and when Vahey formed a new partnership with District Attorney Katzmann, Vanzetti's worst suspicions were confirmed. The Sacco-Vanzetti Defense Committee then turned to anarchists in New York for advice, as well as moral and financial support, to obtain different counsel. The committee concluded that radical defendants could be properly represented only by counsel sympathetic to their clients' beliefs.

Carlo Tresca, a leading anarchist, and his wife, Elizabeth Gurley Flynn, a firebrand agitator for the Industrial Workers of the World, recommended Fred H. Moore, formerly a lawyer for the IWW. Moore's appointment reinforced the public's impression that the defendants were dangerous radicals and that the trial would make radicalism the key issue. The appointment was probably a mistake. Many in Massachusetts found Moore's manner, his clothes, and even his West Coast accent offensive. Worse than an outsider, Moore was a womanizer, a cocaine addict, and often openly offensive in manner. He conducted himself in ways that scoffed at local customs and he made insatiable demands on the defense committee for money to pursue a variety of investigations. Sacco did not like him and the two quarreled frequently. In 1924, during the series of appeals following conviction, the committee replaced Moore with William G. Thompson, a prominent Yankee defense lawyer committed to their cause. After being dismissed, Moore began to express doubts about Sacco's innocence.

Frederick G. Katzmann, district attorney for Norfolk and Plymouth counties, headed the prosecution team. Many who think Sacco and Vanzetti were wrongfully convicted regard Katzmann's conduct as duplicitous, unprofessional, and even criminal. He never missed an opportunity to impugn the loyalty of the defendants and to remind the jury that both men had been draft dodgers, and he appealed in his final summation to native American solidarity against alien peoples and their values. In his 1927 article, Felix Frankfurter charged Katzmann with chicanery in manipulating the testimony of William Proctor, a ballistics expert. In recent writings others have argued that Katzmann connived with Proctor in substituting the crucial fatal bullet. But Katzmann also has his defenders, who see him as upright and honorable, and the trial as fair. Sacco was certainly guilty, according to this group, and probably Vanzetti also.

The trial lasted 35 court days, transcripts of testimony filling six large volumes. Five crucial issues had to be resolved: Could the defendants be placed at the scene of the crime by eyewitnesses? Could the defendants prove, as they contended, that they were elsewhere on the day of the murder? Could the state establish that the gun found on Vanzetti, the .38-caliber Harrington and Richardson, was the gun taken from payroll guard and murder victim Alessandro Berardelli? Could the state prove that Sacco's .32 Colt was the gun that killed Berardelli and that Sacco had pulled the trigger? Finally, did Sacco and Vanzetti show "consciousness of guilt" after their arrest because of their participation in the crime — or because they were radicals and draft dodgers? Did they lie to avoid the penalty for murder or to protect themselves against the mistreatment and deportation that anarchists and slackers could expect?

The crime took place in broad daylight. More than 40 eyewitnesses claimed they saw the shooting, or noticed the bandits in South Braintree earlier in the day, or got a look at the getaway car speeding off. Some of the eyewitnesses at the trial were positive in their identification. Some wavered under cross-examination. Almost three dozen had seen one or two of the bandits but were unable to identify either Sacco or Vanzetti. Some could point Sacco out, but only after being taken to prison to see him, not in a lineup but alone in his cell. Lola Andrews, for example, came into court and identified Sacco in considerable detail. In a later affidavit, pressured by the defense, she repudiated her testimony. Still later, for Katzmann, she retracted her retraction.

More important, and more unreliable as an eyewitness, was Mary Splaine. A bookkeeper, she was working on the second floor of the Slater and Morrill Shoe Company. At the time of the robbery she was facing windows that looked out onto a railroad crossing. When she heard shots, she ran to the windows and saw an automobile crossing the tracks. Watching the scene from a distance of 60 to 80 feet, she caught a glimpse of a man previously unknown to her in a car traveling at a rate of between 15 and 18 miles an hour. She saw him for from one and a half to three seconds. Katzmann relied on her testimony about a man who appeared "between the back of the front seat and the back seat." He weighed perhaps 140 pounds or a bit more and was muscular, an active-looking man. And Splaine saw his hand.

Q. So, that hand you said you saw where?
A. The left hand, that was placed on the back of the front seat, on the back of the front seat. He had a gray, what I thought was a shirt—had a grayish, like navy color, and the face was what we would call clear cut, clean cut face. The forehead was high.

There were more details. In fact, at the end of a year Splaine remembered and described sixteen different details of the person whom she had glimpsed for a period that could not have exceeded three seconds, at a distance of not less than 60 feet. She remembered the size of his hand as well as the length of his hair as being between two and two and a half inches long and the shade of his eyebrows. Such perception and such memory under such conditions are surely extraordinary. But Mary Splaine's description became more detailed and more certain over time. At the preliminary hearing in Quincy she said that Sacco "bears a striking resemblance" to the man she had seen in the car, but she would not swear positively that he was the man. That was on the 26th of May. Four months later, when she appeared before the grand jury, Katzmann chided her for her previous vacillation. "I am determined," he said, "that you shall answer the question directly and that is something you have never done with me before." Despite Katzmann's badgering, she continued for a short while in maintaining that she thought Sacco was the man but that she could be mistaken. At the Dedham trial, nine months later, she gave her detailed and definite testimony. She insisted that Sacco was the man and that her previous uncertainty vanished after she saw the defendant in the courtroom in Quincy.

Frances Devlin was another eyewitness whose uncertainty vanished over time. At the preliminary hearing she refused to identify Sacco positively as the man. At the grand jury she felt that she had not had a good enough view of Sacco. At Dedham she was no longer uncertain. Katzmann heaped praise upon the two women and characterized them as models of Christian righteousness.

Mary Splaine's testimony reveals the evolution of identification which took these two eyewitnesses to certainty. Both had been brought to the Brockton police station to view Sacco. Mary Splaine said, under cross-examination by Fred Moore:

Q. The defendant Sacco that morning did kneel forward in a crouching position in your presence?
A. No, sir, he did not.
Q. Did he take and put on his hat or cap?
A. He took off his hat.
Q. Did he turn around in different positions with the light facing him and in front of him, in back of him and in side of him, as he was directed?
A. No, sir. I walked around him.
Q. You walked all around him?
A. Yes, sir.

Q. With his hat on and with his hat off?

A. Yes, sir.

Q. Did he sit down and stand up during part of that examination?

A. Yes, sir.

Q. Did you at any time, or any one else in your presence there, ask him to take any particular position?

A. Yes, sir.

Q. Was that at you request?

A. No, sir, not at my request.

Q. Whose request was that?

A. Miss Devlin.

Q. But, it was in your presence?

A. Yes, sir.

Q. And the position that he was requested to take he did take?

A. Yes, sir.

Q. Now, you saw him four or five times that day, didn't you?

A. I saw him twice that day—well, three times including when I first saw him at the doorway coming in, but twice when I looked at him afterwards.

Q. All told, the time that you looked him over in these various positions, with his hat on and with his hat off, and walked around him, and so forth, consumed upwards — these various occasions — upwards of a couple of hours, didn't it?

A. I don't think so. I saw him while he passed through the room, and while he was in the room I don't think I took more than five minutes to look at him.

Q. You saw him all you wanted to see him?

A. Yes, sir.

Q. You saw him in every way and every position that you wanted?

A. Yes, sir.

Q. And he was also present in court at the time of the preliminary examination?

A. Yes, sir.

Q. And you saw him there for a matter of I suppose three or

four hours, at the preliminary examination?

A. I couldn't say just how long.

Q. At any rate, when you took the witness stand at the time of the preliminary, you looked right square at the defendant, didn't you?

A. Yes, sir.

Q. And you looked at him during the entire period of your twenty-five or thirty pages of testimony?

A. Yes, sir.

Q. And you haven't seen the defendant from that time since you saw him in the Brockton jail all that you wanted to see him and the time that you saw him on preliminary, you haven't seen him from the day until you saw him in this courtroom, have you?

A. No, sir, I did not.

Q. You availed yourself of every form of opportunity of observation of that young man during the period in the Brockton jail and the police court?

A. Not in jail; in that room. I didn't see him in jail.

Q. And you haven't seen him since?

A. No, sir.

Q. And it was with all those opportunities of observation, which had not in any wise been supplemented since — They haven't been supplemented since? You haven't had any further opportunities of observation?

A. Not since Quincy.

Q. But, it was with those full opportunities of observation to your complete satisfaction that you testified, "I don't think my opportunity afforded me the right to say he is the man"?

A. I made that answer.

A sketchy memory of a bandit momentarily glimpsed in May 1920 had, by June 1921, been replaced by a much fuller recollection not of the bandit but of the prisoner seen in the Brockton police station.

Lewis Pelser was a shoe cutter in the Rice and Hutchins factory, which faced the street where the shooting took place. He, too, was an eyewitness whose testimony changed over time. Pelser was the only witness to identify Sacco as actually shooting Berardelli. At the trial he admitted that when he spoke to the police in May 1920 he told them that he had not seen enough of the shooting to make any identification. Some months later, on March 27, 1921, he told an investigator for the defense that when he looked out of a slightly opened window he saw Berardelli lying on the ground "and I got under the bench." He had "got scared." Still later, he changed his story completely, maintaining that he saw a man shooting and that the man was Sacco. "Well, I wouldn't say it was him, but he is a dead image of him." Pelser took down the license number of the car, 49783. The plates had been stolen from a Ford in the nearby town of Needham. The shoe company robbery was carried out by men riding in a Buick. Or perhaps it was a Hudson. But the confusion over switched license plates and abandoned stolen cars suggests a sophisticated effort to confuse the police and elude detection.

The second major issue at the trial involved the defendants' alibis. Eleven prosecution witnesses had placed the defendants at the scene of the crime. The defense countered with an array of witnesses who put them elsewhere. A large number who testified in Sacco's behalf were fellow anarchists and Italians. From the jury's point of view their statements may have been suspect.

Testifying in his own behalf, Sacco explained how he had spent April 15, the day of the crime. On that pleasant and sunny day he was in Boston, where he had gone to get a passport. Sacco's mother had died in March and he felt the need to return to Italy to visit his father. Late that month or in early April, he made his first inquiry about a passport and was told that he needed a photograph of himself and his family. He made arrangements with his boss, George Kelley, to be absent on April 15 when he planned to go to Boston in the morning and return on a noon train. On the 15th, however, Sacco did not go immediately to the Italian Consulate when he reached Boston. Instead, he loafed the morning away, reading a newspaper and lunching with some journalist friends. When he got to the consulate a little after two o'clock he learned that the photograph was too large for use on his Italian passport. His trip had been a waste of time. He did not return again to the consulate until May 4, when he presented a passport photograph of the correct size. He planned to sail for Italy on the 7th of May.

There were three possible sources of support for Sacco's story. Someone from the Italian Consulate could attest to his presence on the afternoon of April 15. A lunch partner could confirm that Sacco had been at the meal. And another passenger on the Boston–Stoughton train Sacco claimed to have ridden might have seen and remembered him.

As to the first, Giuseppe Andrower, the clerk of the Italian Consulate, deposed that Sacco had come to the "Royal Italian Consulate for information on how to get a passport for Italy." He returned on April 15 with a large photograph and "since such a large photograph had never been presented for use on a passport, I took it and showed it to the Secretary of the Consulate." Andrower remembered that these events took place on the 15th because it "was a very quiet day." The consular official and he "laughed and talked over the incident. I remember observing the date in the office of the Secretary on a large pad calendar while we were discussing the photograph." Neither Sacco's defense nor the police attempted to verify Sacco's alibi immediately after the arrest. Andrower's story seems straightforward enough—but his certainty as to the date is in marked contrast to his inability to recall other dates during testimony. Moreover, since Sacco had had a passport before, he might have been expected to know the correct size for the passport photograph.

Sacco's Boston alibi also involved the lunch he had with two Italian journalists, Albert Bosco, editor of the Italian daily *La Notizia*, and Felice Guadenagi, who wrote for the *Gazetta del Massachusetts*. They had been joined by John D. Williams, an advertising agent who specialized in placing ads in foreign-language newspapers. The lunch took place on April 15 at Boni's restaurant in Boston's North End. In fixing the date of the lunch, Bosco and Guadenagi recalled that they discussed a banquet to be given that evening, the 15th of April, honoring James T. Williams, Jr., the editor of the *Boston Evening Transcript*, for his newspaper's favorable editorial policy toward Italy during the late war. Bosco in particular could not be shaken in his insistence that this was the precise day.

During the period of appeals that followed the trial, Governor Alvan T. Fuller of Massachusetts appointed an advisory committee headed by Harvard president A. Lawrence Lowell to make an impartial review of the trial record. Lowell insisted that he personally had gone through the files of the *Gazetta del Massachusetts* and found no mention of the banquet in the issue for April 15, but he did find a report of a banquet in the issue of May 14, a month later, and after Sacco and Vanzetti had been arrested. Bosco would not concede defeat on what was clearly an important point. He turned out to be correct. Bosco presented to the committee a copy of the April 16 issue of *La Notizia,* which stated that "Yesterday the Franciscan Fathers of North Bennett Street gave a banquet in honor of the new Commandante Williams."

Although the article was written in Italian, Lowell was able to read it for himself, after which he announced that a mistake had been made. He approached Bosco and Guadenagi and extended his hand to them. The court reporter recalled his saying, "Gentlemen, you remember that last night I intimated that I thought you were not telling the truth. I based this upon an examination which I had caused to be made in the files of the *Transcript* and the *Gazetta del Massachusetts.* I find that I was in error, and that the dinner which you testified to as having taken place on April 15, 1920, actually did take place on that day, as you testified. I wish to apologize to you and to express my regret for the mistake that has been made." However, when the minutes of the advisory committee proceedings for the day were printed there was no record whatever of what had occurred except the following notation:

> Investigation resumed with all the members of the Committee present. [The witness Bosco who was on the stand yesterday afternoon again appeared, with editions of *La Notizia,* requested by the Committee, and the Committee, *all* counsel present, and the witness look in the books produced by the witness.]

When Harold Ehrmann, a member of the defense legal team, learned of the omission, he was shocked. He called the court reporter's attention to a significant omission. There was no mention of the Lowell apology in the transcript of the minutes. The reporter replied that Lowell had told him not to transcribe "colloquies." Consequently, the reporter had taken no notes on what had been said. Ehrmann concluded from this that "it would appear the official record of the Bosco–Guadenagi examination was left in such an amputated condition that it ended with Mr. Lowell accusing the two men of lying." The committee report had simply omitted evidence running counter to its conclusion that the trial was error free. In November 1928, after Sacco and Vanzetti had been dead for fifteen months, Lowell finally admitted his blunder.

Against Bartolomeo Vanzetti, the Commonwealth of Massachusetts offered two eyewitnesses who claimed to identify Vanzetti as an occupant of the murder car. Michael Levangie, a gate tender for the New Haven Railroad, was on duty at the South Braintree grade crossing on the day of the murder. According to his testimony, a motor car drove up to the crossing just as Levangie was lowering the gate. A man inside the car then forced Levangie at gunpoint to let the car go through before the onrushing train. Levangie identified Vanzetti as the driver of the car. But earlier he had a different story. Henry McCarthy, a locomotive fireman on the New Haven, testified that three quarters of an hour after the murder he spoke with Levangie. McCarthy related the following:

> He says, "There was a shooting affair going on." I says, "Some one shot?" I says, "Who?" "Some one, a fellow got murdered." I said, "Who did it?" He said he did not know. He said there were some fellows went by in an automobile and he heard the shots, and he started to put down the gates, and as he started to put them down one of them pointed a gun at him and he left the gates alone and ducked into the shanty. I asked him if he knew them. He said, no, he did not. I asked him if he would know them again if he saw them. He said, "No." He said all he could see was the gun and he ducked.

Timothy J. Collins, a reporter for the *Boston Globe*, interviewed Levangie twenty minutes after the shooting. Levangie, according to Collins, "said he saw nobody, he was too damn scared to see anyone." Collins repeated what Levangie told him. "All I saw was the muzzle of that damn gun and I turned and ran for the shanty and they put a bullet through the shanty."

Levangie's testimony embarrassed the prosecution. Without it, Vanzetti might not even have been indicted. Levangie testified that Vanzetti was the driver of the murder car. Even Katzmann was made uneasy by the assertion and specifically disavowed it. Vanzetti did not even know how to drive. In his summation, Katzmann did place Vanzetti in the car. He moved him, however, to a position just behind the driver.

[T]hey say that Levangie is wrong in saying that Vanzetti was driving the car. I agree with them, gentlemen. . . . And can't you reconcile it with . . . the probability that at that time Vanzetti was directly behind the driver in the quick glance that man Levangie had of the car going over when they were going up over the crossing.

On April 15, the day of the crime, Bartolomeo Vanzetti claimed that he was in Plymouth, peddling fish. Vanzetti had no regular job, no steady employment. Because he had no regular daily routine the defense had to work carefully to establish an alibi. When Vanzetti could obtain a supply of fish, he peddled. Sometimes he dug for clams. At other times he worked on construction. But when he was doing none of these things he usually loafed and kept busy with talk. On April 15, however, he was peddling fish, an alibi corroborated by many witnesses, most of whom, unlike Sacco's witnesses, were neither anarchists nor Italians. Angelo Guido Leone, a factory worker from Plymouth, testified that he had bought fish from Vanzetti on the morning of April 15. Joseph Rosen, a cloth peddler, said he had accompanied Vanzetti to the home of Alfonsina Brini between noon and one o'clock on the 15th. Rosen remembered the date because after he left Vanzetti he went to Whitman, near South Braintree, and rented a room for the night. The clerk from the rooming house was able to verify this assertion. Melvin Corl, a fisherman, recalled a social chat with Vanzetti on the afternoon of the 15th and the two of them were joined by Frank Jesse, a Plymouth boat builder. Jesse corroborated.

So spoke the eyewitnesses. But the testimony of eyewitnesses is inconclusive. Both sides claimed to be speaking the truth. Both sides had eyewitnesses. Dealing with physical evidence proved no less difficult. The physical evidence against Vanzetti was the gun he was car-rying at the time of his arrest. It established a clear link between him and the holdup-murder. Vanzetti's .38-caliber Harrington & Richardson revolver, according to the prosecution, had been taken from the murdered guard, Berardelli, as he lay dying in the street. At the trial neither side was able to prove that Berardelli did or did not have his revolver with him at the time of the robbery or that some-thing or nothing had been taken from his body. However, evidence taken from the files of the Massachusetts State Police in 1977 make an answer to this question unnecessary. Vanzetti's revolver was a .38-caliber. Berardelli's was a .32. There is no doubt that the prosecution was aware that the weapons were of different caliber and withheld the information. They wanted a conviction.

The physical evidence against Sacco was his gun and the 32 bul-lets he was carrying the night of his arrest. Eight cartridges were in the gun clip, another was in the gun chamber, and 23 loose cartridges were in Sacco's pocket. They included three Remington, three Winchester, seven U.S., and 16 Peters cartridges. Four discharged cartridge cases, the so-called "Fraher shells," had been picked up at the scene of the murder and turned over to the police by T.F. Fraher, the Slater and Morrill superintendent. Of the six bullets extracted from the bodies of Berardelli and Parmenter, five could not have been fired from the pistols of the defendants. Those five, all with a right-hand twist, had been fired from a Savage automatic .32. But the sixth had been fired from a Colt .32 and had the distinctive Colt left-hand twist. This bullet—a Winchester cartridge known as bullet III—had caused Berardelli's death. The Commonwealth, focusing its attention on the murder of Berardelli, claimed that it was Sacco's Colt that had fired the fatal shot. At trial two expert prosecution wit-nesses, Captain William Proctor of the Massachusetts State Police and Captain Charles Van Amburgh of the Remington Arms Company of Bridgeport, gave their statements. Captain Proctor:

Q. How certain can you be then that . . . [all of the bullets but III were] fired from a Savage automatic .32?
A. I can be as certain of that as I can of anything.
Q. Have you any opinion as to whether bullet III was fired from the Colt automatic which is in evidence [Sacco's gun]?

A. I have.

Q. And what is your opinion?

A. My opinion is that it is consistent with being fired by that pistol.

Captain Van Amburgh was equally clear and direct:

Q. Now Captain, . . . having in mind your examination of No. III, [and] your examination of the six bullets fired by you and Captain Proctor at Lowell, have you formed an opinion as to whether or not the No. III bullet was fired from [Sacco's] Colt automatic gun which you have in front of you? A. I am inclined to believe that it was fired, No. III bullet was fired, from this Colt automatic pistol.

Van Amburgh was "inclined to believe" that the fatal bullet had come from Sacco's gun. Proctor said that the fatal bullet was "consistent with being fired from that pistol." Proctor's statement might very well have meant nothing more than that the bullet had been fired from a .32-caliber Colt automatic pistol, any .32 Colt automatic. Any one of the 300,000 such weapons in existence in 1920 might have been the murder weapon. Proctor later admitted that the prosecution had coached him carefully in the exact wording after he had said that he could not make a positive identification.

The defense argued that neither the bullet nor the shell had come from Sacco's Colt. But little weight can be given to the opinions of the defense witnesses. The comparison microscope, which enables experts to match bullets and weapons with a high degree of certainty, had not yet been developed. Major Calvin Goddard, who pioneered the development of the comparison microscope, in 1927 conducted an informal examination of the crucial bullet. He concluded that bullet III and the shell had been fired from Sacco's Colt pistol. More sophisticated tests in 1935, 1961, and 1983 reconfirmed the opinion that the fatal shot came from Sacco's Colt .32.

The bullet came from Sacco's gun. But did Sacco fire it? All witnesses testified that one man shot Berardelli. This man emptied his pistol and was seen to reload. Four bullets were found in Berardelli's body. Four shells were found near the body. Of the four bullets, three were from a weapon not found on either Sacco or Vanzetti. Of the four shells, only one was from a Colt. Medical Examiner George McGrath had used a surgical needle to mark each bullet with a number on removing it from the body. The Colt bullet, however, seems to have been marked with a different instrument than the other three. Four bullets, one a Colt. Four shells, one a Colt. But one gunman had been seen shooting Berardelli, and one gun.

William Thompson, Fred Moore's replacement as chief defense counsel, became convinced that bullet III and the shell, Fraher Shell W, were not genuine but were fakes. Which meant that Sacco could be innocent only if the State of Massachusetts was guilty of a grave crime. Bullet III, Thompson argued, was a plant, a substitution by the prosecution for the original, and Massachusetts had framed Sacco. The bullet introduced into evidence was certainly fired from Sacco's .32 Colt. Eyewitness testimony—if it can be believed—makes clear that the same gun had to have been used to fire all four bullets removed from Berardelli's body. The bullet, therefore, offered in evidence against Sacco could not possibly have come from Berardelli's body. If the evidence was tampered with, if there was a substitution, there is no further information about it. There is no evidence as to who was responsible, when it was carried out, and whether or not the district attorney and his office were implicated. Was Sacco framed?

And then, what of the "consciousness of guilt" issue? Surely Sacco and Vanzetti behaved like guilty men. When Judge Thayer used the phrase he meant that their conduct during and after their arrest was the conduct of murderers. The judge, in both his charge to the jury and his denial of motions for a new trial, put great stress on this kind of evidence. The accused lied when they were arrested. They were carrying guns. The judge did not believe their story that they had gone to West Bridgewater on the night of their arrest to borrow an automobile in order to collect radical, and therefore incriminating, literature from the homes of five or six associates so they could hide it. In his statements in court Judge Thayer avoided the issue of eyewitness identification. He dealt with the ballistics testimony with dispatch, making a few brief comments that did not address the conflict among the experts. But the judge's emphasis on the defendants' furtive behavior and lack of truthfulness may have left the impression with the jury that the whole case rested on "consciousness of guilt." There can be no doubt that Sacco and Vanzetti had feared arrest and punishment. They had evaded the draft. They were foreigners. They were anarchists. They preached the overthrow of government. They knew what happened to fellow anarchists during the Red Scare.

On July 14 at one o'clock in the afternoon, the jury retired. At seven-thirty that same evening the judge was informed that a verdict had been reached. Sacco and Vanzetti were guilty of murder in the first degree.

Thus ended the first chapter of the Sacco-Vanzetti story. The period between July 14, 1921, when the verdict was returned, and August 23, 1927, when the sentence of death was carried out, was crowded with efforts to obtain a new trial. The defense attorneys filed eight motions for a new trial—all of which were heard and denied by Judge Thayer. They included a motion based on affidavits by one Roy F. Gould, a carnival performer and friend of one of the defense witnesses. Gould claimed that he had seen the shooting and had given his name to the police, but had never been called for questioning by the Commonwealth. He was prepared to testify that the man shooting from the front seat of the car was neither of the defendants. In another motion, Captain Proctor impeached his own earlier expert ballistics testimony. He swore he had told Katzmann that there was no evidence pointing to Sacco's gun as the murder weapon, and that if asked a direct question would answer that there was not. Again the motion was denied, Thayer stating that the jury knew precisely what Proctor meant.

A startling development took place on November 18, 1925. On that day Sacco received a note from a fellow inmate in the Dedham jail that read, "I hear by [sic] confess to being in the South Braintree Shoe company crime and Sacco and Vanzetti was not in said crime. Celestino F. Medeiros." The confession of a criminal awaiting execution for another crime is always, of course, suspect. But Medeiros, in a series of affidavits, provided new evidence which drew the attention of the defense team to a criminal gang operating out of Providence, Rhode Island. Medeiros claimed to be a member of the gang and he reported that it "had been engaged in robbing freight cars in Providence."

The authorities of Providence and of nearby New Bedford, Massachusetts, knew the so-called Morelli gang well as professional thieves. At the time of the South Braintree crime several of them were under indictment in the U.S. District Court of Rhode Island for stealing from freight cars. They were charged with thefts of shoes from the Slater and Morrill and the Rice and Hutchins shoe companies, both of South Braintree. The gang's usual technique of criminal operation strongly suggests that they had a confederate in South Braintree to spot shipments for them. The Slater and Morrill factory was about one hundred yards from the railroad station and an accomplice spotting shipments would have had to pass the paymaster on his weekly payroll trip. The murders and the robbery for which Sacco and Vanzetti were convicted occurred in front of the Slater and Morrill and Rice and Hutchins factories. In the spring of 1920, the Morellis needed money to fight an indictment that was pending. Their only known source of funds was crime. A payroll would be quick and easy. The Morellis had been at large until five weeks after the South Braintree holdup-murder; on May 25, 1920, they were convicted and sent to the Atlanta penitentiary.

Two men had been murdered. Only one bullet and one shell were claimed to have been fired by Sacco and none by Vanzetti. The bullet that killed Berardelli came from a .32 Colt. Joe Morelli had such a weapon at the time of the crime. No one has ever explained who fired the other bullets found in the victims, but Anthony Mancini, one of the gang members, owned a pistol of a type and caliber that might have accounted for them. The murder car was identified as probably a Buick. Medeiros knew, before the matter became public knowledge, that a Buick had been used. The police of New Bedford, one of the gang's bases of operations, had originally suspected that the Morellis committed the South Braintree crime, but they dropped their investigation after Sacco and Vanzetti were arrested. A number of witnesses—prosecution as well as defense—identified Morelli when shown his photograph. Joe Morelli and Nicola Sacco, it turned out, were striking look-alikes. Felix Frankfurter in 1927 believed that there was enough new evidence to warrant retrial:

> The Morelli theory accounts for *all* members of the South
> Braintree murder gang; the Sacco-Vanzetti theory for only

two, for it is conceded that if Medeiros was there, Sacco and Vanzetti were not. . . . The Morelli explanation settles the motive, for the Morelli gang were criminals desperately in need of money for legal expenses pending their trial for felonies, whereas the Sacco-Vanzetti theory is unsupported by any motive. Moreover, Medeiros' possession of $2800 accounts for his share of the booty, whereas not a penny has ever been traced to anybody or accounted for on the Sacco-Vanzetti theory. The Morelli story is not subject to the absurd premise that professional hold-up men who stole automobiles at will and who had recently made a haul of nearly $16,000 would devote an evening, as did Sacco and Vanzetti the night of their arrest, to riding around on suburban street cars to borrow a friend's six-year-old Overland. The character of the Morelli gang fits the opinion of police investigators and the inherent facts of the situation, which tended to prove that the crime was the work of professionals, whereas the past character and record of Sacco and Vanzetti have always made it incredible that they should spontaneously become perpetrators of a bold murder, executed with the utmost expertness. . . .

Celestino Medeiros told his story because, he said, he "felt sorry for Mrs. Sacco and the kids." He wanted to save Sacco, and he thought his confession would do it. Faithful to an apparent gangland commitment to silence, at no time did he name the gang or Joe Morelli. But if he didn't name names, he described the men, and their descriptions fit the members of the Morelli gang.

But once again Judge Thayer denied the motion for a new trial because of the untrustworthiness, which he assumed, of the Medeiros confession. A man who seeks to relieve another of guilt while he himself awaits execution, as Frankfurter pointed out, does not carry conviction. But Medeiros, at the time of his confession, had an appeal pending. Could anything, Frankfurter asked, "be more prejudicial to an effort to reverse his conviction for one crime than to admit guilt for another?" Nevertheless, the motion was denied.

Judge Webster Thayer rejected all motions for a new trial and the Massachusetts Supreme Judicial Court upheld him. By 1927 the case had become an international cause célèbre. Demonstrations on behalf of Sacco and Vanzetti were international in their scope: they took place in South America; in Milan and Turin, Italy; in London; in Berlin; and in various parts of Africa and Asia. In response, slightly more than two months before the scheduled day of execution, Governor Fuller appointed his three-member advisory committee to consider the fairness of the verdict. Chairman A. Lawrence Lowell was a pillar of Boston society and a lawyer by training. His membership in the Immigration Restriction League and the fact that he had, as president of Harvard University, introduced formal quotas to limit the number of Jewish students reveal his capacity for ethnocentrism. The other two committee members were Samuel Stratton, president of the Massachusetts Institute of Technology, a man with no reputation in public affairs, and Robert Grant, a retired judge better known for his attendance at black-tie parties than for his legal acumen.

The committee was dominated by its chairman. For over ten days it heard testimony on the evidence, much of it new. On July 27, 1927, the committee filed its final report, upholding the verdict and the sentence against Sacco and Vanzetti and denying charges of prejudice against Judge Thayer. "Affidavits," it said, "were presented to the Committee and witnesses were heard to the effect that the Judge, during and after the trial, had expressed his opinion of guilt in vigorous terms. Prejudice means, at least in this case, an opinion or sentiment before the trial. That a judge should form an opinion as the evidence comes in is inevitable. . . ." But the witnesses before the Lowell Committee had shown that the judge's expressions of opinion began at the very start of the trial, even before defense testimony. Philip Stong, for many years a feature writer for the North American Newspaper Alliance, reported Judge Thayer as having remarked to a group of his friends, "Did you see what I did to those anarchistic bastards the other day?" On another occasion he heard Thayer refer to the defendants as "Dagoes" and "sons of bitches." Frank Sibley, a reporter for the *Boston Globe*, stopped lunching at the Dedham Court Inn in order to avoid Judge Thayer and his indiscreet remarks. But the committee determined that

> [f]rom all that has come to us we are forced to conclude that
> the judge was indiscreet in conversations with outsiders dur-

ing the trial. He ought not to have talked about the case off the bench, and doing so was *a grave breach of official decorum*. But we do not believe that he used some of the expressions attributed to him, and we think that there is exaggeration in what the persons to whom he spoke remember. Furthermore, we believe that such indiscretions in conversation did not affect his conduct at the trial or the opinions of the jury, who indeed so stated to the Committee.

Despite last-minute appeals to the federal courts, Sacco and Vanzetti were put to death on August 22, 1927. Newspaper columnist Heywood Broun remarked a short time before the execution, "What more can the immigrants from Italy expect? It is not every prisoner who has a President of Harvard throw the switch for him."

In the years since Governor Dukakis' historic proclamation, interest in the matter has not abated, nor has the case of Sacco and Vanzetti finally been resolved. Their guilt has not been established, many people believe, "beyond a reasonable doubt." The Massachusetts governor's proclamation of 1977 judged the trial to have been flawed. It is unlikely that it will ever be possible to determine with reasonable certainty what really happened on April 15, 1920.

2

THE CHICAGO "BLACK SOX"

April 23 was the opening day of the 1919 baseball season and in St. Louis the Chicago White Sox trounced the Browns 13 to 4. Claude "Lefty" Williams pitched for the Sox as Chicago bombarded three Browns pitchers for 21 hits. "Shoeless" Joe Jackson sprayed the field with line drives and Captain Eddie Collins banged out his first homer of the year.

In 1919 baseball was the undisputed national pastime. Around it had developed a reverential dogma promoted by publicists, team owners and baseball heroes. Unlike businessmen and politicians, who might be corruptible, baseball players, in the public mind, were ruggedly honest, their profession untarnished by commercialism. President William Howard Taft had described baseball merely as "a clean, straight game," but many Americans ranked respect for baseball with respect for religion and motherhood.

During the years between the two world wars—baseball's golden age—fans went out to the ballparks in record numbers. While watching this all-American sport, many fans believed that Bolsheviks, anarchists, and other dissenters were a threat to the nation's values. There were, said Attorney General A. Mitchell Palmer, 60,000 dangerous alien radicals in the United States ready to bring the Russian revolution to America. Baseball was welcome relief, and attendance and profits climbed during the decade of the Twenties.

Throughout that decade impressive new stadiums rose in place of simple old ones; steel and concrete structures replaced wood. Forbes Field in Pittsburgh was the first of these, but the 74,000-seat Yankee

Stadium that opened in 1923 was certainly the most impressive. Contributing to the rise in attendance, to the profits, and to the building of the super-stadiums was the defeat of Sunday baseball's opponents. Although liberal churchmen supported Sunday baseball as a diversion for working people, church leaders in general deplored baseball on the Sabbath. Some were fearful that Sunday games were adjuncts to the saloons. Nevertheless, Sunday baseball soon became a fixture.

Baseball reflected American life, and it shared the xenophobia that was an important characteristic of the 1920s. *Sporting News*, the weekly trade newspaper of organized baseball, held that cities were an alien element in American culture. They were filled with large numbers of non-Anglo-Saxons, people who rejected the honest ideal of sports. What the immigrant needed to learn, *Sporting News* urged, was that baseball was not "something for sale . . . that money is not the basis of all games rather than play." Jews, in particular, the newspaper argued after the arrest of six gamblers, were responsible for tarnishing the game. "Do you get their names? . . . [They are the sort who] are generally most active in trying to besmirch baseball with their gambling."

Baseball did, however, share the entrepreneurial spirit of the decade. Business leaders were developing mergers to join together organizations working at related production activities in different communities. The minor league farm system was baseball's version of vertical integration. Originated by Branch Rickey, then with the St. Louis Cardinals, the farm system improved organization and rationalized and articulated player recruitment and development. Less wealthy clubs like St. Louis could not compete in the player market with New York, Chicago, and Pittsburgh—teams with ample resources—so Rickey, who had been born on a farm, decided to grow his own crop on his own land and did so with great success.

The 1920s was a time when Americans made athletes and entertainers into cultural heroes. An adoring public worshiped movie actors like "The Sheik," Rudolph Valentino, and baseball players like George Herman Ruth, referred to admiringly as "The Babe," "The Bambino," "The Sultan of Swat," "The Caliph of Clout," and other endearing terms. Babe Ruth became baseball's greatest star. There may have been better athletes and even better players, but none achieved the adulation that Ruth received. In the 1920s only Charles Lindbergh, "Lucky Lindy," surpassed Ruth in public adoration. Ruth brought to baseball a new style of play: the big bang of the home run. His fame grew not only because of the number of home runs he hit, but also because of how far he hit them. In his first year as a New York Yankee, 1920, he hit 54 home runs, double the number hit by record holder Ed Williamson in 1884. By 1921, Ruth was a national idol who brought fans into ballparks all over the American League, and Yankee Stadium soon came to be known as "The House That Ruth built." The meteoric rise of Ruth was well-timed, because during the middle of that season a jury was empowered to decide whether baseball had been infected with corruption. Eight Chicago White Sox players were standing trial for taking bribes to throw the 1919 World Series.

In 1919 attention had focused on the Midwest. In the fall the Cincinnati Reds were National League champions and the Chicago White Sox had taken the American League pennant. When they faced each other in the World Series, the outcome—to baseball's shame— had been prearranged. Professional gamblers and White Sox players had formed a conspiracy to throw the World Series to the underdog Cincinnati Reds. The fix was on. The White Sox became known as the "Black Sox" in the ensuing scandal.

The scandal should not have struck the baseball world with such force, for neither gambling nor even the fixing of professional baseball games was unknown in 1919, despite the image presented to the world. Even after the appointment of a baseball commissioner in 1920, gambling continued to take place in ballparks. The *New York Evening Sun* in June 1919 noted that gamblers were at work in the Polo Grounds, home of the New York Giants, and in the same article praised the Yankees for trying to clean up the situation at its own park. Even though they constantly cried out against the practice, club owners were remiss in their vigilance and their enforcement, or perhaps they really favored gambling because it brought fans into the ballparks. At their meetings the owners passed resolutions condemning gambling and they sometimes expelled or barred known gamblers from the stadiums. But their actions were more often perfunctory. The efforts of law enforcement authorities to control gambling at racetracks often only diverted the gamblers from the tracks to the ballparks.

What compounded the problem was that baseball men themselves—the owners, the managers, and the players—were not averse to gambling. New York Giants manager John McGraw and "Ban" Johnson, president of the American League, and others as well, were known to have placed more than a few bets. Players often wagered on their own teams. Such gambling might be innocent enough, but what if they bet against their own clubs and then helped bring about the desired results? And inevitably they did.

In 1876 several players on the Louisville Colonels of the National League had confessed to throwing games and were barred from professional baseball for life. The "Louisville precedent" established a lifetime ban against deliberately losing a game. There was, however, no precedent for lesser offenses, for agreeing to throw a game and then double-crossing the conspirators by playing honestly, or for keeping silent about a known fix.

The gambling exploits of Hal Chase, the premier first baseman of the Cincinnati Reds, were widely known. Chase openly and regularly consorted with gamblers; soon he arranged matters for himself and bet accordingly. He learned how to mess up a play and make others look inept. Chase also corrupted, or tried to corrupt, other players as well. Finally he became a full-fledged fixer and gambler, collecting commissions on money he got others to bet on games that he himself fixed. Hal Chase eventually was charged with betting on the Cincinnati Reds in the 1919 World Series and was indicted by the grand jury that also indicted eight Black Sox players.

As World Series time approached in 1919, the Chicago White Sox, with one of the best baseball teams ever assembled, were heavy favorites to win. Eddie Collins, from Columbia University, at second base, and Ray Schalk, behind the plate, were among the very best at their positions. Schalk was eventually elected to the Baseball Hall of Fame. Collins was smart, smart enough to draw a good salary from owner Charles Comiskey, the tightest of tightwads. Many of Collins' teammates resented his salary, distrusted him, and ignored his authority as captain. In left field was "Shoeless" Joe Jackson, an illiterate country boy from Brandon Mill, South Carolina, and one of the greatest natural hitters who ever played. When Jackson left baseball he had a lifetime batting average of .356. The ace of the White Sox pitching staff, Urban "Red" Faber, also a Hall of Famer, was a master of the unpredictable spitball but was unable to play in the Series because of a sore arm. Righthander Eddie Cicotte had had his best year in 1919; he finished the season with 29 victories and was scheduled to pitch the opening game of the Series. Claude "Lefty" Williams was a finesse pitcher, one of the cleverest control pitchers in the game. Williams had won 23 games in 1919 by almost always knowing, people said, exactly what to throw. By all accounts George "Buck" Weaver was the classiest third baseman in the game. The rest of the team—Charles "Swede" Risberg at shortstop, Oscar "Happy" Felsch in centerfield, and Arnold "Chick" Gandil at first base—were journeyman players.

The Sox were managed by William "Kid" Gleason, who was in his first year, and perhaps not quite as knowledgeable or clever as Pat Moran, the Cincinnati manager. The major force in the Sox organization was owner Comiskey, whose sole income came from baseball. The White Sox ballpark, completely rebuilt in 1991, still bears his name. Comiskey became notorious for self-defeating penuriousness toward his players. The money he saved by underpaying stars like Jackson, Cicotte, Weaver, and the others probably cost him the World Series in 1919, the American League pennant in 1920, and many thousands of dollars in uncultivated talent. Because his fortune depended on the support of the fans, Comiskey took pains to treat them well, and he became baseball's most popular owner. Because newspapers were crucial in promoting Comiskey's point of view, he cultivated their writers. Reporters rode in Pullmans as guests of the club owner, all expenses paid. The contrast made his ballplayers feel like dirt.

Comiskey's players were the best and he paid them like the worst — except for Collins, who had a five-year contract at $15,000 per year. Buck Weaver was, next to Collins, the highest paid, although he got less than half of what Collins got: $7250. Joe Jackson never got more than $6000. Eddie Cicotte received only $5000 and a bonus of $2000 for winning 28 games.

The salaries of the Cincinnati Reds made quite a contrast with Comiskey's miserly scale. Ed Roush, the team's leading hitter, was often 40 to 50 points behind Jackson but pulled down $10,000. Henry "Heinie" Groh, at third base, made $2000 more than Weaver. Other salaries were similarly higher than Comiskey's stinginess would permit. But more than stinginess angered the White Sox. There was a general sense of having been cheated and deceived by Comiskey, and it was keenly felt by more than a few of them.

Eddie Cicotte, for example, had been promised a bonus of $10,000 in 1917 if he could win 30 games. As he approached the magic number, Comiskey had him benched, claiming that he was being saved for the World Series. The players believed that Comiskey had promised all of them a bonus if they won the pennant in 1917. They did win, and they hoped for a handsome reward. Then the team learned that the bonus would be nothing but the case of champagne they had enjoyed at the victory celebration. And while all the other teams in the American League allowed their players a minimum of $4 per day for meal money when the teams were on the road, Comiskey permitted no more than $3. In addition to the low morale brought on by Comiskey's tightfistedness, the White Sox suffered from dissension among the players, so serious as to be noticeable even to fans. During pre-game warm-ups the Sox infielders avoided throwing to Eddie Collins and the fans could sense the hostility. The team was sharply factionalized between the players and Comiskey as well as among the players themselves. Kid Gleason could do little about it.

In 1919 the Cincinnati Reds were National League champions for the first time since 1882. Their brightest star, Ed Roush, had won the batting title for the second time and was regarded as the best defensive outfielder in baseball. The Cincinnati pitching staff included Walter "Dutch" Reuther, a smart and daring lefthander with a 19 and 6 won–lost record who was, when sober, as good as any pitcher in either league. Harry "Slim" Sallee had won more than 20 games and righthander Hod Eller had won 19, among them a no-hitter. The Reds were also strong in the bullpen, where the White Sox were weak. Even if the White Sox had a slight edge over the Reds in a position-by-position evaluation, the Reds had been good enough to win the pennant in a league with some strong teams. On the other hand, Chicago had beaten the New York Giants in the 1917 World Series with virtually the same team. The White Sox were favored, but the Reds were not to be underestimated. As October approached, they were sentimental favorites but definite underdogs.

On October 1, 1919, the World Series opened in Cincinnati. The Sinton Hotel, where the players were staying, teemed with gamblers. Before game time a heavy influx of Cincinnati money came in and the odds shifted. From 2-to-1 underdogs the Reds became 6-to-5 favorites. Jack Doyle, whose New York City Billiard Academy was an important post for bookmakers, estimated that more than two million dollars had been bet the night before the opening game. "You couldn't miss it," he said, ". . . the thing had an odor. . . . I saw smart guys take even money on the Sox who should have been asking five to one."

The result of the first game astounded everyone—except the ballplayers and the gamblers involved in the fix. Eddie Cicotte, who had won 29 games, was driven to the showers in the fourth inning. He had seemed tired and his control was bad. The Reds won easily, 9 to 1. The *New York Times*, in its first-page story, showed complete astonishment: "Never before in the history of America's biggest baseball spectacle has a pennant winning club received such a disastrous drubbing in an opening game as the far-famed White Sox got this afternoon." How could it have happened? It was a fluke, said some. Others claimed that the Reds had been underrated. Fans were delighted or dismayed by the triumph of the underdog and recalled the "Miracle Braves" of Boston who, five years earlier, had risen dramatically from last place on July 18 to a championship season. Some observers argued that the star and starting pitcher, Cicotte, was just tired after his 29-game winning season.

The White Sox then lost the second game. Lefty Williams, famous for his control, walked six. The Sox went down three more times, losing the Series five games to three. The Cincinnati Reds were the world champions.

Almost immediately rumors of collusion began to circulate. *Spalding's Guide*, the annual compilation of baseball data and statistics, dismissed the rumors as unfounded and explained that the baseball experts had failed to give the Reds credit for having such a first-rate team. Even Hugh Fullerton of the *Chicago Herald Examiner*, one of the game's most respected reporters, discounted the rumors at first. He had been a journalist for a long time and had learned not to take every rumor seriously. Nevertheless, the day after the Series ended Fullerton began to have serious suspicions. He consulted the great Christy Mathewson and learned about every possible way in which a ballplayer might throw a game. "Matty" described the thin line that separated an effective pitch from a disastrous one and a beautiful play in the field from a spectacular near-miss. A short time later, in

December 1919, catcher Ray Schalk gave an interview in Chicago in which he claimed that he was absolutely certain seven of his teammates who had played in the Series would not be with the team in the 1920 season. When *Sporting News* subsequently asked him to elaborate, Schalk denied the earlier statement and defended the legitimacy of the Series.

Charles Comiskey tried to hush up the whole issue by denying any wrongdoing by his players. "These yarns . . . grow out of bitterness due to losing wagers," he said. "I believe my boys fought the battles of the recent World Series on the level, as they have always done." Comiskey then offered $20,000 (inexplicably halved in later statements) for even a "single clue," at the same time claiming that there was nothing to the rumors. Fullerton believed that Comiskey was naive, but he still had no direct evidence of a fix. "I have no proof that any players are guilty. But one thing is certain: gamblers have stated that they have put over this thing, and that they have solicited capital from others on the ground that they could control players."

From this point on, Comiskey resorted to deviousness as a way of dealing with suspicion. Three days after the Series ended, the White Sox management knew almost as much about the fix as it would ever know, but Comiskey made no attempt to reveal any of this knowledge to Fullerton, even though he invited him in for a confidential discussion. What seemed to be a solid agreement between Comiskey and Fullerton turned out to be only another example of the owner's lack of scruples. At the confidential meeting, Comiskey asked Fullerton to investigate and use the newspaper resources at his command. The two would share their information. If Fullerton got proof of the players' guilt, he was to bring it to Comiskey, who would then make a public revelation. Comiskey was aware that in this way he would be seen as willing to wreck his own team in the name of honest baseball. A selfless hero. On the other hand, if Fullerton found no proof, Comiskey could continue to deny wrongdoing and simply wait for the rumors to fade away. But Comiskey did not tell Fullerton that he had hired a private detective to investigate not only those of his own players whom he suspected but to look for evidence of corruption in other teams as well. Comiskey would then be able to threaten exposure of corrupt activities and prevent other owners from taking action against the White Sox. Fullerton never learned how Comiskey was using him.

Throughout the rest of the year, charges and rumors continued. When the new season opened in 1920, all the White Sox who had been on the World Series team were back, save one. Chick Gandil had held out for a time for more money and finally announced that he was leaving to manage a team in Idaho. By the middle of the season it appeared that the rumors about the 1919 season were over. The baseball public was captivated by a new sensation: Babe Ruth's home-run spree. It was the year of the 54 homers.

The story of the World Series fix of 1919 was only brought to light, almost incidentally, as the result of the investigation of another matter. A Cook County, Illinois, grand jury was looking into charges of a fixed game in 1920 between the Chicago Cubs and the Philadelphia Phillies. Apparently a huge amount of money was bet on the Phillies—money that shifted the odds from 2 to 1 for the Cubs to 6 to 5 for the Phillies. The Cubs management was so suspicious it hired the Burns detective agency to investigate and invited the Chicago Baseball Writers Association to do the same. By the time the grand jury met, on September 22, 1920, the scope of the investigation had been expanded to include the World Series of 1919. This decision followed revelation that White Sox owner Comiskey had delayed sending World Series bonus checks to eight players. Comiskey then announced that he had become convinced after the first game that the Series had been fixed. He said he had told the president of the National League of his suspicions. He and Ban Johnson, president of his own American league, were not on speaking terms. Comiskey was now admitting what he had solemnly denied for a whole year.

A breakthrough in the grand jury hearings came just a few days after they began. James Isaminger of the *Philadelphia North American* wrote a story headlined "Gamblers Promised White Sox $100,000 to Lose." The story was based on an interview with a small-time gambler named Billy Maharg, who had acted as a go-between. There were, said Maharg, some Sox who threw both the first and the second games of the Series. They were promised $100,000. Maharg didn't know anything beyond the third game and nothing about other possible fixes.

The day after the story appeared, September 28, 1920, saw a second breakthrough: Eddie Cicotte and Joe Jackson confessed to the grand jury. Before his appearance Cicotte had spoken to Alfred Austrian, Comiskey's lawyer and also attorney for the Chicago White

Sox. Believing that since Austrian was Comiskey's lawyer, he was his lawyer too, Cicotte followed Austrian's advice. This was to admit his guilt, say he was sorry, and hope for the best. He signed a waiver of immunity, again with Austrian's counsel, without knowing what it meant. Jackson, believing what Cicotte believed, did the same. They told the grand jury that in addition to the first two games, two others were thrown. Even more shocking, they implicated six of their team-mates. According to Cicotte's confession, he lost both the first and the fourth games with carefully contrived actions. He purposely put noth-ing on some of his pitches. He purposely hit a batter, and by doing so gave a prearranged signal that the fix was on. He purposely stopped a throw from the outfield that might have cut off a run. He did all this, he said, for $10,000 that had been secretly placed under his pillow before the first game. He let himself be bribed, he said, for his "wife and kids. I'd bought a farm. There was a four thousand dollar mort-gage on it. There isn't any mortgage on it now." But Cicotte's confes-sion did not identify the gamblers.

According to Cicotte and Jackson, Chick Gandil had orchestrated the fix, feeling out the players and making the offer. Jackson said that for days Gandil had been at him. It was very easy, Gandil assured Joe; all he had to do was to "let the ball drop a few feet in front" of him. He shouldn't hit the big one with men on. He could look good and still play badly. Jackson was troubled. He didn't trust Gandil at all. He decided to see Comiskey to ask that he be benched for the Series. "Tell the newspapers you just suspended me for being drunk," he asked, "or anything, but leave me out of the Series. . . ." Comiskey laughed off Jackson's request. At length Shoeless Joe agreed to go along with the fix. Gandil had talked him into it—and then double-crossed him over the money. Jackson got only part of a promised $20,000. A dirty enve-lope containing $5000 was delivered by Lefty Williams. The rest was to come when the Series was over. But Jackson, still troubled, refused to accept the money from Williams, who just dropped it on the floor and left. The next day, Jackson took the envelope to Comiskey, but Comiskey would not see him. Comiskey apparently wanted to let the rumors that were circulating just fade away. Whether they were crooked or honest, the White Sox players were valuable property, and Comiskey was not prepared to lose them.

Claude Williams, who failed to win the second game, revealed the names of two gamblers who were emissaries for other, bigger, New York gamblers. Happy Felsch, the Sox centerfielder, also confessed, but not to the grand jury. He spoke to a newspaperman. Felsch admitted taking $5000, but he, too, left a doubt about whether he played to lose. "I'm not saying that I doublecrossed the gamblers but I had nothing to do with the loss of the World Series. The breaks just came so that I was not given a chance to do anything toward throwing the games. . . ."

Shortsop Swede Risberg, Buck Weaver, the third baseman, and Fred McMullin, a utility infielder, posted bonds of $10,000 each and protested their innocence. Weaver admitted that he was present at two of the meetings between players and gamblers, but he'd declined to participate, he said, and called attention to his fine performance during the Series. Weaver was never accused of participating in the fix, so far as his playing was involved. Chick Gandil, the alleged leader of the players, skipped out, fleeing to Arizona and refusing to appear before the grand jury.

The scandal shocked the public. Even the news of Attorney General A. Mitchell Palmer's actions against "reds and bolsheviks" took a backseat. Newspaper comment was unanimous. The *Philadelphia Bulletin* likened a player who took part in the fix to "the soldier or sailor who would sell out his country and its flag in time of war." The *Chicago Tribune* bemoaned the fact that the news "almost destroys our faith in human nature." And there was violence. Infielder Buck Herzog of the Cubs was stabbed by an overwrought fan in Joliet, Illinois. He didn't play for the White Sox, but "Chicago" on his uniform was enough to arouse anger.

The grand jury indicted eight White Sox players on charges of conspiracy. Ten gamblers were also indicted for the same crime, including Abe Attell, one-time world featherweight boxing champion and a member of the entourage of notorious gambler Arnold Rothstein. Rothstein himself escaped indictment.

At Charles Comiskey's dictation, Harry Grabiner, White Sox secretary, sent the following telegram to the eight players:

> You and each of you are hereby notified of your indefinite suspension as a member of the Chicago American League Baseball Club. Your suspension is brought about by informa-

tion which has just come to me directly involving you and each of you in the baseball scandal now being investigated by the Grand Jury of Cook County, resulting from the World Series of 1919.

If you are innocent of any wrongdoing, you and each of you will be reinstated; if you are guilty, you will be retired from organized baseball for the rest of your lives if I can accomplish it.

Until there is a finality to this investigation, it is due to the public that I take this action even though it costs Chicago the pennant.

Among baseball men the scandal was more than distressing. They were fearful of its consequences, because working its way up through the court system was an anti-trust case that eventually was decided in baseball's favor. The standard baseball contract's "reserve clause" gave a club an exclusive and perpetual option on a player's services. Every club in organized baseball recognized it and all agreed not to employ any player "reserved" by another club. If baseball were to be found "in restraint of trade," relations between the American and National Leagues and between the major leagues and the minor leagues would be destroyed. Revelations of corruption made a difficult situation worse. Finally, however, in 1922 the Supreme Court ruled that baseball was not "trade or commerce in the commonly accepted use of those words," because "personal effort, not related to production, is not a subject of commerce." Moreover, the travel of baseball teams across state lines was not interstate commerce but merely an "incidental" activity. Baseball was not subject to the Sherman Anti-Trust Act. The owners could continue to depend on the reserve clause for stability.

To the fans generally, the 1919 Series scandal was an outrage. It was not simply a story of betrayal, of eight players who had sold them out. The fans believed that the problem was bigger and more serious. The rumors, the bickering, the dissension and turmoil that seemed to have overtaken baseball appeared to be signs of a malignant inner rot. Something was fundamentally wrong in America. Some of the White Sox players felt they had been betrayed. Following the eight indictments, the "lily white" group (whose play during the Series was collectively far worse than that of the indicted players) said as much. Eddie Collins, captain of the team, explained, "We've known for a long time, but we felt we had to keep silent because we were fighting for the [1920] pennant." Another said, "No one will ever know what we put up with this summer. Hardly any of us have talked with any of those fellows, except on the ball field since the season opened . . . and all the time felt that they had thrown us down. It was tough. . . ."

Professional gambler Arnold Rothstein was the owner of the Havre-de-Grace racetrack and of Saratoga's exclusive resort, The Brook. Newspapers referred to him as a sportsman. Others called him "the financial genius of the underworld plutocracy." His father simply said he was a hoodlum. Rothstein was involved in betting on race-horses, on ball games, on elections, and on prize fights. He would bet, people said, on anything except the weather, because there was no way of fixing that. He not only operated some very plush gambling hous-es, but among his clients he included Charles Stoneham, owner of the New York Giants, and other baseball owners. Rothstein bankrolled the Black Sox fix. When the idea was first proposed, he had been reluctant because he knew what Billy Maharg and others had in mind. He didn't believe it would work and he had little respect for Maharg. But as he learned more he relented, concluding that the number of players involved might provide just the kind of camouflage he want-ed: "If nine guys go to bed with a girl," he said, "she'll have trouble proving the tenth is the father."

Following exposure of the scandal, Rothstein retained well-known criminal lawyer William A. Fallon, who had a reputation for both bril-liance and lack of scruples. Fallon immediately took the offensive and convinced Rothstein to appear before the grand jury voluntarily and assume an attitude of injured innocence. Rothstein blamed the fix on ex-fighter Abe Attell, "who had used my name to put it over. . . . But I wasn't in on it under any circumstances, and didn't bet a cent on the Series after I found what was under way."

The grand jury believed Rothstein and so did the district attorney. Alfred Austrian, attorney for Comiskey and the White Sox, went even further. Rothstein, he said, "had proved himself guiltless." Comiskey hated the grand jury investigation. Like other baseball men, he believed that baseball owners should deal with their own problems; the clubs and their difficulties should not be held up to public scrutiny.

Fallon's method of protecting Rothstein by placing him before the grand jury was calculated. He knew that baseball owners would make every effort to conceal any connection between baseball players and the likes of Arnold Rothstein. Not one would be willing to lay a legal hand on the gambler.

The grand jury continued its investigation. What if other testimony pointed to Rothstein? The law would require that he be indicted. Fallon knew that he had to get his hands on any incriminating testimony, and so did Comiskey. The signed confessions and immunity waivers that had been executed by Cicotte, Jackson, and Williams meant that anything they said could be used to prosecute them—a legal point that Austrian had not bothered to explain to them. These documents would be the basis for any indictment and for any subsequent trial. The documents were critical. Something would have to be done about them.

Even before the grand jury completed its work, plans were afoot to establish a new form of self-governance for professional baseball. The National Commission, which had been established in 1903, was simply not functioning as it should. This three-man body was made up of the two major league presidents and a third member chosen by them to serve as chairman. The Black Sox scandal emphasized the need for a new and stronger form of governance to replace the commission—a need that had already been recognized. Steps toward change were already underway.

A year before the scandal, Albert Lasker, a prominent Chicago businessman and leading stockholder in the Chicago Cubs, had argued that it would be better for professional baseball to be monitored by some group or leader with enough power to punish players as well as owners, and even with the power to declare a franchise forfeit. It was necessary, Lasker believed, that baseball be run by some person or group other than the baseball owners themselves. Lasker's plan called for a three-man committee of eminent citizens without financial interests in baseball who would be given ample and "unreviewable authority" to reprimand, fine, and otherwise punish both players and owners.

The eminent citizens under consideration were General John J. Pershing, who had led the American Expeditionary Force in Europe during World War I; William McAdoo, son-in-law of President

Woodrow Wilson and a leading contender for the Democratic presidential nomination in 1924; federal judge Kenesaw Mountain Landis; Senator Hiram Johnson; and General Leonard Wood, former United States Army Chief of Staff. The plan was strongly supported by the president of the National League and by the owners of the National League teams. Also in support were owners of the American League teams in Chicago, New York, and Boston. The group favoring reorganization thus included four teams from the two biggest money-making cities and three American League teams that were prepared to sever connections with their own league and throw in their lot with the Nationals.

The plan was opposed by the president of the American League, Ban Johnson, and owners of the five remaining American League teams. The schism in the league had begun as early as 1919 with a quarrel over a controversial trade involving a right-handed pitcher that put the Yankee and Red Sox owners on one side and Johnson on the other. Reciprocal hostility between Johnson and Comiskey went back even further. Clashes between them had been occurring since the turn of the century, but a permanent rift resulted from an episode in 1905 when a White Sox outfielder was suspended by the league president without informing the White Sox management until minutes before game time. Comiskey was left shorthanded in the outfield and permanently antagonistic toward Johnson.

The split over reorganizing was healed, in the main, because the Johnson faction did not have the resources to challenge the other eleven clubs. The eleven simply threatened to go their own way without the participation of those that stood with Johnson. Johnson was realistic. He knew that he had no chance to win the battle, especially since his allies had made it clear that they did not want a long contest that would be both useless and wasteful. On November 12, 1920, organized baseball framed the basic governance structure that stands to this day. Judge Landis was confirmed unanimously for a term of seven years as chairman of a new commission. Within a short time the idea of a three-man commission was dropped and the reins of autocratic power were placed in Landis' hands alone. He became the final arbiter in all disputes involving the leagues, the players, and the individual teams. The owners agreed to be "bound by the decisions of the Commissioner" and "to the discipline imposed by him." At the same time, they waived the right to resort to the courts. The commissioner became the court of last resort. Even before the trial of the eight accused players and the gamblers began, the baseball owners—like the movie studio owners a bit later, and like them also following a scandal—found a way for a business engaged in questionable practices to give the appearance of cleaning up its own affairs.

It was Kenesaw Mountain Landis who shored up the image of baseball at this time of grave crisis. Fearing that the disclosure of corruption might turn the public against the game and ruin their properties, the club owners felt the urgency of placing baseball under the custody of a strong leader. They wanted a man whose integrity would not be questioned and who could restore the public's faith in the sport. They also wanted someone whose authority would serve as a bulwark against repetition of the scandal.

Landis was named after the site of a Civil War battle in which his father, a surgeon, had been wounded in the leg. Even though he did not graduate from high school, he attended the YMCA Law School in Cincinnati and completed his legal training at Union Law School (now merged into Northwestern University Law School). In 1893 he served as clerk to Secretary of State Walter Gresham. In 1904 he returned to Illinois to manage Frank Lowden's campaign for governor. President Theodore Roosevelt appointed him to the federal bench in 1905. He became a judge in the United States District Court for Northern Illinois, a district that included Chicago. His record as a federal judge was not without difficulty. During World War I he went after pacifists and anti-war defendants with a vengeance. Many important cases that he decided were overturned by the Supreme Court and Landis was called "heartless." It was charged that he abused power and that he condemned or exonerated according to whim, that when the law did not seem amenable to his desired interpretation he often ignored it. But he was strong.

Judge Landis had come to the attention of organized baseball in 1915 in a case involving an anti-trust suit against the National Commission by some teams calling themselves the Federal League. Landis delayed judgment in the case. The Federal League collapsed and Landis dismissed the suit. Organized baseball benefited significantly and Landis won much appreciation, but even after his appointment in 1920 he continued to try to have his own way. He intended to stay on the bench while serving as baseball commissioner. When he didn't leave the court, there was a movement in Congress to impeach him. Landis then resigned his judgeship and devoted full time to his work as commissioner.

Two weeks after becoming Commissioner of Baseball, Landis faced the issue of the indicted players. They had been suspended and were awaiting trial. A high-powered legal group was retained to represent them. It included Michael Ahern, later to head a defense team for Al Capone. Thomas Nash and Ben Short were prominent and powerful attorneys and they were expensive, too expensive for the defendants. At first the players made some token payments. Soon they realized that their legal fees were being taken care of by others. Comiskey was paying the tab. For Charles Comiskey, the players represented a big investment. He wanted them acquitted. An unusual development occurred when four of the prosecuting attorneys switched sides and joined the defense. Again, the fees were paid by Comiskey.

There were five separate conspiracy charges against the players in one indictment. The same charges applied against the gamblers.

(1) conspiracy to defraud the public;

(2) conspiracy to defraud catcher Ray Schalk (of the difference between the winner's and the loser's share of World Series money);

(3) conspiracy to commit a confidence game (on Charles Nims, a Chicago fan who lost $250 betting on the White Sox);

(4) conspiracy to injure the business of the American League;

(5) conspiracy to injure the business of Charles A. Comiskey.

The defense failed in its motion to have the case dismissed, and so began the tedious job of impaneling the jury. On hand for jury selection were 100 veniremen. Each side was allowed 120 peremptory challenges—an unusually large number. Over 600 prospective jurors were eventually questioned by both sides, with queries ranging from "Do you know any ballplayers and did you see the World Series?" to "What value would you attach to the testimony of a co-conspirator?" It took two full weeks, until July 15, 1921, to complete a jury. Two clerks and two machinists were serving, a telephone repairman, a stationary engineer, a hydraulic press operator, a salesman, a steel worker, a florist, and two foremen, one in a stockyard rendering plant and the other in a motor company. Most of the jurors were under thirty-six years of age and all but two were married. One of them admitted he was a White Sox fan but had bet on the Reds because he believed they were a better team.

By the time the trial opened, only seven of the original eight player indictments remained. The state dropped its case against utility infielder Fred McMullin for lack of evidence. The case against the others was going to rest on the confessions of Joe Jackson, Eddie Cicotte, and Lefty Williams, and on their waivers of immunity. Proceedings had barely got underway when State Attorney George Gorman rocked the court with a revelation that created a host of legal problems and forced Illinois to rely heavily on the testimony of gamblers Billy Maharg and "Sleepy" Bill Burns. Burns, a Texan, had been a third-rate pitcher for a few years but finally left the major leagues in 1917 to go into the oil business. He established connections with some Philadelphia gamblers and was involved in a meeting with Cicotte and Gandil, along with Maharg, to try to fix the Series. Gorman announced that documents containing the confessions of the three ballplayers—Jackson, Cicotte, and Williams—and their waivers of immunity had all disappeared from the files of the grand jury. Gorman had never even seen this evidence, which had vanished before he took office. Although Happy Felsch had also "confessed," it was to a newspaper reporter. His statement had not been given under oath. It lacked legitimacy. There was now a gaping hole in the prosecution's case.

What happened to the evidence? Hartley Replogle, a former assistant state attorney, testified under oath that his boss, McClay Hoyne, Gorman's predecessor, had, just before leaving office, taken a large number of documents from the grand jury files. Hoyne did not deny this, explaining that he had done so only to make copies for his own records. American League president Ban Johnson issued a public statement accusing Rothstein of engineering the theft.

I charge that Arnold Rothstein paid $10,000 for the Grand Jury confessions of Cicotte, Jackson and Williams. I charge that this money, brought to Chicago by a representative of Rothstein, went to an attache of the State's Attorney's office under the Hoyne administration. I charge that after Rothstein had examined these confessions in New York and found that the players had not involved him to the extent of criminal liability, he gave the document to a friend of his, the managing editor of a New York newspaper. I charge that the editor offered these documents for sale broadcast throughout the country.

Rothstein's threat to sue Johnson for libel came to nothing. Johnson's accusation was right on target. But it is not clear whether Johnson knew of Charles Comiskey's role. The theft had been masterminded by William J. Fallon, Rothstein's attorney, and by Alfred Austrian, attorney for Comiskey and the White Sox.

Despite Judge Landis' threat to take "federal action" if any evidence was found missing, nothing was done. The vanished documents reappeared when Joe Jackson sued Comiskey for back pay, four years after the trial. At that time the papers were in the possession of Alfred Austrian. How they came to be there neither Austrian nor Comiskey could or would explain.

State Attorney Gorman went ahead, insisting that the statements contained in the missing confessions and waivers of immunity could be reconstructed from "the testimony of the grand jurors, the court stenographers, and others present when the statements were obtained." But even that seemed to be unnecessary since carbon copies of the confessions were available, although unsigned. Judge Hugo Friend, sitting on the case, asked how the state intended to show that the confessions had been made voluntarily if the carbons bore no signatures. The court, he finally held, would accept the confessions as freely given, if the players had signed the waivers of immunity. To determine this the judge, dismissing the jury, decided to hear what the players themselves had to say on the matter.

Under interrogation by the judge, the three players claimed that they were ignorant of the significance of the waivers; they had merely been assured by Alfred Austrian that it was in their best interests to sign them. Judge Friend then recalled the jury and announced his determination that the confessions had been made voluntarily. They would be admitted into evidence, but each of the confessions was to apply only to the confessor who made it. No one but the confessor himself could be implicated by the confessions. Now the situation seemed perilous only for the three confessors. The charges against the others had to be dropped for lack of evidence.

Since the state's case had been weakened by the missing evidence, the testimony of Sleepy Burns became all the more important. As Burns told the story, he had been approached by Ed Cicotte and Chick Gandil with a proposition. The meeting took place at the Ansonia Hotel in New York City, where, he said, the players offered to throw the Series for $100,000. Further meetings included Lefty Williams, Happy Felsch, Fred McMullin, and Buck Weaver. Under cross-examination Burns also explained the reason for his willingness to testify. He was eager to do so, he said, not to uphold the purity of the game but because Abe Attell and the players "doublecrossed me and I would have been the fall guy for the whole outfit." His testimony was for self-protection. He had been, he continued, promised a cut of the payoff money from both. He got nothing from either. By the time he left the stand, Burns had been a very effective witness.

Billy Maharg's story was essentially the same as Burns's. The White Sox had deliberately lost the first two games of the Series. His firsthand knowledge, however, did not extend beyond the third game. Under cross-examination Maharg was unshakable.

None of the accused players testified. In their final arguments the state's attorneys went after the arguments and tactics of the defense:

There has been so much poison injected into the case by the attorneys for the defense. They have attacked Bill Burns, the man who bared the conspiracy of their clients. They have hit at Billy Maharg, the man who corroborated him. They tell you these men lied. They call Burns an accomplice. By their own words they convict their own clients. If Burns is an accomplice, some crime must have been committed. . . . I tell you, at least three of their clients, Eddie Cicotte, Lefty Williams, and Joe Jackson, have condemned themselves so badly that I don't see how you can acquit them. . . . Thousands of men . . . waited to see the great Cicotte pitch a ballgame. Gentlemen, they went to see a ballgame, but all they saw was a con game. . . . Unless the jury, by convicting the ballplayers in this trial, does its part to stamp out gambling that is corrupting baseball, I predict restrictive legislation for baseball such as has been enacted for boxing and horseracing.

The state asked for five-year jail sentences and fines of $20,000 for each of the three defendants.

The final arguments of the defense were persuasive. The jury had already heard testimony from Harry Grabiner, White Sox secretary, which made clear that the club's profits for 1920 were more than double those of 1919. Ben Short now focused on a strictly legal interpretation:

> The state failed to establish criminal conspiracy. There may have been an agreement entered by the defendants to take the gamblers' money, but it has not been shown the players had any intention of defrauding the public or of bringing the game into ill-repute. They believed an arrangement they may have made was a secret one and would therefore reflect no discredit on the national pastime or injure the business of their employer as it would never be detected.

The defense could not help but be pleased by Judge Friend's charge to the jury. "The State," he said, "must prove that it was the intent of the ballplayers and gamblers charged with conspiracy through the throwing of the World Series, to defraud the public and others and not merely to throw games." This very narrow focus was not what the prosecution had been concentrating on, but the jury was limited to considering a conspiracy to defraud. The jury did so. All defendants were acquitted. The players had intended to throw the Series, but they had not intended to defraud either the public or Comiskey.

The press overwhelmingly responded to the verdicts with displeasure, if not anger. The *New York Times* derided the "legal hairsplitting" angrily: "The Chicago White Sox are once more whiter than snow. The jury has said that they are not guilty, so that settles that. The court instructed the jury to determine whether the defendants intended to defraud the public and others and not merely to throw ball games. To the lay mind, this sounds very much like asking whether the defendant intended to murder his victim or merely to cut his head off." Other newspapers referred to the verdict as "a dangerous lesion in the American moral sense" and "a petty and hollow victory."

Judging from their behavior during the trial, the fans were more sympathetic than were the sportswriters.

The trial was over, but important issues remained unresolved. Arnold Rothstein had been identified as the financier of the fix by the state's star witness, Sleepy Bill Burns. But Rothstein was never indicted and other gamblers also were permitted to escape. Rothstein had agreed to appear voluntarily to testify before the grand jury, and his pose of injured innocence had apparently been convincing. State Attorney Hoyne, who later admitted "borrowing" the confessions and waivers of immunity of the players, announced publicly after Rothstein's appearance that the gambler was not involved. Alfred Austrian, representing Comiskey, also believed Rothstein's testimony; both men were quick to exonerate him—Austrian acting on Comiskey's behalf to protect Rothstein from indictment and to protect Comiskey's valuable investment in his players. Hoyne's reasons can only be guessed at. That Rothstein was indeed the financier of the fix became clear in 1928, when the gambler was gunned down in New York City during a poker game. The FBI in going through his papers found among them reference to payments of $80,000 destined for the Chicago players. (Abe Attell, who handled the money for Rothstein, had put some of it out on bets for himself instead of delivering it as intended.)

Other elements in the whitewashing operation involved the absence of testimony by the accused and the statements of American League president Ban Johnson. The three accused players did not take the witness stand in their own behalf. Their silence was not only for self-protection but also for the protection of Charles Comiskey and baseball. They sat out their trial, kept their mouths shut, and organized baseball—protecting itself—kept quiet to give them protection as well.

Following the revelation of the missing confessions, Ban Johnson in ringing tones had accused Arnold Rothstein of responsibility. Yet earlier, after Rothstein had appeared before the grand jury, Johnson had held the view that the trickster was not involved. Johnson's early vindication of Rothstein occurred after Johnson had interviewed him in New York City. At that time he contended that Rothstein knew about the fix but had not been personally involved. Johnson apparently believed that the grand jury investigating the baseball scandal would bring down his long-standing enemy Charles Comiskey and clean up baseball in the process. Rothstein's participation in the fix was not of any great concern to him. He wanted only to get Comiskey. With the disappearance of the confessions, however, out went Johnson's best chance to nail Comiskey. Johnson's accusation came after the grand jury had handed down indictments, and by then it was too late.

Both Abe Attell and "Sports" Sullivan, another of the shady characters from the New York gambling scene, escaped indictment by leaving the country. Hal Chase went to California and three minor gamblers were acquitted along with the seven players. For the accused White Sox, however, there were still dues to pay.

When the trial ended, the exonerated players were euphoric, celebrating at a local restaurant late into the night and hoping to be restored to good standing in professional baseball. But such was not to be. Judge Landis had made his position clear even before the trial: "[T]here is absolutely no chance for any of them to creep back into organized baseball. They will be and will remain outlaws. . . . It is sure that the guilt of some of them will at least be proved." Certainly a member of the federal bench should have known better than to make such a statement before the players had been tried in a court of law with the protections of due process. Whether or not the players were aware of Landis' earlier statement, they were shocked and felt betrayed by the action he took following their acquittal.

> Regardless of the verdict of the juries, no player that throws a ball game; no player that sits in a conference with a bunch of crooked players and gamblers where the ways and means of throwing games are planned and discussed and does not promptly tell his club about it, will ever play professional baseball again.

The ban applied to all the players acquitted by the jury, to those against whom charges had been dropped, and even to Fred McMullin, who had not been indicted. He had known about the fix but did not report it. The ban's effectiveness was total. Teams refused to play these men. Ballparks were closed to them. Even semi-pro teams were fearful of breaking the ban. Realizing that they would never play again, they gradually faded from public notice and finished their lives in more prosaic occupations.

Buck Weaver was one who fought back. Suing in the courts, he won partial payment on his 1920 contract. It was said that Weaver had been present when the conspiracy was being discussed and that he did not talk. But what should he have done? Had he told of the fix, would he have felt safe in his own career? He appealed six times to two baseball commissioners and he filed a petition bearing 14,000 signatures in his support. Each time he was rebuffed. "Landis wanted me," he said, "to tell him something that I didn't know." In selecting the crusty Landis, the owners had made clear that they wanted the absolutism of a charismatic leader who would bring crowds into the ballparks by restoring their faith in baseball. Landis was chosen democratically but he wielded complete authority.

So there was a fix in 1919. But a nagging question still remains: If the "Black Sox" did throw the Series, why, as individuals, did they play so well? Jackson, for example, led both teams with a .375 average. Weaver hit .324. Neither Weaver nor Jackson made an error in the eight games. Eddie Collins, on the other hand, made two, and hit only .226. In the third game, won by the White Sox, Gandil drove in two of the three runs and Risberg scored the third after hitting a triple. McMullin, as a pinch hitter, batted .500 in two times at bat. Someone looking at the box scores and the play-by-play would have a difficult time finding anything amiss if it were not for revelations off the playing field. And those revelations—the confessions of Cicotte, Jackson, Felsch, and Williams—were given without assistance of counsel and with a poor understanding of the consequences. Still, they seem genuine. Organized baseball survived the scandal of the 1920s in the same way that the movie industry survived the Arbuckle scandal and the Republican Party survived Teapot Dome. Individuals suffered but the institutions came out largely unscathed.

After the troubles of 1919–21, baseball flourished. In addition to the reorganization provided by the creation of a strong commissioner, the game itself was on the verge of a revolution in its style of play. Babe Ruth was the primary agent. The "long ball" delighted the fans, and Ruth's 54 homers in 1920 astonished the sports world. The truth about the 1919 World Series wasn't really known until late in the 1920 season. By that time the mighty figure of Ruth almost blocked from view the shame of 1919. His accomplishments diverted attention from the Black Sox story as it came out in dribbles. The revolution on the field was aided in 1920 when organized baseball ruled out freak pitching deliveries that required tampering with the ball: the spitball, the emery ball, and the ball roughed up with the belt buckle. These changes also encouraged emphasis on the long ball.

In 1920 the American League topped five million at the gate, although before that date four million had been the ultimate aspiration. By the mid-1920s five million had become the usual standard every year. By 1930, professional baseball games accounted for almost 26 percent of paid admissions to all spectator sports. In addition to the new excitement engendered by the heroics of Babe Ruth, there was the increasing popularity of the automobile. The fear that families would prefer picnics and other such outings over Sunday baseball proved exaggerated. Instead, the automobile became the essential means by which suburban and rural fans could get to the ballparks. And the demographic trend that brought about the rapid urbanization of America brought people to the games. Finally, radio broadcasting of play-by-play details stimulated interest. The fears of sports writers that fans would stop reading about baseball when they could hear the details of the game, and the fears of owners that radio broadcasting of the games would harm attendance, proved groundless.

The decade which opened in scandal ended in a series of victories for organized baseball. To promote efficiency and cooperation, business enterprises had been encouraged by Secretary of Commerce Herbert C. Hoover to create trade associations. Voluntary self-regulation was intended to forestall the threat of the anti-trust laws. Organized baseball created its commissioner and vested him with dictatorial powers, also in order to avoid government regulation. And baseball prospered and flourished with the type of farm system developed by Branch Rickey. Despite the changes in the game's governance structure, though, the specter of gambling still haunts baseball. Three-quarters of a century after the World Series of 1919, the gambling activities of Cincinnati star Pete Rose broke into the news. This time, however, the power of the commissioner made swift expulsion possible.

The ugly side of the decade of the 1920s—the preoccupation with one-hundred-percent Americanism, the xenophobia, the grotesque revival of the Ku Klux Klan—also touched the baseball world, but lightly. One club owner in 1921 blamed an increase in unruly behavior at baseball games on the increasing numbers of foreigners attending. Attacks on umpires were blamed on young people who were "born of foreign parents." The Philadelphia Athletics team was torn by dissension between those who were members of the KKK and those who chose not to join. If America was the melting pot, American baseball was selective about what went into that pot. Jews had difficulty melting and blacks never even got near the cauldron. But by and large, *Sporting News* was almost accurate when it pointed out in an editorial that any player could be admitted to the game with the exception of the "Ethiopian," and, simultaneously, that blacks were "some of the greatest players the game has ever known." If so, race relations in the 1920s prevented taking the obvious next step. That didn't come until 1947, when Jackie Robinson put on the uniform of the Brooklyn Dodgers, owned by Branch Rickey.

3

THE TRIALS OF "FATTY" ARBUCKLE

Roscoe Conkling "Fatty" Arbuckle weighed 14 pounds at birth and 266 pounds when he was full grown. He was so popular that in 1919, hoping to enjoy a leisurely European vacation, he found himself instead besieged by newspapermen and cheering crowds wherever he went. By 1921, only 34 years of age, he had completed over twenty feature films and was raking in a million dollars a year. He was at the peak of his Hollywood fame that year, when accusations of rape and murder were leveled against him.

Arbuckle began his career in vaudeville at the age of eight. He began to act in movies, but continued also to work the vaudeville circuits until 1913, when he went off to join the filmmaking community in sunny California. Mack Sennett's Keystone Film Company mixed slapstick comedy and pretty girls with plenty of action. Audiences loved Keystone's prescribed formula of "police, pulchritude, pace, and pursuit—all of which produced pandemonium." Arbuckle did his stint as a Keystone Kop when Mabel Normand, the star at Keystone and Sennett's longtime lover, recognized his extraordinary talent. She convinced Sennett that Arbuckle was not just fat but funny too. Despite his size he was light on his feet, remarkably agile, and a skillful dancer. Ambidextrous and a deadeye with a custard pie, he could hit any target within ten feet. In a number of Keystone films he fired off two pies at once—in opposite directions.

Arbuckle left Keystone in 1916 to work for Paramount Pictures' Joseph Schenck, one of the film industry's most powerful men. Their contract not only gave Arbuckle his lavish yearly salary but also "complete artistic control" of his pictures. With the exception of a few two-reelers, the next twenty-two Arbuckle films were to be feature length. This was truly extraordinary, for no comic actor starred in more than an occasional feature film in those days. Even Chaplin was still making two-reelers in 1922.

In February 1917 Arbuckle began a twenty-three-city promotional tour to publicize his new association with Paramount. Everywhere he was acclaimed as a national hero. In his home state of Kansas—not known either for its exuberance or its enthusiasm for the motion picture industry—almost a quarter of a million people turned out to greet him. The tour ended in Boston, with a final banquet as the grand climax of the trip. Unfortunately, innuendo, mud-slinging, and downright lies have never been absent from reports about the heroes of popular culture, and such distorted stories about the Boston banquet appeared in the press. One account claimed that the star was "caught with his pants DOWN and a starlet's UP." What happened was that when the banquet ended, some of those attending continued to party. And some of those who continued to party turned it into an orgy. But, really, not Roscoe Arbuckle. He was not the kind of man to take part in orgies. More to the point in his defense, he was recuperating from a carbuncle on his leg and had retired for the night several hours before. After a time the Boston story faded from view, only to be resurrected in 1921 to hound Arbuckle during his trials.

By 1919 Hollywood was becoming the center of the world's film industry. Great wealth was pouring into the hands of people who a few years before could not have afforded the price of a dinner. Now they had at their disposal fast cars and fast women, high-priced bootleg whiskey, and drugs. Arbuckle, too, had come a long way from the sod hut in Kansas where he was born. It was not Roscoe's wont to play the Hollywood game, but under Schenck's prodding he began to live in a manner consistent with his astronomical earnings. He bought a house for a quarter of a million dollars and started to fill his six-car garage with a Rolls-Royce, a Stevens-Duryea, a white Cadillac, a Renault, and an extraordinary $25,000 Pierce Arrow.

But Roscoe was not a woman chaser. His first wife, with whom he maintained friendly relations all his life, said there was never the slightest suggestion during their marriage that he played around. He seemed shy with women, possibly because of self-consciousness about his size. After he broke up with his first wife, a strong friendship with co-star Alice Lake developed, but there is no evidence of an affair with her. Arbuckle's inclination to keep his libido carefully in check was more than notable in the movie industry.

That industry in the 1920s embodied much of the spirit of the decade. It seemed to have two conflicting sets of values. One was belief in repectability, gentility, and moral idealism. Movies of the pre-war era with their emphasis on religion, self-sacrifice, duty, and devotion to family life were making their last stand. But the new postwar generation was eager to be free of the old dogmas. The new mood rejected restraint. Sex was exploited by movie producers in their films and in their advertising. No one embodied this change more fully than Cecil B. DeMille. His pictures attacked the genteel tradition, flaunted sex, promoted a new morality, condoned illicit relationships, and signaled the breakdown of the old order. And it wasn't even necessary to see his movies themselves, for advertisements conveyed the same thing.

HER HUSBAND DREW THE GIRL TO HIM AND—
A long, long kiss, a kiss of youth and love and beauty, all concentrating like rays into one focus, kindled from above; such kisses as belong to early dawn. Where heart, and soul, and sense in concert move, and the blood is lava, and the pulse is ablaze!!

Enthusiasm grew for materialism as well as for sex. Racketeering, a new phenomenon in American life and in the movies, also caught the popular interest. Above all, the audiences of the 1920s cared about the stars, the movies' alluring heroines and dashing heroes. For a time, when audiences seemed to be more interested in the off-screen behavior of the performers than the moral nature of the characters they portrayed, there was a call for banning "immoral" players from the screen. But in Hollywood it seemed that bad morality drove out good; people with high moral standards merely stayed away from the movie business. Eventually moralizers gave up and went back to condemning the plots and scenes of the movies themselves, leaving the private lives of the stars to the gossip industry.

Even prior to World War I many middle-class Americans shunned the movies, finding the pictures offensive and the nickelodeons where they were shown disreputable. Hanging over the movie industry from its beginning was the threat of censorship. Movies provided competition for churches, saloons, and the vaudeville theaters of the nation, and attacks came from ministers, social reformers, and theater critics. A number of states passed censorship laws and even federal censorship loomed as a possibility, especially after 1915. In that year the United States Supreme Court lifted from motion pictures the protection against prior censorship offered by the First Amendment. The Court held, in Mutual Film Corporation v. Industrial Commission of Ohio, that "the exhibition of motion pictures is a business pure and simple . . . not to be regarded . . . as part of the press of the country."

Beginning in 1920, a series of scandals focused public attention on the sordid side of Hollywood life. On March 2 Mary Pickford, "America's sweetheart," quietly left California, traveled to Nevada, and divorced her actor-husband, Owen Moore. Concerned about the reaction of her fans, she announced that she did not intend to marry again. Three weeks later "Little Mary" married her male counterpart in innocence and purity: Douglas Fairbanks, star of swashbuckling adventure films. The public was not shocked by the divorce alone, since divorces in Hollywood had become old news. Mary and Douglas had done nothing illegal, but their illicit premarital romance certainly contradicted their on-screen purity. Both Pickford and the movie industry had gotten a black eye.

In 1921, William Desmond Taylor, an English movie director working at Paramount, was mysteriously murdered. After his death he was accused of a variety of crimes ranging from witchcraft and drug trafficking to adultery and sexual perversion. Several female stars' careers were permanently damaged by the publicity they received from the Taylor affair—among them, Mabel Normand. Soon an even more shocking revelation horrified Hollywood and the American people. Wallace "Wally" Reid—handsome, clean living, an immensely popular matinee idol and an all-American hero—was revealed to be a heroin addict and confined to a sanitarium, where he died in 1923. Other prominent stars, including the unfortunate Mabel Normand, were also rumored to be drug users.

There was more to come in 1921. In July newspapers dug up the old Arbuckle story about the Boston banquet of 1917 and the party from which he had really been absent. A new and mysterious detail was now revealed. The district attorney in Massachusetts had received a $100,000 gift right after the party. What, the public wondered, had the district attorney discovered that was worth that kind of money? The temper of the press was unmistakable. The movie industry was a sink of depravity that needed to be exposed. And exposure sold newspapers.

The churches thundered against Hollywood and the press joined in, relishing the opportunity to support traditional values, attack evil, and attract readers. It was in this atmosphere that the three trials of Roscoe "Fatty" Arbuckle were held. Every director, every actor, every producer was a potential object of suspicion and Arbuckle came to symbolize everything the public suspected about Hollywood's supposed moral degeneracy.

*   *   *

On September 3, 1921, the Saturday before Labor Day, Arbuckle, director Fred Fischbach, and Lowell Sherman, an actor, signed into San Francisco's St. Francis Hotel after a 500-mile drive from Hollywood in Arbuckle's Pierce Arrow. He had just finished making six feature films in seven months. Now it was time for a holiday. Despite Prohibition, there was no difficulty getting a drink. In an open city like San Francisco it wasn't even necessary to go to a speakeasy. Refreshments were called for and brought up to the twelfth-floor suite.

While Arbuckle was getting comfortable at the St. Francis, three people booked into the Palace Hotel across town. For the moment, neither group knew the other was in the city. The trio at the Palace were Virginia Rappe, a screen actress, her manager Al Senmacher, and Maude Delmont, a friend of Senmacher's. Neither Arbuckle, Fischbach, nor Sherman knew Mrs. Delmont, but all had some acquaintance with Virginia Rappe. Arbuckle knew her slightly and thought she was "good fun." He did not know, however, that she suffered from gonorrhea and had also been banned from her movie studio. At the time of the Labor Day weekend party in Arbuckle's suite she had not worked for nearly two years.

Partying started at the St. Francis about noon. Arbuckle, Fischbach, and Sherman occupied a three-room suite, numbers 1219, 1220, and 1221. The first served as a reception room and the latter two as bedrooms, each with its own bath. The ongoing party was attended by Virginia Rappe, Maude Delmont, and two showgirls, Alice Blake and Zey Prevon. Several other people, male and female, came and went at various times. When guests started arriving, both Arbuckle and Sherman were dressed in pajamas. Sherman got fully dressed but Arbuckle remained in silk pajamas and a bathrobe. The liquor flowed and a Victrola played popular songs. In two hours Mrs. Delmont downed ten double scotches, and even before the dancing began Virginia Rappe had finished three orange blossoms.

Loosened up by the drinking, Virginia started to tell Arbuckle all her troubles. She was broke and needed money, a lot of money. She was sick. She was pregnant. She needed an abortion as soon as possible. Arbuckle tried to dissuade her, suggesting that she have the baby and either give it up for adoption or raise it herself. In any event, he did not have with him the $2,000 she needed. He told her to see him in Los Angeles during the following week. A few minutes later, about 2:40 p.m., both Zey Prevon and Alice Blake saw her weaving toward room 1221 and Lowell Sherman's bathroom. At the time, Maude Delmont and Sherman were in the bathroom together. Maude yelled to her to go to the other bathroom, Arbuckle's.

A few moments later, Arbuckle, realizing that it was almost three o'clock, got ready to dress. He had promised to go for a drive with Mae Taube, a latecomer to the party. When he went to bathe before dressing he found the bathroom door partially blocked. On the floor, moaning and vomiting into the toilet bowl, was Virginia Rappe. Arbuckle helped her into the bedroom, sat her on the single bed, and gave her some water. She told him she had had similar spells before and needed to lie down for a while.

When Arbuckle returned from his bath he found Virginia on the floor, groaning in pain. No more than ten minutes had passed. Arbuckle sought help. Zey Prevon and Maude Delmont hurried into the bedroom, where they found Virginia now sitting on the edge of the bed, fully dressed and wildly tearing at her clothes. She was frothing at the mouth and moaning, "I'm hurt! I'm dying! I know I'm dying!"

Everyone present was drunk in varying degrees, and instead of calling a doctor immediately they suggested a series of do-it-yourself cures. Ms. Prevon suggested standing Virginia on her head. One of the others recommended dunking her in cold water. And a third favored applying lumps of ice to the painful area. When, after more than an hour, a call was finally made to the hotel physician, he could not be located. Dr. Olav Kaarboe, his alternate, arrived at 4:45, examined Virginia, found a normal pulse, a normal heart reaction, no marks or bruises on her body, and a strong odor of alcohol. He concluded that she just had had too much to drink. He asked if she were hurting, but Virginia merely turned her head away. Kaarboe told Maude Delmont to call if she needed further help, and he departed.

The party at the St. Francis continued into the evening. A few minutes after 7 p.m. the hotel physician, Dr. Arthur Beardslee, having returned, paid a visit to the patient. Virginia was in great discomfort. She complained of severe pain in her lower abdomen and cried out at the slightest touch. In order to complete the examination Beardslee gave her an injection of morphine and atropine. While waiting for it to take effect, he asked Maude Delmont what had happened. When Maude charged that Arbuckle had attacked the girl, Virginia interrupted and declared clearly and without hesitation that Arbuckle had neither attacked her nor even attempted sexual relations with her.

The following morning, September 5, Virginia awoke with severe abdominal pains. After his earlier examination Dr. Beardslee had decided that he was dealing with a problem that would require surgery. Now he administered morphine and atropine once again and catheterized his patient, who had not urinated since the previous day. The procedure produced a small amount of urine tinged with blood. "I knew," said Beardslee later, "I was dealing with a lesion of the bladder, and from the signs and symptoms . . . I knew that her internal condition was at least complicated by bladder trouble. A ruptured bladder, I suppose."

Having made this determination, the doctor continued to administer sedatives, although they only masked the symptoms. At no time did he tell either the patient or Mrs. Delmont that hospitalization was called for or that an operation was needed. Despairing of Dr. Beardslee, Maude Delmont called in a third doctor.

During his examination, Dr. Melville Rumswell asked Virginia if she had been suffering from a vaginal infection. Although she admitted only to leukorrhea, a vaginal discharge with a number of possible causes, Dr. Rumswell concluded that Virginia had gonorrhea and required immediate hospitalization. She was taken to the Wakefield

Sanatorium, although it was only a maternity hospital and was not equipped to deal with her condition. When that condition worsened, Dr. Rumswell called in still another physician for consultation. Dr. Emmett Rixford, professor of surgery at Stanford University, determined after examination that the patient was suffering from peritonitis. It had been caused by a "ruptured pus tube" brought on by the fulminating gonorrhea. Her condition was extremely dangerous and the disease too far advanced for surgery. An operation would probably kill her. There was, he concluded, little that could be done. The diagnosis was accurate. Virginia Rappe died on September 9, four days after Labor Day and less than a week after the party.

About an hour and a half before Virginia's death Rumswell, for some undiscoverable reason, arranged for an illegal postmortem examination. The postmortem confirmed the Beardslee and Rixford diagnoses: a ruptured bladder and peritonitis. The bladder was removed and placed in a specimen jar. Astonishingly and mysteriously, so were the uterus, part of the rectum, and the ovaries and fallopian tubes.

Maude Delmont, despite Virginia Rappe's denials, continued to charge that Roscoe Arbuckle had raped Virginia. So long as the girl had remained lucid and coherent she denied such charges. What motivated Maude Delmont? Maybe she believed that Arbuckle had rebuffed her. At one moment he had actually called the hotel detective to remove Maude because of her drunken and offensive behavior. But perhaps there is an answer less dependent on hurt feelings. Maude sent two identical telegrams to two different attorneys, one in San Diego and the other in Los Angeles: "WE HAVE ROSCOE ARBUCKLE IN A HOLE HERE CHANCE TO MAKE SOME MONEY OUT OF HIM."

Whatever her reasons, newspapermen certainly found Maude Delmont cooperative. Headlines blared:
ACTRESS DIES AFTER HOTEL PARTY
GRILL FOR ARBUCKLE ACTRESS DEATH QUIZ
FATTY ARBUCKLE SOUGHT IN ORGY DEATH
Maude gave her version of what happened in an interview:

... Arbuckle took hold of her and said, "I have been trying to get you for five years. ...." During the afternoon the party began to get rough and Arbuckle showed the effects of drinking. Virginia and I were in our room. Arbuckle came in and pulled Virginia into his room and locked the door. From the scuffle I could hear and from the screams of Virginia, I knew he must be abusing her. I made every effort I could to get in the room, but I could not get through the door. Arbuckle had her in the room for over an hour, at the end of which time Virginia was badly beaten up. Virginia was a good girl. I knew that she had led a clean life, and it is my duty to see this thing through.

Maude Delmont's later statements provided embellishments for this one. At times she referred to her "lifelong" friendship with Virginia, whom she had actually met only two days before the party. The press played the Rappe affair for all it was worth. Selling papers was the game and the Hearst papers were among the leaders.

William Randolph Hearst had perfected sensationalism as far back as the 1890s and there was almost no limit to what he would do for circulation. But it may have been more than sensationalism that Hearst was after. In 1921 Hearst's relationship with a "certain actress" was a closely guarded secret even though rival newspapers had begun digging. Perhaps the Arbuckle case provided Hearst with an opportunity to deflect attention from his relationship with Marion Davies. And there was also Hearst's special relationship with San Francisco, his beloved city by the sea. Hearst was personally affronted by the alleged crime. How dare Arbuckle, or any actor from Hollywood, use San Francisco as a playground for immoral activities?

From coast to coast, newspapers and periodicals of every description painted Arbuckle as a libertine. They "revealed" that he had inserted either a Coke bottle or a champagne bottle into Virginia Rappe's body during his sadistic sexual assault. They made her into a paragon of virtue and health, a clean-living victim of rapacious lust. In fact, however, by the age of sixteen Virginia Rappe had already had several abortions. Hearst portrayed Rappe, against all evidence, as a woman of wealth acquired through shrewd and careful investments in oil and real estate. The evidence, on the contrary, was that her total assets at time of death came to less than $200.

Religious organizations took up the cry immediately. Less than three days after Virginia's death, Sunday sermons in churches through-

out Los Angeles provided variations on a theme. "Moral Degeneration" was the subject at the First Congregational, "Movie Stars and
the Ten Commandments" at the Immanuel Presbyterian, and "Is
Arbuckle a Sample or a Warning?" at the Westlake Methodist.

Roscoe Arbuckle had returned to Los Angeles on Tuesday,
September 6. Rappe died on Friday and Arbuckle immediately went
back to San Francisco. There he discovered that the custodians of the
city's morals, the club women, had already mobilized their forces.
They had telephoned officials of the grand jury, the district attorney's
office, the police chief, the mayor, and many others in positions of
influence. They sought, they said, justice. At both the Palace Hotel and
the St. Francis, Arbuckle had been declared persona non grata and
was unable to get a room. On September 10, the day after Virginia's
death, two movie houses withdrew Arbuckle films. By the time his
first trial was underway, his films had been banned across the nation:
in Memphis, in Pittsburgh, in more than 600 theaters in New York, in
Pennsylvania, in Missouri, and so on and on.

Arbuckle brought with him to San Francisco Joseph Schenck's
own attorney, Frank Dominguez. In the foyer of the Palace Hotel
police detectives ordered Dominguez to take Arbuckle to the Hall of
Justice immediately for questioning. Having just enough time to advise
his client to say nothing, Dominguez was physically removed from the
room and for the next three hours—before the Miranda ruling, without his lawyer present—the police grilled Arbuckle. Assistant District
Attorney U'Ren told Arbuckle that if he did not answer all questions
put to him, he would be charged with murder. Arbuckle answered as
best he could, but his account differed greatly from Delmont's. He was
then charged with murder under the section of the penal code providing that a "a life taken in rape or attempted rape is considered
murder."

Matthew Brady, the San Francisco district attorney, was not in the
city when Virginia Rappe died or when Arbuckle was arrested. When
he finally did speak to the press, his account of the matter was Maude
Delmont's account. In addition, he had already decided to try
Arbuckle in the newspapers. For a man with political ambitions,
achieving a murder conviction in a case like this was an opportunity
not to be missed; even conviction on a lesser charge would not satisfy
a public lusting for blood. Arbuckle, as instructed by Dominguez,

remained silent.

There was little to give Arbuckle much hope. Here was a manufactured scandal, aided and abetted by the press. No newspaper questioned the statements of Maude Delmont. The results of the postmortem performed on Virginia Rappe's body should at least have
raised a doubt. A public statement by Dr. Ophuls, who performed the
postmortem, was virtually ignored: "The post mortem examination
showed a ruptured bladder, the rupture being due to natural causes.
There were no marks of violence on the body, no signs that the girl
had been attacked in any way." Nor was much attention given to the
statement made at the coroner's inquest by Dr. Rumswell: "At no time
. . . did anything in connection with this case lead me to believe that
any violence had been done whatever."

Very few people who knew Arbuckle thought he was responsible
for Virginia's death. Minta Durfee, Arbuckle's first wife, claimed that
he'd been sexually impotent as early as 1917. Buster Keaton never
doubted Arbuckle's innocence. When he heard the incredible story, he
opened his purse generously. Charlie Chaplin also believed in Roscoe's
innocence. The murder charge, he said, was preposterous. "I know
Roscoe to be a genial, easy going type who would not hurt a fly." But
not a word of Chaplin's opinion was printed.

Aside from Buster Keaton, few in the Hollywood world came to
Arbuckle's assistance. Some surrendered to the fear of box-office losses. Sid Grauman, long a personal friend, withdrew Arbuckle's latest
picture, *Gasoline Gus*, from circulation. William S. Hart, a popular
cowboy star, denounced the Arbuckle–Rappe affair as "disgraceful"
and insisted that he and the movie industry were blameless. "The
crime was not committed because the man was a motion picture star.
The same man would have done the same thing whether he was a
manufacturer, hod carrier, bank president or minister of the gospel."

The first hurdle faced by District Attorney Brady was the coroner's
inquest. Maude Delmont's statements were full of conflicts and inconsistencies, but Brady could not avoid having her testify. The best he
could do was delay her appearance as long as possible so that he could
coach her about what to say. Brady succeeded in arranging a change
in the order of calling the witnesses.

The second hurdle was getting an indictment for murder from the
grand jury. The most important evidence for Brady was Maude

Delmont's statement that when she rushed into Arbuckle's bedroom, she heard Virginia scream out, "I'm dying! I'm dying! He killed me!" For this statement to be allowed in testimony the rule of evidence required that the accused be present at the time it was made. Maude Delmont had placed Arbuckle in the room and had him saying in reply to Virginia's accusation, "You're crazy. Shut up or I'll throw you out of the window." But this statement had to have been heard by someone other than Maude. Brady needed it heard by either Zey Prevon or Alice Blake. Both women had been interviewed shortly after Virginia's death and both denied having heard the statement. Brady got to work.

Playing one off against the other, threatening them with perjury, Brady wore them down. Ms. Blake, Zey was told, had testified that Virginia had said Roscoe had assaulted and raped her. "I never heard her say that," Zey retorted. "If Alice says that, then her ears hear differently than mine." Brady, however, discovered that Alice Blake had an illegitimate child. She was warned that unless she cooperated with the authorities the child would be taken from her. The woman crumbled, but she only agreed to state that Virginia had said, "I'm dying. He hurt me." When Zey Prevon got the news, she replied, "I never heard Virginia say it, but if you want me to say I did, I will."

Maude Demont's testimony to the grand jury was given, as was customary, in a closed hearing. Neither Arbuckle nor his attorney was present to contest her statements. Delmont told the grand jury what she had told the press and the police: that Roscoe Arbuckle had pulled Virginia into his bedroom saying, "I've waited five years for you and now I've got you." When she entered the room, Delmont said, Virginia was naked, her clothing torn to shreds and scattered all around. At the coroner's inquest, a public affair where she faced both Arbuckle and his attorney, Delmont said that when she entered Arbuckle's room Virginia was fully clothed. And she made no mention of the lascivious "I've got you" statement. It was because of these inconsistencies, District Attorney Brady later claimed, that Maude Delmont was never called to give evidence during the trial itself.

The grand jury, despite Brady's efforts, failed to return an indictment for murder, but it did indict for manslaughter. Under California law Brady was not obliged to accept the grand jury's finding. He could "file an information," charging the defendant with murder. If a lower court concluded that the D.A.'s charge was warranted, the defendant would be made to answer for it in a superior court. Police Judge Sylvain Lazarus determined that a murder charge was not warranted by the evidence, but a charge of manslaughter could be brought.

Both sides were upset by the decision. Brady was furious because he did not get the murder charge. Paramount Pictures, footing the bill for legal expenses, believed that Dominguez should have gotten the matter dismissed. He was replaced by Gavin McNab, a successful San Francisco lawyer and a major political force in that city, whose own investigation convinced him that Arbuckle was innocent. Roscoe Arbuckle was released on bail after eighteen days in jail. He returned to Los Angeles to await trial; it was scheduled for November 14, 1921.

Three trials took place in the matter of *California* v. *Roscoe Arbuckle*. At one level they were criminal trials for rape and manslaughter. In a much larger sense they were a trial at the bar of public opinion, a trial of California and the rest of the United States against Hollywood. After seven months, Arbuckle was acquitted of any crime. Nevertheless, Hollywood discarded Arbuckle, threw him away, purged him for its own good.

Before the first trial, both sides made strenuous efforts to uncover helpful information. Brady hired the famous Pinkerton Agency to do a nationwide search for material that would reveal Arbuckle as a moral degenerate. The defense tried to find out all it could about the people who attended the party, about Virginia Rappe's past, and about Maude Delmont. Among other things, the defense learned that Maude had committed bigamy. Brady learned it as well, but he quietly arranged that she not be arrested until after the Arbuckle trial. Some information gained by the defense could not be used at trial. To have revealed that Virginia had five abortions between 1908 and 1910 might have alienated the jury, might have caused its members to resent an attempt to defame the memory of the dead starlet.

It took five days to select seven men and five women for the jury. The prosecution's case focused on showing that when Virginia arrived at the party she was healthy and that it was Roscoe's assault that caused her bladder to rupture. Virginia's housekeeper and her masseuse testified that she regularly took three-mile walks, tossed medicine balls around the living room, and devoted herself to dancing. Virginia, they said, "was a powerful and resistant woman with a fine pair of lungs." Alice Blake and Zey Prevon did not turn out to be good witnesses for the prosecution. McNab succeeded in getting their grand jury testimony read into the record, and it was this testimony that revealed how they had been browbeaten into accepting the words "He hurt me."

Dr. Arthur Beardslee, also called by the prosecution, described Virginia's condition as critical. She was suffering, he said, from a "surgical abdomen." Beardslee was not, however, permitted to testify about his conversation with Virginia in which she denied that Arbuckle had hurt her. The court ruled that such testimony was hearsay. But if Virginia Rappe's condition was so serious, if she had a "surgical abdomen," why was no operation performed? Why did Beardslee do nothing? Why was Virginia sent to a maternity hospital to treat gonorrhea? Why was an illegal postmortem performed at the maternity hospital? Why wasn't official permission obtained and why were attempts made to keep it secret from the coroner's office? Virginia had been pregnant, she had asked Arbuckle for money for an abortion, and she had asked one of her nurses for the name and address of an abortionist. Was there an abortion? Was the postmortem performed to hide the abortion? A charge of malpractice was raised against Dr. Rumswell but the district attorney's office never proceeded with the matter. Was there collusion?

The defense set out to establish that Virginia Rappe had suffered for many years from inflammation of the bladder. Chronic cystitis had finally caused the bladder to rupture. A number of witnesses were called to describe past episodes in which Virginia had suffered from agonizing abdominal pains. Her medical history was introduced to show that she had had severe attacks in 1913 and again in 1914. Witnesses testified that when suffering from such attacks Virginia would tear off her clothes. McNab succeeded in showing that Roscoe was in the room with Virginia for no more than ten minutes by using evidence the prosecution had elicited from its own witnesses. Finally, although his legal staff was divided on the wisdom of doing so, Roscoe Arbuckle took the stand in his own defense. In both direct testimony and cross-examination he maintained his composure and told his story as he had told it before.

McNab's closing arguments were powerful. He asked why the district attorney had not produced the complaining witness. "Why has he not placed this witness on the stand, so you, the jury, might see and hear her? Why substitute for Maude Bambina Delmont?" He showed how the evidence of Zey Prevon and Alice Blake had been fabricated by the district attorney and his staff, and he chided the D.A. for not allowing the three doctors to testify about what Virginia had said to them. All three were prepared to swear that she had not blamed Roscoe for her condition. All were prepared to repudiate the statement of Maude Delmont.

Finally, McNab brought up Virginia Rappe's alleged physical abilities, her athletic vigor. Surely, he said, someone as athletic as Virginia could have managed a shout if Arbuckle had tried to rape her in the small bedroom. But none of the partygoers had heard her shouts. He concluded by summarizing what he believed to be the crux of the matter:

> This man went into the room, and either he found the giantess that has been described by the prosecution, or he found a sickly, broken woman, as has been testified to [by several witnesses] in convulsions. . . . And that woman, lying there, writhing and vomiting, would not have excited the passions of the lowest beast that ever was called man. You have to take one theory or the other; there isn't any escape from it. If she was in that condition, no man would have touched her. And if she was in the condition of a giantess and an athlete, no man could have touched her without the knowledge of everybody in that part of the building, and in the period of ten minutes nothing could have been done.

After a number of ballots the jury was declared hung. It had not been able to break a deadlocked vote of 10–2 for acquittal.

On January 11, 1922, the second trial of Roscoe Arbuckle began. The prosecution made no major change in its strategy. The defense produced more witnesses who testified to Virginia's predisposition for stripping after she had been drinking. Confident this time of an acquittal, defense attorney McNab made two serious mistakes. He decided that it was not necessary to have Arbuckle testify again since the prosecution had his entire testimony read into the record. More seriously, he felt so confident that he made no closing statement. In the minds of the jurors, this was tantamount to conceding defeat. Again, the jury was hung. This time, however, it was 9–3 for conviction.

The third trial began on March 13, 1922. Both prosecution and defense proceeded much as they had earlier. This time, however, the prosecution erred seriously in making public Virginia Rappe's life story. Her early years had been hard and perhaps an effort was made to evoke the jury's sympathy. It failed in that. The jury deliberated for no more than five minutes, and those five minutes were spent in writing an eloquent statement of acquittal.

> Acquittal is not enough for Roscoe Arbuckle. We feel that a great injustice has been done him. We feel also that it was only our plain duty to give him his exoneration, under the evidence, for there was not the slightest proof adduced to connect him in any way with the commission of a crime.
>
> He was manly throughout the case, and told a straightforward story on the witness stand, which we all believed. The happening at the hotel was an unfortunate affair for which Arbuckle, as the evidence shows, was in no way responsible.
>
> We wish him success, and hope that the American people will take the judgment of fourteen men and women who have sat listening for thirty-one days to the evidence, that Roscoe Arbuckle is entirely innocent and free from all blame.

Arbuckle's vindication, unfortunately, did not restore his career. The jury ruled on April 12. On April 18, Will Hays, just four months after having been appointed to head the movie industry, banned Arbuckle from the screen. Hays had been invited to become "czar" of the motion picture industry, the movies' counterpart to baseball's commissioner Kenesaw Mountain Landis. Hays was an elder of the Presbyterian Church, a crony of the president of the United States, a man of inflexible morality. "What is immoral is always immoral," he wrote in his *Memoirs*. Arbuckle had been acquitted. He had even received an apology from the jury. But he was still controversial. Hays, acting for the Motion Pictures Producers and Distributors Association, imposed the ban at the request of Adolph Zukor and Paramount Pictures. Zukor argued, "That will show that the Association means business."

The public clamor over Hollywood depravity had not been stilled. Calls from the pulpit and expressions of outrage from women's and civic groups did not abate. A scapegoat would surely be useful. Better for the Association to make a sacrifice of Roscoe Arbuckle. Acquittal meant simply that he had been freed for lack of evidence—not for lack of guilt. Arbuckle (and most of Hollywood) were guilty of dissipation and loose living. Arbuckle had to go.

Shortly before Christmas, 1922, Will Hays lifted the very ban he had imposed before Easter. "In doing this," he said in his *Memoirs*, "I was not acting without long deliberation. Of the criminal charges against him, Arbuckle had been acquitted; he had been leading an orderly life ever since." Hays "refused to stand in the man's way of earning a living in the only business he knew." Besides, Arbuckle's movies were always "clean and brought laughter to millions." Perhaps it was simply the Christmas spirit that moved him, for Hays could have offered the same explanation in April.

The anti-Arbuckle forces around the nation reacted vehemently to the lifting of the ban. The mayor of Boston said he would continue the ban in that city. The mayor of Indianapolis determined that "it [was] a big mistake to make a hero out of a man who did the thing he did." The California State Church Federation wired Hays: "The announcement that Roscoe Arbuckle is to reappear is incredible. . . . Our children have rights we must safeguard." As an elder in the Presbyterian Church, Hays was warned by some of his fellow elders: "Your failure to maintain the ban on Arbuckle will mean a forfeiture of the confidence and respect of all God fearing, decent men and women."

Arbuckle's acquittal and the lifting of the official Hays ban mattered not a whit. His career as an actor was over. The *New York Times* called lifting the Hays ban a serious blunder—a view endorsed by the New York State Federation of Churches. The Catholic Welfare Council urged all its affiliates "to prevent the showing of Arbuckle films." Banning Arbuckle in the first place implied that he had done something wrong. Lifting the ban didn't change that.

The few remaining years of Arbuckle's life were not happy ones. He turned to directing films, but he had to change his surname. He became William Goodrich, adopting his father's surname. Still itching to entertain, Arbuckle performed in revues in nightclubs and on the stage, but even there he experienced hostility. Nevertheless, the hope that glimmered within him was finally rewarded. In 1932 Arbuckle was at last invited by Warner Brothers to return to the movies as an actor. He finished a successful series of two-reelers and on June 28, 1933, signed to make a feature film. The following day, June 29, Roscoe Arbuckle was felled by a heart attack in his hotel room.

The movement to censor films did not originate with the Arbuckle affair, nor did efforts at self-regulation of the movie industry. By 1907, nickelodeons—"five cent theaters"—had proliferated throughout the United States. The *Chicago Tribune* attacked them as ". . . without a redeeming feature to warrant their existence . . . ministering to the lowest passions of childhood . . . influence is wholly vicious. . . ." Later in that year the city of Chicago established a board with power to censor the pictures shown in its nickelodeons. Between 1909 and 1922 seven states enacted censorship legislation and various groups advocated federal action.

The series of scandals that hit Hollywood in 1920 and 1921 led religious groups of all denominations to condemn the sinfulness of the movies. Nearly 100 bills calling for censorship were introduced in the legislatures of 37 states. Moreover, between 1915 and 1940 approximately 60 bills that would have provided some measure of federal supervision of the film industry were introduced in Congress. Senator Henry L. Myers of South Dakota, for example, called for an investigation of the movies and on the floor of the Senate he referred specifically to Arbuckle. "At Hollywood, California," he thundered, "is a colony of these people, where debauchery, riotous living, drunkenness, ribaldry, dissipation, free love seem to be conspicuous." Representative Theodore F. Appleby of New Jersey regarded censorship as important to the welfare of children and illiterates because of the lasting impressions films left on their minds. Since no two state censor boards would ever agree, federal legislation seemed preferable and was badly needed. In 1925 Representative William D. Upshaw of Georgia introduced a bill to ban all films showing illicit love, vice, white slavery, and scenes of "exaggerated" sex and nudity. But no federal legislation was ever enacted. The only official censorship of motion pictures in the United States came through passage of state and municipal laws. Fortunately for the movie industry, the advocates of censorship were not as well organized as the industry itself. In fact, these same advocates were often so lethargic after a measure did pass that they failed to make use of the law until some sensational film aroused their fury.

It was the formation of the Motion Pictures Producers and Distributors Association on March 11, 1922, that largely neutralized the enforcement of censorship laws. The Hays Office, as it came to be called, at once began a massive public relations campaign to improve the image of the movies. As Hays himself put it, "The flow of scandals was telling at the box office. . . . It was more than a question of mild censorship. It was a question of self-regulation or prohibition."

Will Hays was chosen because he seemed to be the ideal man for the job. Until his retirement in 1945 he remained the industry spokesman, and he worked closely with the MPPDA, which was created precisely to provide for self-regulation within the industry. Hays was an adept administrator. His church affiliation and his friendship with the president were well known. He had been Republican National Chairman and Postmaster General. He could provide, with his considerable political clout, a bulwark not only against federal censorship but anti-trust action as well (always a Hollywood phobia). Hays was a non-smoker, a teetotaler and, as Postmaster General, an avowed opponent of smut. For those vast numbers of Americans concerned about Hollywood morality, Hays was the perfect choice.

The MPPDA created a Committee on Public Relations to review movies intended for public showing, promote those it approved, and report back to the Association its objections to those not approved. In 1924, MPPDA proposed the "Formula," a voluntary agreement not to produce pictures that were suggestive in "theme, title or advertising." There was to be nothing that was legally binding among the members; rather, there would be cooperation among producers, enforced only by the persuasive powers of Will Hays. That, as it turned out, was often not enough to deter movie companies in search of profit.

In October 1927, the same month that saw the introduction of sound film, the movie producers in their effort at self-regulation adopted a series of "Don'ts" and "Be Carefuls"—in effect, a code—without a single negative vote. Eleven "Don'ts" were listed, matters that were not to appear in movies.

pointed profanity;

any licentious or suggestive nudity—in fact or in silhouette;

illegal traffic in drugs;

any inference of sexual perversion;
white slavery;
miscegenation;
sex hygiene and venereal disease;
scenes of actual childbirth—in fact or in silhouette;
children's sex organs;
ridicule of the clergy;
willful offense to any nation, race or creed.

The list of "Don'ts" was followed by a smorgasbord of "Be
Carefuls," subjects that needed to be treated with special care so that
"vulgarity and suggestiveness be eliminated" and "good taste may be
emphasized." Producers had to take care in treating

the use of the flag;
theft, robbery, safe cracking and dynamiting of trains;
brutality and possible gruesomeness;
techniques of committing murder;
sympathy for criminals;
sedition;
the sale of women, or of a woman selling her virtue;
rape or attempted rape;
first night scenes;
a man and woman in bed together;
surgical operations;
deliberate seduction of girls;
the institution of marriage;
the use of drugs;
titles or scenes having to do with law enforcement or law enforcing officers;
excessive or lustful kissing, particularly when one character plays
a "heavy."

Although the Code was created by the MPPDA itself and not by a
government agency, much of it was drawn from the censorship laws of
states and municipalities. Self-censorship, of course, raised no First
Amendment issues. It was not until 1952 that the Supreme Court
granted First Amendment protection to motion pictures. By the latter

part of the twentieth century, with the Code long gone, perhaps 90 percent of films shown would have been in violation.

From the very beginning there was tension between the producers' wish to circumvent the Code and their recognition of the need for self-regulation. The introduction of sound film intensified the strain. When Hays discovered, for example, that the word "damn" was used several times in a picture, he said that he personally was not offended by "this mildest of 'cuss words,'" but "as a matter of policy we ought to avoid expressions that rub any notable section of the public the wrong way." In 1930 a new Motion Pictures Production Code superseded the Code of 1927, but it still lacked an adequate enforcement mechanism. Adherence to the Code was voluntary, and producers knew that many of the things prohibited were the very things the audience wanted.

The MPPDA at length determined to set up a more efficient means of enforcing the Code—largely at the prodding of American Catholic bishops. All scripts and completed films were to be submitted to the Production Code Administration within the Hays Office. Under the leadership of Joseph Breen, a strong-willed former newspaperman, the PCA acquired significant power. No producer in the MPPDA could, without risking a $25,000 fine, release or distribute a picture unless it had a certificate of approval from the PCA. To this the producers agreed as if they had signed a contract. By the middle of the 1930s the content of the movies had been cleaned up to an extent that, earlier, would have seemed impossible.

The artistic and aesthetic cost of the cleanup can be seen in two examples. When MGM decided to film Leo Tolstoy's classic *Anna Karenina* it realized that there would be trouble. A central element in the story is adultery, a topic which the Code said should be avoided. After extensive consultations with the PCA, the studio agreed that the illegitimate child who appears in the novel would be eliminated, that the "matrimonial bond" would be "positively defended" by prominently featuring two happily married couples, that Anna's lover, Vronsky, would be portrayed unfavorably and would be miserable, and that no scenes would be played in Anna's bedroom. So much for Tolstoy.

In 1940 David O. Selznick set out to produce the film *Rebecca* from the Daphne Du Maurier novel. In the novel Rebecca's husband, Max, murders her. He then takes her body to their boat, which has had holes drilled in it, pushes it out into the water, and lets it sink. Max commits an immoral act, and the Code required that he be punished for it. The original script, true to the novel's story line, lacked the "evil must be punished" quality, and the Hays Office revised it to conform to the Code. Now Rebecca, in a confrontation with Max, trips and kills herself in falling. Max takes the body—dead now by accident—to the boat and sets it adrift.

The constraint on freedom of expression imposed by the Hays-Breen Office went beyond script revision. Hays' feelings were so strong against Sacco and Vanzetti, for example, that he ordered destruction of all copies of the film, shot years before, which showed the men's gigantic funeral procession through Boston. Ultimately, the power of the Hays Office diminished with the changes in American society that followed the Second World War.

Perhaps the movies and the movie players in the 1920s serve as a reflection of the greater American society. Public interest in the private affairs of the stars remained keen throughout the decade and the fantasy world of the silver screen presented a picture of hedonism and self-indulgence to many moviegoers. It may be that the general loosening of sexual restraints in American life has some cause-effect relationship with what was happening, earlier, in Hollywood. More likely, the two were reflections of a larger social change that affected them both.

Roscoe "Fatty" Arbuckle saw his movies banned from public showing, but they were not censored because of content. It was Arbuckle himself who was banned—the victim of a blacklist. In the summer of 1922 the Hays Office prepared a list of nearly two hundred people whose reputations for drug use, drunkenness, and debauchery contributed to the image of Hollywood as a city of sin. They were to be removed from participation in the movie industry, eliminated to improve the public perception of filmdom's capital. The blacklists of the 1940s and 1950s were the direct descendants of the blacklist of 1922. The later blacklists focused on politics, however, rather than on personal morality. Whatever the reason, freedom to work at one's chosen profession still remains vulnerable to public whim.

4

THE PEOPLE vs. AL CAPONE

At a time when the Prohibition Amendment was still pending before the American Congress, former president William Howard Taft announced that he opposed it, purely on practical grounds. "I don't drink myself at all, and I don't oppose prohibition on the ground that it limits the liberties of the people." But, he believed, there was too much sentiment against prohibition. Opportunity for crime and graft would increase. Federal law enforcement would reach out in new directions and federal power would grow. The enterprise was too large and the political consequences dangerous. "[A]ll over the United States . . . elections will continuously turn on the rigid or languid execution of the liquor law, as they do now in the prohibition states." The conservative former president (1909–12), soon to be appointed Chief Justice of the United States Supreme Court, understood clearly what was coming. There would be anger at the methods used by the Drys to win public support, growing awareness of the impossibility of enforcing the Volstead Act, and a general distaste for any government regulations dealing with personal habits of eating or drinking.

Neither the eminence of former president Taft nor the prescience of his statement had any impact on the adoption of the Eighteenth Amendment. Although in the House of Representatives the measure barely managed the required two-thirds majority, in the Senate it passed by a vote of more than three to one. Ratification was achieved within fourteen months. Eventually forty-six states ratified; only Connecticut and Rhode Island never formally approved the amendment.

In a society in which individual rights are a matter of major concern, prohibition posed a philosophical as well as a real problem. Was prohibition an affirmation or a repudiation of democratic principles? The functioning of ordered liberty requires acceptance of laws established by a majority in accordance with well-defined procedures. But if such laws invade the privacy of individual citizens, they go too far. Sumptuary laws governing the use of food, drink, and dress, most civil libertarians agree, subvert democracy. Those who supported prohibition denied that it was sumptuary legislation. It was social legislation, they asserted. The distinction between them, according to clergyman and civil libertarian John Haynes Holmes, was clear.

> The State hasn't any right to dictate to you what you shall drink, provided that what you drink affects yourself alone. . . . If any man should prove to me . . . that the drinking of a cup of coffee does to society what the drinking of a glass of whiskey does, then I should say that legislation against coffee . . . was justified—justified by its social effects, justified by the fact that the safety and happiness of all must be protected. . . . [C]ertain types of individual freedom are inimical to the freedom of others and thus should be curtailed in the interests of social progress.

Widespread concern about the consumption of alcohol was not new in the United States. As early as the 1820s the temperance movement sought ways to limit if not abolish the use of spirits. At that time, temperance usually meant avoiding drunkenness. By the end of the nineteenth century, however, temperance came to be identified with prohibition of the liquor traffic and the closing of saloons. By general reputation, and with some justification, these parlors of sin were thought to be the scene of all kinds of debaucheries. They stayed open seven days a week and profaned the sabbath. They served minors, even young children. Some were dens of prostitution. In the twentieth century, national prohibition represented a victory for the Protestant, rural, nativist majority over changes brought by industrialization, urbanization, and immigration. It was a temporary victory in a culture conflict in which the political power of generally rural populations brought Dry supremacy.

The Southern states provided the greatest single source of Dry political strength, but there were elements in the urban middle class that supported prohibition as well. Social workers believed that prohibition might alleviate deep-seated poverty in industrial areas. Some professionals and members of the small-business class believed that the drinking immigrant was a threat to continuation of a sober and disciplined society. Old Progressives, veterans of many campaigns against political bosses and political machines, believed that abstinence might help bring an end to political corruption. Many physicians and health officials were convinced by the scientific and medical data presented by the Drys showing that alcohol was destructive and debilitating. And many employers were concerned about safety and the maintenance of production in their factories and mines.

There is rarely a completely uniform division of voters in any respect, and many voters in highly urban areas voted Dry; indeed, and some rural districts polled Wet. The controversy over prohibition also involved an immigrant–nativist conflict. As a general rule, voters in the Wet districts were working-class immigrants or at least identifiably "ethnic." Not only did the voting split develop as Wet–Dry, urban–rural, and immigrant–nativist but also along lines of Catholic–Protestant and working class–middle class.

The Anti-Saloon League was established in Ohio in 1896. Its great contribution to the fight for prohibition was the merging of its campaign to abolish the saloon with the use of pressure politics to do it. The Eighteenth Amendment could not have been enacted without the work of the Anti-Saloon League. The wording of the amendment represented a compromise between the radical, "bone dry" prohibitionists and those who were more moderate. The first section of the amendment prohibited the "manufacture, sale, or importation of intoxicating liquors." The word "intoxicating" displeased the radicals, who wanted the more inclusive word, "alcoholic." "Intoxicating" prevailed in part because most Catholic, Episcopal, and Jewish spokespersons wished to avoid any implication that sacramental usage involved intoxication. And for the time being at least, there was no constitutional definition of "intoxicating."

Section 2 of the amendment called upon Congress and the "several states to enforce this article by appropriate legislation." The Volstead Act, drawn up by Anti-Saloon League attorney Wayne B.

Wheeler and sponsored by Representative Andrew Volstead of Minnesota, was designed to provide for enforcement. The act defined "intoxicating" beverages as those containing .5 percent alcohol (making "alcoholic" and "intoxicating" almost synonymous). The .5 standard had its origin in what the experience of several states had found to be measurable and not in any effort to judge what was in fact "intoxicating." The act, like the amendment, contained no prohibition regarding purchase or consumption of intoxicating beverages. If the amendment had been motivated by a desire to protect people from their own impulses, this was a curious omission. Just as curious was another provision which allowed people to "possess" such liquors as they possessed before January 1920. This clause permitted those with wealth and foresight to anticipate the alcoholic drought to come. The Yale Club of New York, it was said, had a fifteen-year supply of wet goods to please its wealthy private membership.

The law also provided generous concessions concerning liquors sold for medicinal, sacramental, or industrial purposes. The manufacture of industrial alcohol was to be licensed and the alcohol produced denatured to render it unfit for human consumption. Beverage alcohol was limited to physicians' patients, communicants at religious services, and makers of ciders and vinegars. The law also allowed individuals to produce ciders and wines in their own homes for their own use. The Volstead Act thus had some striking contradictions: It was designed to kill off the liquor business in general and the saloon in particular; at the same time, neither the Volstead Act nor the Eighteenth Amendment prohibited the possession and drinking of alcoholic beverages.

Who, precisely, was going to enforce the new moral code? And how? Section 2 of the Eighteenth Amendment gave Congress and the states "concurrent power to enforce this article by appropriate legislation." It had been worded this way to mollify the sensitivities of states-righters because, as Congressman Webb of North Carolina put it, "Nobody desires that the Federal Congress shall take away from the various states the right to enforce the prohibition laws of those states." In addition to this deference to states' rights, there was the practical problem of enforcement. Few federal laws were aimed directly at individuals and few federal agencies existed to enforce those laws. The federal government was not really prepared to set up massive blockades in order to prevent the operation of trucks carrying kegs of beer. At the very least, it lacked the necessary manpower, and few Americans were ready to pay to assemble it.

The Commissioner of Internal Revenue of the Treasury Department was put in charge of enforcing the Volstead Act. He and his assistants were empowered to investigate offenders and report them to United States attorneys, who would prosecute in the federal courts. For a first offense a bootlegger could be fined a maximum of $1,000 and jailed for six months. Second-offenders were treated more harshly and could receive a fine of $10,000 and a jail sentence of five years. A "padlock" law enabled the authorities to close for one year any establishment illegally selling liquor. And the law authorized the government to seize and sell at public auction automobiles, boats, and airplanes used for the illegal transportation of liquor. The money earned from the sale of such goods would help defray the expenses of law enforcement.

Most of the states enacted laws to supplement the Volstead Act. Evasion of the dry law became both a state and a federal crime. Sixteen states defined the word "intoxicating" even more strictly than the federal statute and some even criminalized the possession of liquor. But state appropriations never adequately supported the need for additional police to enforce the laws. Moreover, state resentment of federal interference often prevented federal prohibition officers from doing their duty. There were many instances in which zealous federal prohibition agents were transferred or removed because state officials were annoyed by their efficiency.

The Volstead Act's exceptions also made for difficulties. The exception of prescription or sacramental alcohol, for example, tempted medical professionals and even clergymen to dabble in bootlegging for their friends. The demand for sacramental wines increased by 800,000 gallons during the first two years of Prohibition. A spokesman for the Federal Council of Churches in America observed that "not more than one-quarter of this is sacramental — the rest is sacrilegious."

Smuggling was another major problem. To seal off the 3,000-mile border between the United States and Canada would have required a border patrol of massive proportions. To close the thousands of miles of shoreline on both coasts would have required a naval presence of enormous size. In the Prohibition Bureau's District 20 there were twenty agents assigned to police an area that included the edge of the Pacific Ocean, Puget Sound and its numerous islands with their secluded and wooded coves, and the adjacent mainland. District 20 was a haven for rumrunners, who from it could supply bootleggers from Seattle to California. For the lawbreakers the risks were slight, the rewards great.

The Drys provided little help in making law enforcement more effective. For many it was more important to have prohibition as a symbol than to enforce it as a reality. The law of the land condemned alcohol and all of the cultural values that it represented. When violations of the Volstead Act were pointed out, some Dry leaders did not respond by demanding more troops or more guns, or more prisons; they asked simply for "more respect for the Constitution."

Enforcement of the Volstead Act was weak and ineffective. At the same time, prohibition was responsible for bringing about a sharp decline in per capita consumption of alcohol and in diseases and deaths related to alcohol. Consumption fell to one-half the rate prior to World War I. A sharp rise in the price of liquor caused by prohibition had the effect of limiting the number of purchasers. In 1928, for example, the average price of a quart of bootleg beer was 80 cents, 600 percent more expensive than beer in 1916. Gin was $5.90 a quart, up 520 percent. Whiskey at $7 was up 310 percent. The average annual family income was about $2,600. Wage earners—the greater part of the population—who normally drank beer, drank less during Prohibition. As for hard liquor, it was associated with affluence, with those who wanted it and could afford to pay for it. Outside the larger cities most people never knew or came into contact with a bootlegger and probably never saw a speakeasy. The notion that "everyone drank, including many who never did before" was a myth created by journalists and writers.

The number of arrests for drunkenness fell off remarkably during Prohibition. Alcoholism disappeared as a topic from American medical journals. Social workers reported that the working class drank very much less than before, even taking into account those urban areas where immigrant populations openly flouted the law. On balance, social workers believed, conditions among low-income Americans had been improved.

* * *

Alphonse "Scarface" Capone began his criminal career before the Eighteenth Amendment was added to the Constitution. Without the Volstead Act and the Eighteenth Amendment he might have become just as prosperous, just as influential, and just as ruthless. Without prohibition there would have been no bootlegging industry, but prostitution and gambling formed an ample basis for a successful career in crime.

Al Capone was brought from New York to Chicago to function in the organization of "Big Jim" Colosimo and Johnny Torrio. Their basic source of revenue came from the houses of prostitution that flourished in Chicago even before prohibition presented new opportunities. Jim Colosimo had been a bootblack, a pickpocket, a pimp, and a bagman for the aldermen who controlled the vices and votes in their Chicago districts. He married a brothelkeeper and was soon managing scores of bordellos and saloons. By the end of the first decade of the twentieth century, Colosimo was the biggest vice operator in the city of Chicago and possessed great political influence. In 1909 Colosimo brought his nephew, Johnny Torrio, from Brooklyn. Torrio—sometimes called "the father of modern American gangsterism"—was to help Colosimo in the management and operation of his growing prostitution business. Furthermore, Colosimo needed Torrio's assistance with the Mafia and the Black Hand, which had been extorting money from the now wealthy racketeer. Torrio dealt with the problem expeditiously—with hired gunmen. Torrio also helped organize saloons and gambling dens, and he paid off politicians and policemen who were on the take. When Colosimo branched out into the protection racket, Torrio worked with collections.

While he was tending to his uncle's domain, Torrio quietly built his own organization. Late in 1919 he sent to the East Coast for Capone, not yet a leading figure. Capone was to be a bodyguard, a chauffeur, a bartender, and a "capper" to bring customers to a new brothel known as the Four Deuces on the fourth floor of a building at 2222 Wabash Avenue. On the second and third floors there were rooms for gambling and on the first floor was a saloon and an office.

When the the Volstead Act went into effect at 12:01 a.m. on January 17, 1920, Johnny Torrio wanted to get in on the ground floor of the illicit liquor trade. Colosimo ridiculed the idea, however. Big

Jim had fallen for a pretty nineteen-year-old who had come to Chicago for a career in opera. Colosimo hired her to sing in his cafe and nightly she entertained his customers with a repertoire of light classics. Torrio was unable to rouse the amorous Colosimo to a recognition of the possibilities for profit in the new era. Most of the existing saloons, beer gardens, and roadhouses had stayed open in the expectation that somehow they would be able to get supplies. Torrio wanted to meet that expectation, but Colosimo repeatedly told him that prohibition would not amount to much. There was no money in bootlegging, he said. "Stick to women. That's where the money is."

Big Jim Colosimo paid the price of his intransigence. There is little doubt, although it was never proved, that Torrio paid $10,000 to Frankie Yale, a well-known hit man from New York, to get rid of his Uncle Jim.

By the middle of May, 1920, Torrio set about organizing the Chicago liquor trade. He put Al Capone in charge of field operations and made him manager of the Torrio headquarters at the Four Deuces. Capone was to get 25 percent of the brothel profits and half of the net yield from bootlegging. Although he was then no more than twenty-three, Capone was already known as a gunman and slugger. When he was only nineteen and a member of New York's Five Points gang, he had been under suspicion for armed robbery and murder. Capone had an impressive curved scar that ran from the top of his left ear to the corner of his mouth, earned in a fight over some remarks he had made about a girl. Because no hair grew through the scar tissue it presented a sharp contrast to his darkish cheek and jaw. He was self-conscious about the scar and sought to reduce the contrast with liberal applications of talcum powder, and he was careful to offer his right, unscarred profile to news photographers when he could.

Together, Torrio and Capone expanded the business. They worked well in concert. Torrio—older, wiser, more conservative—condoned violence only when other strategies were unsuccessful. Capone—younger, more gregarious, and fearless—had a temper with a low flash point. Within two years the two were working as partners. They brought Al's brother Ralph into the business. They moved south and west, pushing into the controllable suburbs of Cicero, Burnham, and Stickney. There they established a variety of liquor enterprises. Their breweries openly and without police interference turned out real beer, as distinguished from the legally permissible "near beer," a beverage from which nearly all alcohol had been removed.

Torrio and Capone also established rumrunning depots and gambling parlors fully equipped with roulette wheels, slot machines, and dice tables. They accomplished this expansion without bloodshed, using bribery as their chief tool. They bought town and village officials, and protesting property owners near the site of a prospective dive became quiet when Torrio opened his purse. By 1923, Capone and Torrio were the undisputed rulers of Cicero. In the municipal elections in the spring of 1924 their man was elected mayor and they were able to name the chief of police. So successful were the two that their combined operations grossed an estimated two to five million dollars a year. Other gangsters could not help but be attracted to what was obviously a bonanza. This was particularly true of Dion O'Banion, who, as a boy, had sung in the choir of Holy Name Cathedral on Chicago's North Side and been remarkable for his piety and obedience to the Sisters. As an adult, however, O'Banion was a racketeer and murderer. He loved flowers and habitually wore a carnation in his buttonhole as well as three pistols carefully concealed in his specially tailored suits. In Chicago he was only slightly less important than Torrio and Capone.

In the early days of Prohibition the three men worked in partnership, until activities of operators allied with Torrio and Capone caused O'Banion's defection. He charged specifically that the Genna brothers were selling bad beer in his territory, Chicago's North Side. He wanted something done about them, but Torrio explained that no one could order the Gennas around. Outraged, O'Banion declared his independence and announced contemptuously, "To Hell with the Sicilians!" On November 10, 1924, while O'Banion was working contentedly in his flower shop with some newly arrived chrysanthemums, three well-dressed gentlemen entered, apparently to purchase some flowers. The men, later said to be "Italians," fired six shots. There were no arrests and no one was ever prosecuted for the murder. But in the Chicago underworld it was widely believed that the assassins were the Torrio-Capone gang. In the war that followed, about an equal number from both gangs lost their lives. At one point, a barrage of shots from a passing car left Torrio with four bullets in his jaw and neck and one in his shoulder. For weeks he was near death. Torrio was so frightened that, once recovered, he fled with his wife and belongings to Italy, where he remained for several years. The organization was effectively now in the hands of Al Capone.

The gang wars did not end when Capone took over, nor did the business stop expanding. Capone extended his operations beyond Chicago and its environs to St. Louis, Newark, New Orleans, and Atlantic City. He also acquired an interest in a number of dog tracks in the Chicago area, and went into the labor union racket, taking over unions and using this power to shake down employers in several industries. Capone even extended his "protection" business to laundries and cleaning and dyeing establishments, imposing on them compulsory insurance payments against bombing. Such "protection" seemed necessary. In one calendar year Chicago had 115 mysterious bombings and no prosecutions for any of them. From all his operations Capone's take in 1928 has been estimated, probably without exaggeration, at $105 million.

Capone, applying the lessons Torrio had taught him, forged a highly centralized, strongly disciplined, heterogeneous business enterprise, organized and structured like other big business organizations. With Capone at the head of the organization was a business manager, a treasurer, and the director of liquor sales. On the next level was a manager for the distribution of liquor, another who managed off-track race betting, and a third who ran the whorehouses. Below them were those who provided special services. Louis Cowan, for example, who operated a newspaper kiosk in Cicero, was the organization's chief bondsman. Every member of Capone's organization had Cowan's name and telephone number in case of arrest. Cowan would appear before the magistrate equipped with documentary proof of real estate holdings which he put up as security for bail. Still further down the hierarchy were bodyguards, sharpshooters, goons, and musclemen.

The gang wars continued. Between 1923 and 1926, the newspapers reported, there were 135 gang killings. Of these, some 70 involved what the papers called "big shots."

Al Capone lived in the shadow of the gun. He went nowhere without bodyguards. When he attended the theater, he often bought entire sections of seats to surround himself with trustworthy friends and insulate himself from possible assassins. In 1928 he spoke of retiring, of finding a peaceful place where he could live as a rich citizen rather than as a target. Finding such a place was not easy. He liked Los Angeles, but when he arrived two plainclothesmen met him at the station to tell him that he was "undesirable" and would not be permitted to stay. The residents of St. Petersburg, Florida, decided that having Capone in their midst would ruin property values. He made his journey to that city in the sun but did not stay long. British authorities in Nassau declared him persona non grata and the same thing happened in Miami, where he was "officially requested" to leave. Finally, on Palm Island, just off the Florida coast opposite Miami but not within that city's jurisdiction, Capone managed to buy a villa. When he told the authorities that he would resist any attempt to deny him the right to live there, that he would fight them in every court, they backed down. He had no convictions under Florida or federal laws that could be used to label him as undesirable.

While Capone was on Palm Island in 1928, his close friend Tony Lombardo was gunned down in Chicago. Lombardo was at that time president of the Unione Siciliana, later renamed the Italo-American National Union. Originally a lawful fraternal organization devoted to advancing the interests of Sicilian immigrants, it had come under gangster domination. The presidency of the association was a valuable prize because it meant control of thousands of "alky cookers" as well as wine, beer, and liquor distributors. Much of the carnage that resulted from gangland rivalry involved struggles for control of the Sicilian association. With Lombardo's death, control passed to Joseph Aiello, who was allied with "Bugs" Moran, now the leader of the O'Banion mob. Aiello held the presidency for less than a year, when he was murdered. It appeared that the gangs were now realigning themselves mainly, although not entirely, according to ethnic ties. The Irish, Polish, and Jewish gangs fought the Capone people, and as Capone expanded and diversified his operations he met challengers attempting to block his way. His most relentless foes were Moran and his North Siders, who challenged his every move. They hijacked trucks carrying liquor on consignment to Capone. They bombed saloons selling Capone's beer. They murdered Capone's associates. And they went into the cleaning and dyeing racket.

While still in Florida, Capone decided on violent retaliation. Soon the greatest mass gangster murder in history took place, on St. Valentine's Day, 1929. As one writer put it, "The firm of 'Bugs' Moran and Company was found operating outside the zone that had been agreed upon as their sales and merchandising territory, and seven executives died in defense of free enterprise." Moran himself and two of his men, however, escaped death by a matter of minutes. No one was ever charged with the crime, but for Moran and the survivors there was no doubt as to responsibility. "Only Capone kills like that."

The St. Valentine's Day Massacre and the murder of Alfred "Jake" Lingle, a journalist concerned with the activities of the underworld, brought a public outcry led by Lingle's former employer, the *Chicago Tribune*.

> Murder has become the accepted course of crime in its natural stride, but to the list of Colosimo, O'Banion . . . [and] the seven who were killed in the St. Valentine's Day Massacre, the name is added of a man whose business was to expose the work of the killers. The *Tribune* accepts the challenge. It is war. There will be casualities. . . .

Colonel Robert McCormick, publisher of the *Tribune*, posted a reward of $25,000. Hearst's *Chicago Herald and Examiner* matched that sum, and the *Evening Post* added $5,000 more. The Chicago citizenry, at least some of them, were stirred to action. A group called the Secret Six—important business figures headed by Colonel Robert Isham Randolph—took the lead. The group was sponsored by the Chicago Association of Commerce Sub-Committee for the Prevention and Punishment of Crime and was plentifully supplied with funds, all privately contributed. The Six prepared to fight to clean up Chicago, which Randolph described as having "the most corrupt and degenerate municipal administration that ever cursed a city—a politico-criminal alliance formed between a civil administration and a gun-covered underworld for the exploitation of its citizenry."

Colonel Randolph was the only known member of the Secret Six; he declined to name the other five, lest their lives be endangered. The group was both realistic and practical. They knew they had to seek federal help from the Department of Justice because they could not rely on either their local or state governments. Prosecutions for racketeering, extortion, or even murder were impossible because the politico-criminal alliance pervaded local government and extended to the state level. It was difficult to find an official, local or state, who was not in Capone's back pocket.

At this time agents of the federal Department of Justice and of the criminal investigation division of the Bureau of Internal Revenue had begun seeking evidence of violations of the Volstead Act and of the income tax laws. The investigations had been encouraged by newly elected President Herbert Hoover at the urging of Colonel Frank Knox, publisher of the *Chicago Daily News*. A two-pronged attack emerged as a result of the federal investigations. One was led by Eliot Ness and his Department of Justice raiders. Ness operated with a great deal of publicity. He kept the press informed of his operations and was delighted to welcome a cameraman to the scene of the action whenever he went after a Capone brewery. Ness's penchant for publicity rather than secrecy severely limited his effectiveness.

The second thrust involved federal investigators who were looking for violations of the income tax law. Proving anything against Capone would not be easy. He kept no personal books and had no bank accounts in his own name. He had never made a financial statement or filed an income tax return. But he had property. He had full or partial ownership of brothels, gambling houses, bookie joints, dog tracks, and breweries that were connected to over 1,200 speakeasies. In Cook County, whenever liquor was moved, bets made, or whores laid, Capone had a piece of the action. The problem was that federal agents had no proof of Capone's ownerships and other business interests. He lived regally. He spent large sums on personal wearing apparel. He maintained a retinue of henchmen and bodyguards. He kept his estate on Palm Island and a well-appointed home on Prairie Avenue in Chicago. He ran a fleet of high-powered and strongly armored automobiles, among them a custom-built $20,000 Cadillac with plush upholstery, a half-ton of armor plate, a steel visor over the gas tank, and thick, bullet-proof glass. Capone entertained lavishly and he lost vast sums gambling. But documentary proof was needed.

To help trap those taxpayers who concealed their income, the Internal Revenue Bureau had developed two methods of indirect proof. Both were based on circumstantial evidence. According to the "net worth" method, the taxpayer's scale of living was analyzed. The difference between reported income and indications of accumulated assets was deemed to be an increase in net worth. Such an unreported gain in net worth was then declared taxable. Acording to the second method, "net expenditure," investigators applied the same yardstick to the taxpayer's expenditures. Those in excess of reported income were deemed taxable. Both "net worth" and "net expenditure" were applied to the Capone case.

Federal agents scoured Chicago and Miami for businessmen and establishments of any kind with which Capone might have been involved—hotels, real estate agents, merchants. For the years 1926 through 1929 they compiled a partial list of expenditures for goods and services and an evaluation of those possessions which they could identify as his. They learned from two Chicago furniture companies that Capone bought chairs, sofas, tables, beds, and rugs for his two homes and office priced at $26,000. He spent $20,000 at two Chicago jewelers' for silverware, a gold-plated dinner service, and thirty diamond belt buckles. From Marshall Field & Company he obtained his custom-made suits, monogrammed shirts, underwear, and other items at an outlay of $7,000. His hotel bills in Chicago ran about $1,200 a week and his telephone bills totaled $39,000. On the night of the Tunney–Dempsey fight Capone threw a party that cost $3,000. Federal agents were able to account for expenditures of $165,000, although this was a pittance compared to what they believed flowed into his hands from illicit sources.

A 1927 decision of the United States Supreme Court gave the enforcement branch of the Bureau of Internal Revenue a powerful weapon to use against gangsters like Capone. The case was an appeal by a bootlegger named Manley Sullivan. Sullivan had filed no income tax returns because, he claimed, income from illegal transactions was not taxable. Moreover, to be forced to declare such income would violate the Fifth Amendment's privilege against self-incrimination. The Court found neither argument convincing. There is no reason, the Court declared, "why the fact that a business is unlawful should exempt it from paying taxes that if lawful it would have to pay." The argument that the Court violated the Fifth Amendment was similarly given short shrift. "It would be an extreme if not extravagant application of the Fifth Amendment to say that it authorized a man to refuse to state the amount of his income because it had been made in crime."

Internal Revenue agents worked on the Capone investigation for almost two years. They ran into countless blind alleys. Agent Frank J.

Wilson got the first major break. A one-time Buffalo real estate operator, later to become chief of the United States Secret Service, he was so unflappable that he was said "to sweat ice water." Challenged to find evidence of Capone's gross income over the standard exemption of $5,000 for the years in which he had failed to file returns, Wilson began searching through properties allegedly controlled by Capone. While rummaging through documents relating to The Ship, a Cicero gambling house reputed to be one of Capone's holdings, Wilson found a cashbook containing handwritten records of the house's income. With great care, Wilson and his assistants examined handwriting samples from every known or suspected Capone associate or employee. They looked at voting registers, police court bail records, and other written documents they were able to obtain. They were rewarded by matching the handwriting on a Cicero bank deposit slip with entries in The Ship's cashbook. The handwriting was that of Lou Schumway, a Capone henchman and once a bookkeeper at The Ship. The agents located Schumway in Florida. His reluctance to talk was understandable, but agents were able to persuade him to cooperate with the government. He went to California under protective custody and remained there until he was needed at the trial.

In Cicero, agents pursued a mysterious "J.C. Dunbar," whose real name, they discovered, was Fred Ries, a former employee in one of Capone's gambling houses. Between 1927 and 1929, "Dunbar" had brought to the Pinkert State Bank nearly $300,000 in cash to purchase cashier's checks. Agent Wilson had him held as a material witness.

It was learned that Ries had a pathological aversion to vermin. After four days in a particularly unwholesome jail cell, probably swarming with insect life, Ries gave in. Agents sneaked him into the grand jury room, where he gave his testimony. The Secret Six then provided money for Ries's protective custody in Latin America, where he remained until needed for the trial.

On June 5, 1931, a federal grand jury, acting on the evidence of Schumway, Ries, and a good deal more, returned indictments. Alphonse Capone—alias Al Brown, alias "Scarface" Brown, alias "Scarface" Capone, alias A. Costa—was charged with 23 separate violations of the internal revenue laws during the years 1924 through 1929. His income for those years—probably only a fraction of it—was said to total $1,038,655. The tax assessment plus the penalties came

to $383,705. Capone was released on $50,000 bond pending the outcome of his trial.

A week later, the grand jury returned an additional indictment
against Capone and 59 others based on evidence compiled by Eliot
Ness and his investigators. The charge was conspiracy to violate the
Volstead Act. The indictment cited five thousand offenses, four-fifths
of them consisting of beer deliveries. The sixty names in the grand jury
indictment constituted a Who's Who of the Chicago illicit liquor trade.
But it was the income tax case that was central in the proceedings
against Capone.

From the day the indictment came down, the American press was
convinced that Capone would get a light sentence. The *Louisville
Courier-Journal* complained: "It is not conducive to American pride
that gangsters, guilty of every abomination . . . should be found guilty
only of failing to pay taxes on their ill-gotten gains." Even in this
major respect the government's case against Capone was shaky. The
United States Circuit Court of Appeals had recently ruled that there
was a three-year limitation on tax evasion cases. The government
argued in favor of six years. If the Supreme Court rejected the government's argument, it meant that the Capone prosecution would be
ended for all the years in the indictment save one. Moreover, apparently Capone's attorneys believed that they had struck a bargain with
the United States Attorney for the Northern District of Illinois, George
E.Q. Johnson. Capone would plead guilty in exchange for a light sentence. Johnson was said to have agreed with Capone's lawyers on a
recommendation of two and a half years after having consulted Agent
Wilson, Internal Revenue's enforcement branch chief Elmer Irey,
Attorney General William Mitchell, and Secretary of the Treasury
Ogden Mills. But Judge James H. Wilkerson had other ideas about
such a compromise.

> The Court will listen . . . to the recommendation of the District
> Attorney. The Court will listen to the recommendation of the
> Attorney General. . . . But the thing the defendant cannot
> think, must not think, is that . . . the Court is bound to enter
> judgment according to that recommendation. It is time for
> somebody to impress upon the defendant that it is utterly
> impossible to bargain with a federal court.

Michael Ahern, Capone's attorney, was quick to respond. He moved to withdraw the original guilty pleas, telling the court that if he had had any inkling that the court would not follow the recommendation of the prosecution he would not have entered such pleas. Judge Wilkerson permitted the plea withdrawal and scheduled trial for October 6, 1931. The income tax cases were consolidated, one for the year 1924 and a second for the years 1925 through 1929. The indictment charging Capone with violations of the Volstead Act was never brought to trial.

As preparations were being made for trial, Agent Frank Wilson heard that somehow Capone had obtained a list of the veniremen from which the jury was to be chosen. Capone's men were busy trying to bribe some of them with jobs or cash offers. Others were threatened with mayhem or death. Wilson brought ten of the names to U.S. Attorney Johnson, and together they took their list to the judge. "Bring your case into court as planned, gentlemen. Leave the rest to me," Wilkerson told them. Jury selection began, but the names of the veniremen were not the names on the list that Capone had obtained. Judge Wilkerson had eliminated the possibility of a suborned jury by simply exchanging his list of panel members with another judge. From that point on, jury selection proceeded with dispatch. It took only half a day to select three retail grocers, two journeyman painters, a pattern maker, a real estate broker, a stationary engineer, a hardware merchant, an insurance agent, a farmer, and a clerk. As was customary, they all swore that they harbored no prejudice against Capone and had no wish to see him imprisoned.

The attorneys for both sides represented what contemporaries called "the cream of the bar." The prosecution team consisted of U.S. Attorney George E.Q. Johnson, Assistant U.S. Attorney Dwight H. Green, and a competent staff. (Green became governor of Illinois in 1940.) The leading defense attorney was Michael Ahern, who represented most of the top-ranking gang lords and was regarded as one of Chicago's most erudite trial lawyers. He was joined by Albert Fink, a trial lawyer who had enjoyed many notable successes. Judge James H. Wilkerson had an enviable reputation for integrity, ability, and impartiality.

But most of the attention of the curious onlookers was upon Al

Capone, sitting impassively, tonsorially perfect, his sturdy frame garbed expensively, his colored silk shirts making a striking contrast with his face, its scar carefully powdered over.

Prosecutor Green's opening statement informed the jury that the government did not need to prove the exact amount of income earned. It was necessary only "to prove that the defendant had earned taxable income during one or more of the years in question on which he had paid no tax." There followed a procession of witnesses. Some came from the Bureau of Internal Revenue to testify that Al Capone had filed no tax returns for any of the years in the charge. Some who had sold things to Capone—butchers, bakers, real estate brokers, furniture dealers—contributed to the picture being created of the accused's net expenditures and net worth.

The first "star" witness, Louis Schumway, testified as to the profits of five or six gambling houses in Cicero during the years 1924 through 1929. "I often saw Capone in this rear room [of the Hawthorne Smoke Shop]," he said, "when we were going over the books and the money." He continued: "Capone was always interested in the daily take and was always worried about a stick up." Schumway, however, had no proof that Capone had received any of the profits—about $550,000—which his responses had revealed. Nor did Fred Ries, brought back from South America where he had been kept under wraps, see Capone "handle any of the money of the enterprises . . . [or] do anything to indicate that he was in charge of or financially interested in the places."

Most crucial in the government's case was the testimony of four employees of the Bureau of Internal Revenue, who were called to testify about the activities of Louis B. Mattingly. Mattingly, a tax expert and attorney, had been engaged by Capone in March 1930 to try to negotiate a "compromise" with the government over its tax claims. Mattingly had conceded during one of his conversations with bureau personnel that his client's businesses had produced income, although the sum was modest. To the surprise of agent Frank Wilson, Mattingly had agreed at that time to specify in writing just how much Capone's businesses had profited. The letter provided indisputable corroboration that although Capone had never filed a return, he had earned a taxable income. Mattingly wrote:

> Re Alphonse Capone
>
> Taxpayer became active as a principal with three associates at about the end of the year 1925. Because of the fact that he had no capital to invest in their various undertakings, his participation during the entire year of 1926 and the greater part of 1927 was limited. During the years 1928 and 1929, the profits of the organization of which he was a member were divided as follows: one-third to a group of regular employees and one-sixth to the taxpayer and three associates. . . .
>
> I am of the opinion that this taxable income for the years 1926 and 1927 might be fairly fixed at not to exceed $26,000 and $40,000 respectively, and for the years 1928 and 1929, not to exceed $100,000 per year.

A dispute broke out immediately as to the admissibility of the letter. Defense attorneys Ahern and Fink objected strenuously. In attempting to work out a compromise, Mattingly had had several interviews with bureau officials and once even allowed them to interrogate Capone. Stenographic notes had been taken. Ahern and Fink argued that the letter and whatever was said during the negotiations were privileged and therefore inadmissible. But they were ignoring the fact that both Capone and Mattingly had been warned before they made their statements that nothing said at the meetings would be regarded as privileged and that everything might be used as evidence.

Judge Wilkerson ruled the statements admissible. A compromise in the legal sense, he said, "meant a meeting of opposing interests, where both sides, properly authorized, come together to settle a genuinely disputed claim." Those elements were not present in this case because Capone and Mattingly, both uninvited, had approached officials and made statements, although they had been warned that any statements they made might be used against them.

On the fifth day of the trial, an episode occurred which added a measure of excitement to the proceedings. Throughout the trial Phil D'Andrea, Capone's bodyguard, had sat behind him, keeping a vigilant watch over his boss. Government officials, however, had become suspicious of "a bulging breast pocket in the bodyguard's flashy sportscoat." By prearrangement, a bailiff notified D'Andrea that a messenger in the corridor had a telegram for him. Once in the corridor, agents grabbed D'Andrea and hurried him to the judge's chambers, where a search revealed a fully loaded .38-caliber revolver. The judge ignored the protests of Ahern and Fink that D'Andrea had a permit to carry a concealed weapon. He did not know, they argued, that the permit did not extend to a federal court building. D'Andrea remained in custody for the duration of the trial. He was then charged with contempt of court and sent to jail for six months.

Capone's central argument focused on his gambling losses. According to witnesses, Capone was a chronic loser. His bad luck cost him $24,000 in 1924, $47,000 in 1925, $55,000 in 1926, and $90,000 in 1927. The point that the defense was trying to make was that Capone's net income was far less than the government had contended. It was, in any event, a futile argument. Taxpayers may deduct gambling losses only from gambling winnings. The Capone defense had been grasping at straws. Testimony by bookmakers clearly showed that Capone must have received income totaling thousands of dollars. Nor could the substantial income evidenced by Capone's possessions and expenditures be plausibly explained. Probably for these reasons neither Capone nor John Torrio, who had been in the courtroom since the opening day, testified.

In summation for the prosecution, Jacob I. Grossman and Samuel G. Clawson, members of the team headed by U.S. Attorney Johnson, recapitulated the government's evidence. Clawson ridiculed Mattingly's contention that Capone had no taxable income in 1924 and 1925, a time when Capone claimed that he was working for Johnny Torrio at $75 per week. "Remember," Clawson pointed out, "that in those same years, if you are to believe his witnesses, he was losing five times that much at the racetrack."

Albert Fink presented the first of the defense summations. He launched into a two-hour argument that faced an overwhelming weight of adverse evidence.

> There are two principal questions involved in this case—one in which the defendant alone is interested, another which interests you and me, the present generation and future generations. The first question is whether there is any evidence at all which rises to the dignity of hearsay indicating guilt on the part of the defendant. The second and most important ques-

tion is whether, if there be no evidence of guilt, a jury can be persuaded and conned by the prosecution to bring in a verdict of guilty merely to appease a public clamor.

All the counts against Capone, Fink reminded the jury, charged him with "willful intent" to evade the payment of income tax. "Suppose," Fink continued, "Capone believed that the money he received from so-called illegal transactions was not taxable. Suppose he discovered to the contrary and tried to pay what he owed, would you say he had an intent to defraud the government?" Or, as Fink continued with a second example, "If I were sick on the day my income tax was due and failed to make a return, that would be no crime. And there are other circumstances in which one may fail to make a return and still not be guilty of an attempt to evade the tax." There was simply no evidence that Capone willfully evaded taxes for the years charged, Fink asserted. Then he attacked the principle of net worth: that the amount of Capone's income could be deduced from the amount of his spending. "We don't know what his losses were. How do you know that the money spent wasn't borrowed?" All the government had proved, Fink conceded, was that Al Capone was a spendthrift. He concluded with a question that has been asked many times since:

> Is the government merely prosecuting this defendant for evasion of income tax, or is not this prosecution being used as a means by which to stow Al Capone away. . . . If this defendant's name were not Al Capone, there would be no case. You would be laughing at this so-called evidence.

U.S. Attorney Johnson, speaking at great length, completed the government's closing argument. Sarcastically, he noted that the defendant claimed no income, yet he spent lavishly. "Did this money represent gifts, inheritances or the proceeds of life insurance? . . . You can draw your own conclusions." Then, in answer to Fink's charge that the trial was really an attempt to find a way of ridding society of a public enemy:

> They say we prosecute because of the name Alphonse Capone, but can you imagine a federal case the result of public clamor?

Consider the thousands of little men and women who can only earn a little more than $1,500 a year and pay their taxes. Is it public clamor to demand taxes due in a time of national financial stress and treasury deficit from a man who buys two hundred and fifty dollar belt buckles and twenty seven dollar shirts?

It was not the defendant's name, Johnson insisted, but what he did that was significant. "Future generations will not remember this case because of the name of Alphonse Capone, but because it will establish whether or not a man can go so far beyond the law as to be able to escape the law."

It took Judge Wilkerson more than an hour to instruct the jury. The government did not have to prove the exact amount charged, he said. All that the government had to prove was that in any of the specified years Capone had had an income large enough to be taxed. He expounded on the principles underlying the terms "net worth" and "net expenditure." Insofar as the Mattingly letter was concerned, the jury had only to find that the admissions in the letter were freely made by an authorized agent of the defendant.

It took the jury only eight hours to reach a verdict. In some ways it is a confusing one. The indictment for 1924—for alleged tax evasion committed in 1925—had been handed down by the grand jury only days before the statute of limitations would have run out, but the trial jury found Capone not guilty. He was guilty of the charge in the second indictment: tax evasion for the years 1925, 1926, and 1927. He was found guilty of only a misdemeanor for failure to file returns in 1928 and 1929. It is difficult to understand how he could be found guilty of failing to file returns in these two years yet be innocent of tax evasion.

For his convictions on the felony tax evasion charges, Capone was sentenced to serve ten years and pay fines totaling $50,000 and costs. After the felony counts had been served, he was to serve an additional year in the county jail on the misdemeanor charges.

Capone served less than eight years. He was released in November 1939, suffering from advanced paresis caused by untreated syphilis. He died on January 25, 1947, of an apoplectic stroke.

* * *

Criminal activities during Prohibition are the stuff of legend, and Al Capone was the most notorious of the gangsters of that remarkable era. During Prohibition, bootlegging became an industry of major importance, employing many thousands of people and serving a great many more. Committing murders, bribing officials, and suborning jurors cannot be blamed on the Eighteenth Amendment and the Volstead Act. They resulted from the pursuit of criminal ambition. Capone seized the opportunities that came his way and soon regarded himself simply as a successful businessman whose methods of consolidating and centralizing many small operations into a large organization matched those of American big business generally. That he murdered in order to do so seemed to him no more than a method unique to business organization in criminal circles. As Capone himself put it, "Why can't they let me alone? I don't interfere with them any. Get me? I don't interfere with their racket. They should let my racket be." He supplied, he said, a legitimate demand. "Some call it bootlegging. Some call it racketeering. I call it a business."

Prohibition reflected some of the major themes of the 1920s. In many ways it was a manifestation of the anti-urbanism, the nativism, and the religious fundamentalism of that era. It played a role in the 1924 convention of the Democratic Party and in the defeat of Al Smith in the 1928 presidential election. As former president Taft had predicted, prohibition led to a big step in the centralization of federal power, for it involved the national government in the problem of criminal law enforcement as it had never been involved before.

5

DAVID C. STEPHENSON

The Ku Klux Klan in the 1920s was unlike its predecessor, the Klan of the post–Civil War Reconstruction era. The first Klan, organized in 1866 by Confederate veterans, was southern, rural, and committed solely to maintaining white supremacy. The second Klan was national in scope, with a membership of 3 to 6 million during its heyday. Its greatest strength lay in California and Oregon in the West, and in Oklahoma, Texas, Arkansas, Ohio, and Indiana, reaching perhaps 10 percent of the latter state's entire population. The Klan was not merely a movement of the back country and small towns. It had great support in many of the nation's cities. Nevertheless, despite its urban strength the Klan represented an older, agrarian angle of vision. Many city dwellers had only recently migrated from small towns or villages and their view of life remained as it had been before their change of address.

The 1920s were marked by a widespread climate of resistance to social and cultural change and by urgent attempts to hold back any alteration of a mythic American tradition. The KKK was a leader in these efforts, proclaiming itself the prime defender of "Americanism" and the protector of Christian ideals. The Klan of the Twenties saw the black man as an enemy, of course, but it was more concerned with other enemies: Catholics, Jews, foreigners, immigration, integration, and internationalism. It fought not just for a white America but for a white Protestant America founded on "traditional" Protestant morality. The KKK regarded itself as a guardian of public virtue and private morality, striking out, it said, against "bootleggers, speakeasies, rumrunners, syphilitic gangsters, organized gambling, open prostitution, lurid movies, salacious literature, Sabbath sports, easy divorce, family disintegration, sexy dances, purchased politicians, [and] bought policemen." Klansmen often regarded themselves as agents of purification and they frequently turned to vigilantism. The Klan was ever ready to purge society of "evil."

The millions who flocked to the Klan tended to feel a sense of loss and bewilderment. The values they shared and the Americans they knew—Americans of "pioneer stock"—were succumbing to a world they neither understood nor wanted. Unassimilable aliens were invading the country and undermining the moral and religious values of the Nordic race, "which, with all its faults, had given the world almost the whole of modern civilization." "We are demanding," announced Hiram Wesley Evans, the Imperial Wizard of the Ku Klux Klan, "a return of power into the hands of the everyday, not highly cultured, not overly intellectualized, but unspoiled and not de-Americanized average citizen of the old stock." Members of the KKK proudly admitted that they were "hicks" and "rubes" and "drivers of second-hand Fords." The Klan's *Weekly Newsletter* pointed out the targets: Catholic office holders in New England, Catholic power in the Midwest, Jewish predominance in the large cities, opponents of white supremacy in the South, the International Workers of the World in the Northwest, the "yellow peril" in California, Mexicans in Texas, and, everywhere, employers of union labor.

In Indiana the Klan achieved its greatest power. It was the only state where the Klan elected the governor, the only state where a Klavern was chartered in every county, Indiana having 92. At the height of its power, from 1922 through 1925, Klandom in the Midwest regarded Indianapolis as the unrivaled bastion of the Invisible Empire. Indiana's early settlers had included large numbers of homesteaders from Kentucky, Tennessee, and the Carolinas. During the Civil War its large population of southerners made it a replica of the divided nation. Even though almost three-quarters of the male population capable of bearing arms enlisted in the Union cause, Indiana was also a center for "Copperheads"—Confederate sympathizers who lived north of the Mason Dixon Line. Following the war, the original Ku Klux Klan found a friend in Indiana's Thomas Hendricks, who served in the United States Senate and later as vice president under Grover Cleveland. Between 1880 and 1915, the anti-Catholic, anti-immigrant American Protective Association made considerable progress in Indiana.

The First World War cut off large-scale migration from Europe. One consequence was that great numbers of black Americans began leaving the rural South for the cities of the North, now that they had access to railroad and industrial work that formerly went to immigrants. They also sought greater personal freedom and better educational opportunities for their children. Between 1910 and 1930 the black population of Indiana doubled, most of the newcomers settling in urban areas. In earlier years, black migrants had come from the upper South, largely from Kentucky; those coming in the 1920s came in increasing numbers from the lower South, especially from Mississippi. From the first, such a rapid increase in the black population created new tensions in a state with a long tradition of racism.

Until 1869, black children had not been admitted to public schools. Thereafter state law permitted local school authorities to opt for segregation if they wished, and in the 1920s the practice was widespread. Intermarriage between whites and others with as little as one-eighth black "blood" was prohibited. Despite a law that forbade discrimination in public accommodations, "White Trade Only" signs were common. Some rural communities prohibited blacks from settling or even spending the night. Klan propaganda, hostile to blacks, merely reflected traditional racial feeling. As black migrants continued to arrive in Indianapolis, white property owners faced the prospect of black neighbors. Fearful of a decline in property values, they organized local protective associations to keep the newcomers out, using force if necessary. All prospective Klan members had to vow to "faithfully strive for the eternal maintainance of white supremacy."

But the desire to maintain white supremacy was only one element in the Ku Klux Klan movement. In many of the areas in which the KKK was powerful the black population was inconsequential. If many whites feared the rising tide of color, an even greater number trembled over the menace of Catholicism. In Muncie, local Klansmen announced that they would remove their masks "when and not until the Catholics take the prison walls down from about their convents and nunneries." Robert and Helen Lynd reported in their famous sociological study of Muncie, lightly disguised as "Middletown," that

Klan membership zoomed when rumors made the rounds that the Pope intended to move the Vatican to Indiana.

> "Lady," exclaimed an earnest woman to one of the staff inter-
> viewers. . . . Do you belong to the Klan?" To a negative reply
> she continued, "Well, it's about time you joined the other good
> people and did something about this Catholic situation. The
> Pope is trying to get control of this country, and in order to do
> it, he started the old Klan to stir up trouble among the
> Protestants, but instead of doing that, he only opened their
> eyes to the situation, and now all the Protestants are getting
> together in the new Klan to overcome the Catholic menace. I
> just want to show you here in this copy of the Menace—look
> at this picture of this poor girl—look at her hands! See, all
> those fingers gone—just stumps left! She was in a convent
> where it was considered sinful to wear jewelry, and the Sisters,
> when they found her wearing some rings, just burned them off
> her fingers.

The Fiery Cross, an Indianapolis-based Klan weekly of considerable influence, was responsible for circulating some remarkable stories
about Roman Catholics and their church. It reported that, in Indiana,
every time a male child was born to a Catholic family the local Knights
of Columbus donated a rifle to the Catholic Church. More than that,
the high steeples on Catholic churches were to enable sharpshooters to
rain down gunfire on helpless citizens when the Pope declared war on
the Protestants.

A crucial factor in this fear of Catholicism was the identification
of Protestantism with Americanism. After all, the argument went, the
Protestants had been primarily responsible for the establishment of the
American colonies, for the creation of the American nation, and for
the attainment of its greatness. "We want," said the leader of the Ohio
Klan, "the country ruled by the people who settled it. This is OUR
country and we alone are responsible for its future." The authoritari-
an structure of the Catholic Church, the Klan warned, threatened a
society with democratic institutions. Even where the Catholic population numbered less than two percent of the total, as it did in Indiana,
the Ku Klux Klan was able to capitalize on anti-Catholic attitudes.

Patriotic Protestants feared for the future of "their country." Conflict arose over parochial schools, censorship, and prohibition. Although such issues created sharp tensions in many communities, the Klan spoke for only one segment of American Protestantism. Leading ministers and theologians among American Protestants denounced the Klan, as did almost every national governing body of the larger denominations.

The Klansmen themselves were almost all fundamentalists—both religious and social. The Klan stood in defense of stability and order. No infraction of the traditional code was too petty for concern. In this the Klan often had the support of the "best people," who were said to be genuinely alarmed by what they perceived as deteriorating standards and values, civic corruption, and moral decay.

The second Ku Klux Klan came into existence in 1915, the brainchild of Colonel William Simmons, an Alabaman. Simmons had, he said, long dreamed of founding a fraternal order based on the ideals of the original Klan of the Reconstruction period. He picked the moment for launching the organization to coincide with the showing in Atlanta of D.W. Griffith's film masterpiece, *Birth of a Nation*, an electrifying motion picture based on Thomas Dixon's angry novel *The Clansman*. Dixon had asked President Woodrow Wilson to view the film because he wanted to "revolutionize Northern sentiments by a presentation of history that would transform every man in my audience into a good Democrat!" Dixon was also aware that motion pictures were "the mightiest engine for moulding public opinion in the history of the world." The film glorified the ideals of the South's Lost Cause and of the Ku Klux Klan, and it made heroes of the Klansmen.

The revived Klan reached Evansville, Indiana, a river town on the Ohio, in the latter part of 1920. There David Cortis Stephenson joined in 1921, the same year the Klan secured a charter from the State of Indiana. Under Stephenson's leadership the Klan used an old law to build its strength. In 1852 the state legislature had authorized a voluntary constabulary for the apprehension of "horse thieves and other felons." Early development of the Klan in Indianapolis now took place in connection with the "Horse Thief Detective Association."

According to the 1852 law, any group of men could band together, apply for certification, and then act as bona fide policemen. They could carry arms and detain suspects. At the same time, they were under no bond—as police were—for the legal and faithful performance of their duties. This law was still on the books in 1922. Stephenson dusted it off and revived the Association as a legal adjunct of the Klan. It no longer confined itself to searching for horse thieves. It raided "vice dens" and enforced the prohibition laws. Under Indiana's stringent "smell law," anyone caught with an empty liquor bottle could be arrested for illegal possession of an alcoholic beverage, and Klansmen indiscriminately stopped and searched automobiles on the highways. The KKK also stopped roadside "petting parties." On primary election days Klan members drove through the black neighborhoods of Indianapolis with their guns on display. When the Klan held its meetings, armed Klansmen took control of adjacent highways to assure privacy. The horse thief statute provided for nothing less than legalized vigilantism.

The rise and fall of David Curtis Stephenson is the story of one type of American self-made man. Shrewd and unscrupulous, he became not only the dominant figure in the Indiana Klan but was significant in the Klans of twenty-three northern states. Stephenson was born in Texas, probably in Houston, and attained no more than a grade school education. His earliest schooling, curiously, was in a Catholic parochial school. Stephenson began working at sixteen years of age in printing shops and newspaper offices in Texas, Oklahoma, and Iowa. In Oklahoma he joined the Socialist Party and wrote articles and made speeches on behalf of its principles and its candidates. He married in 1915 but deserted his wife the same year, shortly before the birth of his only child, a daughter. In 1917 he was commissioned an Army second lieutenant and assigned to active duty. Stephenson never got to France, however, despite later boasts to the contrary. Two years later, he married again and lived with this wife less than a year. Sometime in 1920 he appeared in Evansville, selling securities in a coal mining company in which he had an interest. In Indiana he left the Socialist Party and registered as a Democrat. Stephenson entered the 1920 Democratic congressional primary as a Wet and was defeated through the efforts of the Anti-Saloon League. Having learned a lesson, he switched to Dry Republicanism.

Physically, Stephenson was unimpressive. He was short, overweight, and heavy jowled, with blond hair and steel-gray eyes. He had, according to contemporaries, a friendly smile, and he was an impeccable dresser. After he joined the Klan, his rise in the organization was meteoric, even as his later downfall was swift and bitter. With native wit and a special penchant for organization and leadership, he was a tireless worker. His speeches were rousing and persuasive. In less than two years he brought over 300,000 new members into the organization. Imperial Wizard Hiram Evans was so impressed with Stephenson's ability that he appointed him to leadership in Indiana.

On the Fourth of July, 1923, 200,000 Klansmen gathered in Melfalfa Park, Kokomo, to hear Imperial Wizard Evans and to celebrate Stephenson's inauguration as Grand Dragon of the Invisible Empire for the Realm of Indiana. Robert Coughlan, onetime member of the board of editors of *Life* magazine and a native of Kokomo, recalled the day of Stephenson's installation in office. That day had a special significance for the Coughlans, a Catholic family living in an almost entirely Protestant neighborhood.

. . . [A] great crowd of oddly dressed people clustered around an open meadow. They were waiting for something; their faces framed in white hoods, were expectant, and their eyes searched the bright blue sky. Suddenly they began to cheer. They had seen it: a speck that came from the south and grew into an airplane. As it came closer it glistened in the sunlight, and they could see that it was gilded all over. It circled the field slowly and seesawed in for a bumpy landing. A bulky man in a robe and hood of purple silk hoisted himself up from the rear cockpit. As he climbed to the ground, a new surge of applause filled the country air.

Stephenson headed for the speaker's stand, raised his hand to quiet the crowd, and spoke to his followers.

My worthy subjects, citizens of the Invisible Empire, Klansmen all, greetings. It grieves me to be late. The President of the United States kept me unduly long counseling upon vital matters of state. Only my pleas that this is the time and place of my coronation obtained for me surcease from his prayers for guidance.

Stephenson launched into his prepared speech—a reiteration of his persistent theme of "One Hundred Per Cent Americanism." Few people, according to some observers, could hear what he was saying that day. But at the conclusion of his speech someone tossed a coin onto the platform. Soon more coins and then rings, stickpins, watchfobs, and other jewelry descended. It was an astonishing display of enthusiasm. The Grand Dragon had told the crowd that he was ready to start "kluxing Indiana." And he proceeded to do so.

Stephenson was probably not personally a bigot. Anti-Catholicism was rife in Indiana, it sold well, and Stephenson didn't argue with success. He was particularly successful in his appeals to fundamentalist clergy, making every one of them an honorary member of the Klan. Under his leadership the Indiana Klan also extended honorary membership to all law-enforcement officers. It subsidized the Horse Thief Detective Association and urged Klansmen to report law violations to its "detectives." In addition to honorary memberships, clergymen and policemen enrolled frequently as regular members of the Klan. Both occupations were dedicated to upholding the law—the sacred law and the profane. In their dual roles as clergymen/Klansmen and policemen/Klansmen these members saw themselves as chosen agents to punish those who did not measure up to their purified version of Americanism. The police worked with their billy clubs, the clergy with threats of hellfire and brimstone.

By the end of 1923, the Indiana Klan had become the largest and strongest in the nation. In the 1924 state elections Republicans, many of them closely allied with the Klan, swept into office. Ed Jackson, the newly elected governor, was a close friend of Stephenson. A majority of the elected members of the Indiana House of Representatives were beholden to the Klan for their nominations and elections. Anti-Klan Progressive Albert J. Beveridge lost his United States Senate seat to Samuel Ralston. And Stephenson could look about and pronounce, "I am the law." The power he attained included patronage: The Indiana secretary of state, for example, received the following telegram from Stephenson: "Permit no selection to be made and permit no one to be named until I have had an opportunity to confer with you." The secretary of state heeded Stephenson's message.

The Grand Dragon adopted a flamboyant way of life. He lived in bacchanalian ostentation on a spacious tree-lined estate in a suburb of

Indianapolis. For a time he maintained a yacht, on which he entertained municipal officials, governors, and even United States senators. His suite in the Kresge Building in downtown Indianapolis had a bronze bust of Napoleon in the outer office, while inside was a battery of eight telephones (including a fake direct line to the White House). Stephenson's ambition knew no bounds. He wanted not only to lead the Klan but to run for the United States Senate in 1926 and then press for the Republican presidential nomination in 1928.

This ambition led inevitably to conflict with Hiram Evans, the Imperial Wizard. The many points of friction between the two involved access to power. Evans feared losing his own authority in the face of Stephenson's phenomenal success. A major conflict erupted over the latter's wish to purchase Valparaiso University, a "people's university" near Gary, Indiana, that had successfully educated thousands. It operated with no frills, no fraternities, and no athletics; it had no entrance examinations and no formal degree requirements. Its motto announced that it was "Where Theory Squares With Practice." All this had been managed with a cost to students of not much more than a hundred dollars per year. In 1920, however, Valparaiso was on the verge of bankruptcy and extinction. It could not meet the challenge of competition with the state universities and improved professional standards in many fields. Stephenson had long cherished a plan to create a university and run it as a "one-hundred-per-cent American institution." He hoped that Evans would commit Klan funds for the purchase of the school, but national Klan headquarters in Atlanta refused. Stephenson was furious. He complained publicly in *The Fiery Cross* that Evans was willing to spend Klan funds freely for southern projects but not for projects in the North:

> They donated $100,000 to erecting a monument at Atlanta to a memory of the rebels who once tried to destroy America, yet they refused to give a single dollar for Valparaiso University to help educate the patriots of the north who saved the Union to posterity unsullied from the contamination of southern traitors.

Control of the weekly *Fiery Cross*—the northern voice of the Klan, with a circulation of nearly half a million—was a point of bitter contention between the two men. Stephenson used it to further his bids for power. Editorials characterized southern Klansmen as "igno-ramuses," "thieves," and "rebels," and charged Evans with having mishandled Klan funds. Stephenson also complained that Evans pur-posely underrepresented the northern Klaverns in the Klan's Imperial Kloncillium, or grand council, since any increase in the number of northern council members would be a threat to Evans' leadership. Other issues of contention involved control over Klan auxiliaries for women and allocation of profits from the sale of Klan regalia. The net result of this internal friction was Stephenson's resignation in September 1923 from his state and national Klan offices.

Despite his resignation, Stephenson sought to maintain his influ-ence in the Klan and its affairs. Both Stephenson and Evans, eager to see the Klan gain strength in the 1924 primary elections, made some effort, for a time at least, to conceal the friction between them. But with Klan-sponsored candidates receiving overwhelming support, Stephenson became convinced it was the moment to make a complete break with national headquarters. At the same time, keeping control in Indiana required a different strategy. Speaking at a statewide meet-ing of the Indiana Klan in May 1924, Stephenson said of Evans that he was "an ignorant, uneducated, uncouth individual who picks his nose at the table and eats his peas with a knife. He has neither courage nor culture. . . . The only thing he was ever known to do was to launch attacks upon the character and integrity of men eminent in talent and virtue." The assembled delegates voted unanimously to reinstate Stephenson as Indiana's Grand Dragon.

Stephenson and his faction had bolted from the national Klan, but for a short time longer the two contending groups glossed over their differences and cooperated for the purpose of winning Indiana for Klan principles. In 1924 pro-Klan forces swept the state, electing sher-iffs, court officials, district attorneys, school boards, a majority of the mayors, a majority of the state legislators, and the governor. But the victory was a complicated one that would render ineffective most Klan-sponsored legislation. Most of the Klan-minded members of the lower legislative house retained their ties to Imperial Wizard Evans and to the national organization. The governor, the state senators, and the new state and city officials were loyal to Stephenson. In spite of the conflict, it was clear that Stephenson was now the single most powerful man in the state. Before the election, for example, he had squeezed the successful mayoral candidate in Indianapolis and got the following written promise:

> In return for the political support of D.C. Stephenson, in the event I am elected mayor of Indianapolis, I promise not to appoint any person as a member of the Board of Public Works without [sic] they first have the support of Stephenson.
>
> I fully agree and promise to appoint Claude Worley as Chief of Police and Earl Klinck as Captain.

Wrangling between Stephenson and Evans and their factions prevented the enactment of laws which the Klan had long desired. Petitions from the Indiana Klaverns to ban the teaching of evolution could not get out of legislative committee. Compulsory Bible reading in the public schools did not get through the Indiana House. The only piece of Klan legislation enacted was a law requiring high school students in Indiana to study the United States Constitution. One of the bills that Stephenson helped kill would have eliminated a minor position in the office of the State Superintendent of Public Instruction; it received almost no publicity but later had great impact on his life and career. The job he saved belonged to twenty-eight-year-old Madge Oberholtzer.

Stephenson's actions had disrupted the Klan's legislative program, but for him there was no question of creed or ideology involved. It was authority that mattered, and he enjoyed the role of power broker. Within three months after the legislative session had begun, Stephenson was at the very height of his power. He was only thirty-four years of age.

*   *   *

In April 1925, Stephenson was arrested for the rape and murder of Madge Oberholtzer. The two had met that January at the inaugural ball held for Governor Jackson. Miss Oberholtzer was a pleasant-looking woman about five feet four inches tall. Somewhat plump at 145 pounds, she was hardly the outstanding beauty that some newspapers later described. Madge was unmarried and a manager of one of the state's welfare activities. She lived with her parents in Irvington, about two or three blocks from Stephenson's mansion. Her father was a clerk in the post office and her mother took in roomers to supplement the family income.

At first, Madge Oberholtzer refused Stephenson's requests for a date, but when she learned that Stephenson had been responsible for saving her job she changed her mind. She was flattered by his attention and accepted a dinner invitation. For the next three months they saw one another from time to time. On all these occasions, according to Madge's later story, Stephenson was a perfect gentleman.

On Sunday, March 25, 1925, three months after they had met, Madge received a message from her parents that Stephenson had been calling her all evening. He had left an urgent request that she return the call, for it involved a matter of great importance to her. When she did so, he asked her to come to his house without delay. It pertained, he repeated, to a matter of concern to her, but he would not explain over the telephone. She agreed, and Stephenson sent one of his bodyguards, Earl Gentry, to escort her. Madge probably believed that the important matter concerned her job and the failed legislation that would have affected her status as a state employee. She left the house with neither her purse nor her hat, expecting, apparently, to be gone only a short time.

Madge had not returned home by the next morning, and her parents were worried. A telegram arrived from Hammond, Indiana: "We are driving through to Chicago. Will be home on the night train." When Madge was not on the night train, Mrs. Oberholtzer made a fruitless trip to Stephenson's home. Neither Stephenson nor her daughter was there.

On Tuesday morning, the 27th, an automobile stopped at the Oberholtzer home and a man lifted Madge from the car and brought her, groaning wretchedly, into the house. The man was later identified as Earl Klinck, whose appointment as captain of police had been secured by Stephenson. Mrs. Schultz, a roomer in the Oberholtzer home, was making lunch for her son. They were the only ones in the house. When Mrs. Schultz asked Klinck if Madge had been badly hurt, he indicated that she had been in an automobile accident, but "I don't think any bones are broken." Before Mrs. Schultz could question him further, he said he was in a great hurry and left.

Mrs. Schultz called the Oberholtzer family physician, Dr. Kingsbury, who arrived at nearly the same time as did Mrs. Oberholtzer. His examination showed that Madge was in a state of shock. She had a rapid pulse and her body was cold. There were no broken bones, but there were bruises and lacerations all over her body. The skin on her left breast was torn and also on her right cheek. There were enormous contusions on her left hip and buttock. Tissue on her genitals had been torn off. Between sobs and groans, Madge told what had happened to her. It turned out to be her dying declaration, later formalized in a signed statement drawn up by Asa Smith, an Indianapolis attorney. Smith had been brought in by Madge's father during her disappearance. When it became apparent that Madge was not going to recover, Smith wrote down her story to be used as evidence. Madge Oberholtzer's formal statement became the basis of the state's case against David Stephenson.

When Madge arrived at Stephenson's house he was quite drunk, having been at the bottle for some time. With him were his chauffeur, "Shorty," and Captain Klinck. Stephenson forced Madge to drink "some kind of liquid." According to her story, she "became ill almost immediately, vomited profusely, became confused and could scarcely move." When she asked to be taken home, Stephenson said, "No, you can't go home; you are going with me to Chicago; I love you more than any woman I have ever known." He and the other men blocked all her efforts to call her home.

Stephenson and his men half-carried Madge into a car and from there into a drawing room on the midnight train to Chicago. She was still unsteady from the drink but recalled that Gentry, the bodyguard, climbed into an upper berth and that immediately afterward Stephenson attacked her in the lower berth.

He took hold of the bottom of my dress and pulled it over my head. I tried to fight but was weak and unsteady. Stephenson took hold of my two hands and held them. I had not the strength to move. What I had drunk was affecting me. Stephenson took all my clothes off and pushed me into the lower berth. After the train started, Stephenson got in with me and attacked me. He held me so I couldn't breathe. I don't know and don't remember all that happened. He chewed me all over my body, particularly my neck and face, chewed my tongue, chewed my breasts until they bled, my back, my legs, my ankles, and mutilated me all over.

They got off the train the next morning, in Hammond, Indiana, just short of the Illinois state line, to avoid violating the federal Mann Act. Registering in the Indiana Hotel as "Mr. and Mrs. W.B. Morgan," Stephenson allowed Madge to send her mother the telegram of March 26. He dictated the contents and she signed it. Madge prevailed upon Stephenson to give her some money and let her go out to buy a hat, for she had none with her. Shorty drove her to a milliner's shop, where she purchased a small black hat. She then convinced Shorty to stop at a drugstore so she could get some rouge. It was there, out of Shorty's sight, that she bought a box of bichloride of mercury tablets.

When Madge was brought back to the hotel, Stephenson was again in a drunken stupor. The box containing the bichloride of mercury held eighteen tablets; Madge took six of them at once. "I only took six because they burned so," she related. She became violently ill immediately, and started to retch blood, after which she told Shorty what she had done and Shorty told his boss. Stephenson wanted to drive Madge to a hospital and register her as his wife so that her stomach could be pumped, but she would not let him do that and she also refused his proposal of marriage. During the long drive back to Indianapolis, Madge was in agony and at length begged Stephenson to take her to a doctor.

> I said I wanted a hypodermic to ease the pain but they refused to stop. I said to Stephenson to leave me along the road some place, that someone would stop and take care of me if he wouldn't. I said to him that I felt he was more cruel to me than he had been the night before. He said he would stop at the next town but he never did. Just before reaching a town he would say to Shorty, "Drive fast and don't get pinched." I vomited in the car, all over the back seat and grips. Stephenson didn't try to make me more comfortable in any way. He thought I was dying at one time and said to Gentry, "This takes guts to do this, Gentry. She is dying." I heard him say also that he had been in worse messes than this before and he

would get out of it. Stephenson and Gentry drank liquor during the entire trip. I remember Stephenson said that he had power . . . that he was the law.

When they reached Indianapolis they drove to the Oberholtzer home immediately but, noticing Madge's mother at the front door, they drove by without stopping. Instead, they took Madge to Stephenson's place, to a loft above the garage. The next day, after making sure that her mother was absent, Klinck took Madge home, carrying her into the house and upstairs to her bedroom.

Realizing that Madge had gone too long without medical attention, Dr. Kingsbury did what he could for her, trying every recognized treatment for elimination of the poison from her system. He also tended to all the wounds and bruises on her body. Madge's general condition did not improve, however. The bichloride of mercury had now been completely absorbed into her system and had caused nephritis, an acute inflammation of the kidneys. In addition, one of the deep bites in her breast had become infected. Other physicians called in for consultation declared her condition hopeless. On April 14, 1925, Madge Oberholtzer died.

More than ten days earlier, Madge's father had filed a sworn criminal complaint against Stephenson, Gentry, and Klinck, charging the three with assault and battery with intent to commit a criminal attack, malicious mayhem, kidnapping and conspiracy to kidnap. After Madge's death, Mr. Oberholtzer filed a new criminal complaint charging the three with murder. They were arrested and held without bond.

Throughout the nation, the scandal and subsequent trial dominated the headlines. Editorials were unanimous in their outrage. They were appalled by the hypocrisy of the Klan and especially by its claim to be the champion of Christian morality. "There's Mud on Indiana's White Robes," said one editorial. The press adopted the label "Stephensonism" as a synonym for the Klan. Those who knew Stephenson—particularly those in the top positions of the Klan hierarchy—were aware of his long history of outrageous behavior. He had committed numerous "immoralities" before, in Columbus, Ohio, in Atlanta, Georgia, and on the way to and from these cities and others, on trains and in boats.

Before the trial began, the defense moved successfully for a change of venue, alleging that "general excitment and prejudice . . . precluded the possibility of obtaining a fair and impartial trial." There was ample justification for the change. A week after Madge Oberholtzer died, five hundred of her neighbors in Irvington held a mass meeting amid great excitement, demanding immediate prosecution and punishment of the murderers.

The trial of Stephenson, Gentry, and Klinck began on October 12, 1925, in Noblesville, county seat of Hamilton County, about thirty miles from Indianapolis. Both prosecution and defense questioned with great care the members of a panel of 400 veniremen. They looked into personal histories, inquired about business and social connections, and sought to uncover bias and prejudice. The attorneys wanted to learn how much the prospective jurors knew about the case and the parties involved in it, and they asked about opinions, impressions, and points of view that might have been formed from news stories or other sources. Challenges eliminated all who were even suspected of affiliation with or sympathy for the Klan. It took eleven days to select a jury. All had heard of Stephenson, but none knew him personally and none had come, they said, to a conclusion as to the guilt or innocence of the defendants.

The two legal teams were fairly well matched. The prosecution was led by Marion County attorney William H. Remy, who, although young, was a man of cultured background and good education, and had a strong sense of morality and integrity. He was also solemn, serious, and hard-working. Assisting Remy was a former city judge, Charles Cox, assigned to present medical evidence and to cross-examine defense experts. All three of the attorneys who made up the defense team were experienced trial lawyers. "Eph" Inman, who headed the team, was an impressive figure at well over six feet in height. His assurance of manner reflected his many successes. Floyd Christian and Ira Holmes were both highly esteemed in the Indiana bar and both had had wide and varied experience.

Much of the defense strategy depended on the results of the autopsy. What had been the cause of death? If Madge Oberholtzer had died as a result of bichloride of mercury poisoning, then she had died by her own hand. But if, rather, she had died of infection caused by the lacerations and bites on her body, Stephenson was responsible for her death. All of the state's expert winesses were in agreement as to the effects of ingestion of bichloride of mercury, and they agreed on what constituted the proper course of treatment for such poisoning. Two or three grains might constitute a fatal dose, but death would depend on whether the poison was eliminated or absorbed. Absorption could be slowed by induced vomiting and purging. The experts acknowledged that there had been recoveries from bichloride of mercury poisoning in cases in which as many as 100 grains had been taken. Generally, however, a substantial dose without treatment would cause death within as little as a few hours or as long as twelve days. Madge Oberholtzer lived for twenty-nine days after swallowing the poison. Medical testimony explained how Madge could linger:

> If death occurs within the first four days, it is because of the corrosive action of the poison on the stomach and the bowels; if after five but within twelve days, it is the result of the action of the poison on the kidneys, causing an acute nephritis. After the twelfth day nature begins a process of absorption of the dead kidney tissue and replacement of it with new tissue. Thereafter, in the absence of new complications, the prospects of recovery improve with each passing day.

The autopsy showed that damage to the kidneys from the bichloride of mercury was nearly healed and the damaged tissue had been almost completely replaced. But twenty-four hours had passed between the time Madge swallowed the poison and the treatment to try to eliminate it from her body was begun. There was no doubt in the minds of all of the state's medical experts that the delay had lessened her chance of recovery. And there was no doubt that "death resulted from the complications of a secondary blood-stream infection, with pus-forming bacteria, superimposed on the nephritis which was the direct result of the bichloride poisoning."

What could cause such an infection? A human bite. The infection was probably introduced into the bloodstream through the lacerations caused by the bites on Madge's left breast, for the breast had become infected with pus-forming bacteria. In view of the fact that she lived for twenty-nine days after taking the poison and when the restorative process in the kidneys was far advanced, she would probably have recovered—except for the secondary infection. On the basis of this testimony, the jury could find Stephenson guilty of murder. The prosecution argued that the "secondary staphylococci infection which manifested itself in the lung abcess and kidneys was advanced as the direct result of a bite which Stephenson in the course of his assault had inflicted on the girl's breast."

Defense attorney Inman's cross-examination of the medical experts faced difficulty from the start. The recognized eminence of the state's experts eliminated any possibility of discrediting them. But perhaps a cause other than Stephenson's assault had led to the secondary infection? One of the new facts elicited under cross-examination was that an abcess of the lung might follow pneumonia. Moreover, influenza could cause some degeneration of the kidneys, heart, and lungs. And more than that, various bacteria, particularly staphylococci, are commonly found in all human organs. Unfortunately for the defense, the autopsy had revealed no indication of pneumonia or influenza.

The experts called in by the defense therefore pressed the point that the cause of death was bichloride of mercury poisoning, and that any delay greater than six hours in beginning treatment to eliminate the poison was simply too long. No subsequent medical treatment, they argued, could have saved Madge Oberholtzer. Medical experts for the defense rejected the charge that Madge had died as a result of the secondary infection caused by the bite on her breast. They provided an alternative explanation: After swallowing the bichloride of mercury, they said, Madge had vomited. Accordingly, "the expelled vomit struck the breast, abdomen, and other parts of the . . . body and remained there for some time." The tendency to "inflame and corrode those surfaces" was in the nature of mercurial poisoning. "The bichloride of mercury," they said, "is readily absorbed from any of the bodily surfaces, and it is quite common to find that women have been poisoned by using concentrated solutions . . . as [in] a vaginal douche."

Cross-examination of the defense's first medical expert was brilliant. Prosecutor Cox was able to reveal that the defense "expert" had never seen or treated Madge, that he had not seen the autopsy report, that his knowledge of toxicology had begun no more than a month and a half before the trial, and that one of the "authorities" he had cited was a book on veterinary practice. The unfortunate witness also had to admit that he had treated Stephenson for alcoholism and that Stephenson's condition had bordered "upon delerium tremens."

Sacco and Vanzetti being escorted from the courthouse after a
day of their trial by a phalanx of formidable police.

Prosecutors William G. Thompson, Herbert B. Ehrmann and
Thomas O'Connor on the Massachusetts State House steps in
1927, after Sacco and Vanzetti's guilty verdict had been upheld.

The mugshots of Nicola Sacco and Bartolomeo Vanzetti just after their arrest on May 5, 1920, for the armed robbery and murder of two men in South Braintree, Massachusetts.

The two Italian immigrants attracted many supporters prior to their being executed. Above, the funeral procession for Sacco and Vanzetti winds through the rainy streets of Boston

Ty Cobb (left) chats with his young rival, "Shoeless" Joe Jackson in 1915. Although Cobb is considered to be the nastiest player in the history of baseball, it was Jackson who became banned from the sport.

An amiable Al Capone enjoys a breath of fresh air during a
break in his trial, and (below) shares a light moment with his
lawyers, Michael Ahern and Albert Fink.

"Only Capone kills like that!" said "Bugs" Moran after the St. Valentine's Day Massacre in 1929. No one was ever tried for the murders, but Al Capone was eventually caught for income tax evasion.

Samuel Insull, onetime assistant to Thomas Edison, helped
start General Electric. The personal toll paid for the collapse
of his financial empire is evident below.

Colonel Billy Mitchell at his court martial. More visionary than diplomatic, he had few friends in high places.

The board that passed judgment on Mitchell, including (fourth from left) Douglas MacArthur.

Billy Mitchell getting out of a bomber (top) and his vison of aerial warfare: a white phosphorus bomb explodes over a moored target ship. He had seen the future, but failed to tactfully present it.

The defense questioned Madge Oberholtzer's reputation, trying to show that her relationship with Stephenson had been much more intimate than was to be inferred from the woman's dying declaration. Those who testified to this were all friends of Stephenson or members of the Klan who had been associated with him in Klan activities.

This was all the testimony offered in Stephenson's behalf. He did not take the witness stand himself because he was confident of acquittal. He believed, according to information he had received, that the jury had been "fixed." Stephenson also claimed later that he did not take the stand because he feared for his life: Klan assassins had threatened him. Finally, he claimed, he did not take the stand because he was unwilling to reveal the name of a woman with whom he had spent the night in question.

Both summations were highly emotional. Inman for the defense tried to dissipate the atmosphere of prejudice in which the trial had been held. He argued that the defendants should never have been indicted. The "state's attorney and those privately employed to reap the vengeance of hate" were responsible. They were responding to "the unreasoning element of hostility which aims to bring Stephenson to destruction." Stephenson had committed no crime at all, Inman continued:

Can suicide be murder? Can suicide be homicide? . . . This so-called dying declaration—this lawyer-made declaration designed as poisonous propaganda to be used in an effort to gain money—if it declares anything it is a dying declaration of suicide and not homicide. She, by her own concealment of taking the poison for six hours, made medical aid of no avail. She, by her own wilful act or conduct, made it impossible for these men to save her life. The dying declaration was made by the girl herself for the justification of herself, to free herself from the fault and place the blame on others, to put her right with her family and friends.

The point was telling. It was the strongest argument made by the defense.

Charles Cox and Ralph Kane shared the state's final arguments. Cox replied to Inman: "Are you," he asked the jury, "going to permit this unparalleled, this unequaled painter of words, this man of stately bearing and melodious voice, are you going to allow him to take the brush of scandal and write the scarlet letter on Madge Oberholtzer's tomb? . . . In the name of the law, in the name of virtuous womanhood, in the name of justice, I call upon you to write your verdict in a way that will put a stop to tragedies like this one."

And Kane added:

> When these defendants unlawfully abducted Madge Oberholtzer, attacked her and dragged her to Hammond, they made themselves criminals, and by that very act drove that poor girl, honored and respected in her community, loved by all, drove her into a position where she had lost all, where she was bereft of all she cherished, and forced to take the poison of death. By those acts D.C. Stephenson and his cohorts became murderers just the same as if they had plunged a dagger into her throbbing heart. . . .

Kane praised Asa Smith, who had had the foresight to take down Madge's dying statement. "He brought the evidence into this courtroom which clinches this case and will send these men to the place where they belong." Kane ridiculed the notion that Madge had gone willingly with Stephenson. If she had done so, "she would have worn a hat. If I understand anything at all about women, when they start on a 250 mile Pullman ride they take along their clothes, their hats, their cosmetics, their lingerie, and other things. . . . If she was a willing companion, why bring her home looking like she had been in a fight? . . . These fellows are guilty of murder, staphylococci or no staphylococci."

Judge Will B. Sparks explained to the jury that under Indiana law it might return any of three verdicts: First degree murder, defined as "the killing of a human being purposely and with premeditated malice, or in the perpetration of or an attempt to perpetrate rape, arson, robbery, or burglary," carried a penalty of death or life imprisonment. The penalty for murder in the second degree was imprisonment for life. Manslaughter, "the killing of a human being without malice, expressed or implied, or unlawfully upon a sudden heat, or involuntarily in the commission of some unlawful act," was punishable by imprisonment for not less than two nor more than twenty-one years.

It took the jury less than six hours to reach a verdict. Stephenson was found guilty of second degree murder. The jury believed Stephenson had killed Madge Oberholtzer purposely and maliciously but without premeditation. Klinck and Gentry were found "Not guilty," and Shorty had fled the jurisdiction and was never prosecuted. But David C. Stephenson, the most powerful political figure in Indiana, was sent to the Indiana State Prison for the rest of his life.

Stephenson had been confident of acquittal. Upon conviction he claimed that he had been framed by Hiram Evans and the Atlanta-based Klan hierarchy. Madge Oberholtzer had simply been the trap to ruin him, and Asa Smith had been bribed to "compose the alleged dying declaration and obtain her signature."

Once convicted, Stephenson remained confident that Ed Jackson, for whose election to the governorship he had been largely responsible, would set him free. In the meantime, Stephenson made endless but vigorous efforts to obtain a new trial, to secure a pardon, or to obtain release on parole. In his appeal to the Supreme Court of Indiana his attorneys argued skillfully but unsuccessfully as to the reason for Madge Oberholtzer's death. Was it the direct result of Stephenson's acts? They argued that "after the assault had taken place the girl was able to leave the train at Hammond and walk a block to the hotel, to drink a cup of coffee, to worry that she had no hat, to accompany Stephenson's chauffeur to a millinery shop to buy one, to get in and out of the automobile and to return to the hotel." She "could at any time have summoned help or escaped from Stephenson and his agents. . . . [T]he essential 'causal connection' between the assault and the suicide [is] lacking," the attorneys insisted.

Four of the five judges rejected this argument: "When suicide follows a wound inflicted by a defendant, his act is homicidal, if deceased was rendered irresponsible by the wound and as a natural result of it." The court continued, "[A]ppellant by his acts and conduct rendered the deceased distracted and mentally irresponsible. . . . [A]ppellant was guilty of murder in the second degree as charged. . . ."

In 1927, after having served for a year, Stephenson had not yet received the pardon from Governor Jackson that he had been confident he would get. The governor was in an unenviable position. Freeing Stephenson would have been politically disastrous, but it was equally dangerous to keep Stephenson in prison. Stephenson spoke often of releasing the contents of a certain "little black box." The governor and the warden tried to keep Stephenson isolated but, realizing he had been abandoned, Stephenson finally struck back, revealing to the press that he had several "little black boxes" that contained material that would embarrass and incriminate some Indiana officeholders. The resulting exposure of corruption astounded the nation. Among the juicier items were affidavits and handwritten or typed political IOUs as well as signed pledges bearing witness to agreements made by mayors, congressmen, and police officials to trade offices in return for campaign contributions. The disclosure of these political promises led to a special investigation by the United States Senate into corrupt tactics and unreported funding by Klan-sponsored Indiana politicians. The investigations painted a grim and ugly picture of the national Ku Klux Klan as well as its branch in Indiana. An independent investigation was launched by Indiana's attorney general, bent on revoking the Klan charter and driving it from the state completely.

Stephenson got his revenge. The contents of the little black boxes sent the mayor of Indianapolis to prison for violating the Corrupt Practices Act. He was accompanied by the sheriff of Marion County, a congressman, the city purchasing agent, the city controller, and many lesser officials. Further, the entire city council of Indianapolis resigned in a body after bribery was exposed. Judge Dearth of Muncie was impeached. Only Governor Jackson and George Coffin, a Republican political boss, evaded criminal trials; the two were saved by the statute of limitations.

The trial and conviction of David C. Stephenson and its aftermath killed the Ku Klux Klan. Within a year, membership in the Indiana Klan had shrunk from 350,000 to 15,000. In Washington, DC, in 1925, 60,000 Klansmen were expected to participate in a march down Pennsylvania Avenue—a show of numbers that would scotch rumors that the Klan was dying. Imperial Wizard Hiram Evans spared no expense for what was to be an elaborate affair, but only half the expected number appeared. By 1926, there were even more defections as hundreds refused to pay the dues that would have continued their membership. How could people continue to believe in the moral authority of the Klan after Stephenson's imprisonment? "He [Stephenson] just chewed that poor girl to pieces." Nowhere did Klan leadership again prove strong or charismatic.

The Klan was in decline by 1926, but many of its aims had either been realized or no longer seemed pressing. The door of immigration had been swung nearly shut by the legislation of 1924—a victory for Protestant nativists. Many southern states outlawed the teaching of evolution in favor of a fundamentalist explanation of life. Prohibition seemed here to stay. The League of Nations and the internationalists had been held at bay. The decline of the Klan did not put an end to the kind of thinking it represented. Many Klansmen recognized that they had misplaced their faith in the Invisible Empire, Knights of the Ku Klux Klan, but the dream of an older, purer, and better, traditional America did not die. The ideals for which the Klan claimed to be an agency of redemption in the "moral sink" that America was becoming were ideals still cherished in the hearts of many.

There is a bit more to the story of David Curtis Stephenson. In 1950, his repeated efforts brought a measure of success. In March he was released by the governor and paroled to his daughter in Tulsa, Oklahoma. At the end of 1951, however, he was back in prison for another four years for parole violation. Stephenson was finally released in 1955 after having served thirty-one years.

6

―――――――――――

THE SCOPES TRIAL

―――――――――――

The 1925 trial of teacher John Scopes for violating a Tennessee anti-evolution law was the high spot of a long-simmering controversy, one that began with the publication of Charles Darwin's work, *On the Origin of Species*, in 1859. After some initial resistance, acceptance of Darwin's theory of evolution by most American scientists was rapid. Acceptance by the nation's major religious groups, however, was another matter, and in the decades following the Civil War controversy over the teaching of evolution continued in colleges and universities. Of course, whatever losses the most extreme anti-evolutionists sustained did not touch the vitals of their faith: Few "true believers" attended college, and those who did so sought out backwater schools that had not been tainted by Darwin's work.

In the years after World War I a resurgence of the controversy took place. By that time increasing numbers of Americans were attending public tax-supported high schools. For the upwardly mobile, breaking into the middle class without a diploma was growing more and more difficult. And by the 1920s, the teaching of evolution in American high schools had become standard educational fare.

The theory of evolution had provided its advocates with an optimistic view of life and a belief in the inevitability of progress. Nothing, it was believed, except humanity's own follies could prevent it from achieving a world that would get better and better. The First World War, however, gave rise to powerful disillusionment and to a massive distrust in the future. To many Americans, even those who had supported United States participation in it, the war had failed to "make

144

the world safe for democracy." Its brutalizing and dehumanizing carnage revealed the power for evil that modern science had put into the hands of mankind. After the war came revelations of secret treaties that exposed the Allies' greed for territory. American disillusionment became directed at all things European, but most emphatically at all things German. Americans rejected the German materialist philosophy and especially the teachings of Friedrich Nietzsche. These were foreign ideologies, many Americans felt, that lay at the root of Germany's murderous grasping for power.

Also at this time, revolutionary developments were taking place in science, technology, and psychology. The world of Ford, Einstein, and Freud sharply changed the way men and women viewed themselves, their universe, and the ways they earned a living. Movies, radios, and automobiles affected American culture profoundly, altering both manners and morals; social and cultural changes threatened traditional values, and all this was fertile ground for a revival of religious fundamentalism. For fundamentalists, the global conflict had been a sign that the world was coming to an end. They placed their faith and hope in the Second Coming of Christ. The war, they believed, had not only exposed the fallacy of the optimism of Darwinism but also of the modernists: those Christians who accepted evolution and believed that the Bible could be reconciled with modern science. If progress were inevitable, if the world were constantly and inevitably improving, asked the fundamentalists, how explain the recent catastrophe? Fundamentalists had a better explanation. The evil days were a period of foreordained devastation before Christ's reappearance.

Throughout World War I, Americans had been told to hate Germany as a barbaric state. The wartime Committee on Public Information fed Americans a steady diet of atrocity stories that blamed the "Huns" and spread rumors of German espionage. To fundamentalists, this German behavior was a logical product of that country's materialist philosophy. The Germans, in following the theory of evolution's general concept of "survival of the fittest," had tried to prove themselves the most fit by a conquest of Europe. Moreover, modernism—that unholy movement which disparaged the Scriptures and treated God as some kind of intangible cosmic force—was responsible for having produced the most destructive war in history. In addition, it had made of the Germans a godless nation, a nation capable of any crime. Bolshevism was another product of the materialist philosophy. It, too, ridiculed the Scriptures, rejected God, and was responsible for the skepticism, the infidelity, the agnosticism and, naturally, the atheism which were sweeping the United States. One Louisiana clergyman observed, "I would say that a modernist in government is an anarchist and Bolshevik; in science he is an evolutionist; in business he is a Communist; in art a futurist; in music his name is jazz; and in religion an atheist and infidel."

By the 1920s, all those who considered themselves modernists were basically agreed as to the significance of science and were prepared to accept whatever was useful among its findings. To fundamentalists, on the other hand, science was inadequate to explain the origins of man. It had failed to prove evolution, and it was dangerous in its implications. As one fundamentalist put it bluntly, "To hell with science if it is going to damn souls." For fundamentalists a literal reading of the Bible was central to faith. The problem was not that they did not grasp the idea of a gradual development of species, or of a possible reconciling of evolution with the Book of Genesis, or that evolution might have purposefully been the process by which God created man. A literal reading of the Bible proved that man was the product of God's fiat creation, not the result of development over untold eons. There was no room for compromise.

The fundamentalist anti-evolution movement began its crusade to drive Darwinism from the public schools early in the 1920s. William Jennings Bryan—three times an unsuccessful Democratic nominee for the American presidency—became an acknowledged leader in the fight, which had its greatest success in the South and in the Border States, although it was indeed not negligible in the Midwest and California. By 1923 the Florida legislature passed a joint resolution declaring that it was "improper and subversive for any teacher in a public school to teach Atheism or Agnosticism, or to teach as true, Darwinism, or any other hypothesis that links man in blood relationship to any other form of life." In a school district in Kansas, fundamentalist parents voted to burn *The Book of Knowledge*. The Board of Education of Carroll County, Tennessee, burned Hendrik Van Loon's recently published *Story of Mankind* and threatened to dismiss any teacher simply for believing in evolution.

Leila Scopes (John Scopes's sister) had an excellent record as a math teacher in the Paducah, Kentucky, schools. When she applied for a new position in a Paducah high school, she was asked to state publicly, as a condition of employment, that she disagreed with her brother. She refused to do so and a member of the school board explained, "Miss Scopes' presence in the high school faculty might embarass the public school system." In one high school in Tennessee the principal, a fundamentalist himself, was fired because he gave a student a definition of evolution. Stories of such harassment can be recounted endlessly. Perhaps even more important were the numerous but uncounted occasions when teachers or textbook writers censored themselves to avoid conflict with the anti-evolutionists.

Oklahoma joined Florida in banning the teaching of evolution in 1923, and Tennessee did so in 1925. Tennessee was neither more conservative nor more fundamentalist than many other states, but its anti-evolution bill swept through the legislature by astonishing margins: votes of 71 to 5 in the lower house and 24 to 6 in the senate. John Washington Butler, the author of the Tennessee anti-evolution law, was a member of the state legislature from Macon County. Butler is said to have run for the legislature because he became alarmed when he heard that a girl from his hometown had returned from college with a belief in evolution but not in God. Butler's two daughters were married, but his three teenaged sons were still young enough, he believed, to have their faith endangered; in fact, they did not even need to go to college to be infected by dangerous thoughts. Evolution, Butler discovered, was taught in the high schools of Tennessee. His campaign for the legislature called for a law to prohibit the teaching of evolution in the public schools because, "In the first place, the Bible is the foundation upon which our American government is built. . . . The evolutionist who denies the Biblical story of creation as well as other Biblical accounts, cannot be a Christian. . . . It goes hand in hand with Modernism, makes Jesus a fakir, robs the Christian of his hopes and undermines the foundation of our Government."

The bill Butler drafted prohibited the teaching of "Evolution Theory in all the Universities, Normals, and all other public schools of Tennessee, which are supported in whole or in part by the public school funds of the state. . . ." It became unlawful in such schools "to teach any theory that denies the story of the Divine Creation of man as taught in the Bible and to teach instead that man has descended from a lower order of animals." Violation of the statute constituted a misdemeanor and called for a fine of not less than $100 nor more than $500 for each offense.

Why the overwhelmingly lopsided vote for the Butler bill, which no one, it seems, except a small bloc of Baptists, took seriously? Some legislators believed that the governor intended to veto it and hoped he would do so. The governor had told one of the senators that he thought the bill absurd, and the senate willingly passed the buck. Governor Austin Peay was highly regarded as a progressive. He had an ambitious program for the State of Tennessee and needed the votes of rural legislators like John Butler to help him enact it. His program was expensive, calling for major construction for highways, schools, hospitals, and prisons. Peay also wanted increased expenditures to inaugurate an eight-month compulsory school year and to raise the pay of elementary school teachers above the meager $634 per year average salary. Furthermore, Governor Peay hoped to make the largest appropriation in the history of the state for the University of Tennessee. The governor got the votes for his reform program and he signed the anti-evolution bill. But he made clear that he did not intend to enforce it. "Probably," he said in a special message to the legislature,

> the law will never be applied. . . . Nobody believes that it is going to be an active statute. But this bill is a distinct protest against an irreligious tendency to exalt so-called science, and deny the Bible in some schools and quarters—a tendency fundamentally wrong and fatally mischievous in its effects on our children, our institutions and our country.

Major support for the Butler bill came from the Baptists, some ministers seeing it as a means of embarrassing their chief rivals, the Methodists, who were generally inactive in the anti-evolution movement. Opposition to the bill might have been expected from officials and faculty of the University of Tennessee, but it was not forthcoming. Having suffered from financial starvation until 1918, the university had begun to receive substantial grants from the state. Neither the faculty nor the university officials wanted to alienate their benefactors. When the Butler bill was under consideration in 1925, the president of the university opposed it in private, but he would say nothing publicly.

Nor did officials of the state department of education make their opposition public: the legislature was considering the bill for a compulsory eight-month school year and the department was eager to see it pass.

A case to test the constitutionality of the Butler Act was the brainchild of George Rappaleyea, a mining engineer born in the East who had been living in Dayton, Tennessee, for three years prior to 1925. The son of a Baptist father and a Catholic mother, he was no infidel. Only thirty-one years old, Rappaleyea directed 400 employees, but with his slight build, horn-rimmed glasses, and bushy hair, he cut an unimpressive figure. In the words of one Dayton local, he was "an untidy little person with rather ill-tended teeth." Despite determined efforts to become a full-fledged member of the community, he was still looked on as an outsider—a "fringer," in the local idiom. Rappaleyea learned that the American Civil Liberties Union was offering to finance a test case and was seeking a client. He approached F.E. Robinson, head of the local school board and a druggist in whose store pupils purchased the state-approved biology textbook. He also asked Walter White, superintendent of schools for Rhea County, of which Dayton was a part, to join in a suit to have the law overturned. Two days later, John Scopes was invited to join the drugstore discussions and he agreed to act as defendant in a test case. Rappaleyea's motives in promoting the test were, no doubt, mixed. He opposed the Butler Act because he thought it silly; he regarded the Bible as "mere history." Perhaps most of all, he was interested in promoting Dayton, in putting the town in the news and bringing business to the local community.

John Thomas Scopes taught science in Rhea County High School. At the time of the trial he was twenty-four years old, described by Mrs. Bryan in a letter to her son as "a grinning, long-jawed mountain product with pale blue eyes and yellow hair which he brushes back from his rather receding forehead. He carries himself wretchedly. . . . His whole appearance is simpering, weak and gawky." Scopes had been born and reared in Salem, Illinois, and had regarded William Jennings Bryan as one of his childhood heroes. He earned his bachelor of arts degree at the University of Kentucky in 1924 and took his first teaching job in Dayton, as a substitute biology teacher and football coach. Scopes was a popular teacher, even though some people disapproved of a hint of looseness. He smoked cigarettes, he danced, and he had even been known to swear out on the football field. As an instructor, his views on evolution were clear: "I don't see how a teacher can teach biology without teaching evolution," was his opinion. His purpose in participating in the case, however, was not to defend Darwinism but to promote academic freedom and freedom of thought.

With only this cast of characters, the Scopes trial would not have become one of the most sensational of the twentieth century. But when rural folk hero and former presidential "also ran" William Jennings Bryan agreed to aid in prosecuting Scopes, he elevated a local difficulty into a national and perhaps even international affair. When Roger Baldwin, national director of the American Civil Liberties Union, agreed to cooperate in Scopes' defense, the stage was set for what Bryan would call a "duel to the death." Waiting to confront Bryan was Clarence Darrow, fresh from his great performance the year before in the Leopold–Loeb case. Darrow actively sought a role in the Scopes case: "For the first, the last, the only time in my life, I volunteered my services in a case . . . because I really wanted to take part in it."

Clarence Darrow was a complex man and a highly controversial figure. His services were almost not accepted, even after he agreed to waive a fee and pay his own expenses. Also, within the ACLU there was disagreement over Darrow's participation. The problem, according to Scopes, was that some of the members "felt Darrow was a headline chaser, and as a consequence, the real issue would be obscured. . . . [T]he trial would become a carnival and any possible dignity in the fight for liberties would be lost." There were other reasons as well, substantial ones. Many in the ACLU believed that considerable hostility would rise against Darrow in the South because of his reputation for infidelity, his supposed atheism, and his criticism of white supremacy. His attitude was reflected in his conception of the lofty Anglo-Saxons, whom he described as ". . . the greatest race of sons of bitches that ever infested the earth." And: "If there is such a race, I am one of them. . . . But I do not brag about it, I apologize for it." Darrow was a maverick, generally. His attitude toward criminals was far from censorious. He favored a welfare state, generally supported the most radical of the anti-monopoly movements, and even approved of public ownership of basic industries. Darrow's participation in the Scopes trial was grudgingly accepted because Dudley Field Malone, another first-rate criminal lawyer, refused to serve on the defense team without him.

Darrow's interest in the trial was in large part motivated by his anti-religious bent. He regarded Christianity as a "slave religion" because it encouraged what he believed was acquiescence in injustice and complacency in the face of the intolerable. It had become, he believed, an adjunct of business. Businessmen financed Billy Sunday's tabernacle, Darrow asserted, "because they thought it was cheaper to pay working men in religious dope than to give them money." In addition to his views on religion, Darrow was impatient with rural America, its narrowness, and its efforts to resist change. He associated rural America with the Klan, prohibition, and immigration restriction, as well as with religious fundamentalism. Bryan was the embodiment of rural America, and Darrow believed that Bryan had caused confusion at every national convention of the Democratic Party since 1896. Bryan's support of bimetallism, prohibition, and pacifism had led to defeat in every election in which he had been the presidential candidate. Darrow objected to control of the national party by Bryan-led agrarian forces. And Darrow was a Democrat.

The prosecution's William Jennings Bryan was more famous than Darrow. He had commanded the respect of a large segment of the public over an extended period of time. Nevertheless, he was often the victim of supercilious comment by those who should have known better. As early as 1900, after his second presidential campaign (his first was in 1896), Bryan became convinced that he had spent too much of his time and energy in politics and had failed in his duty to serve God. From that point on, Bryan was a familiar figure at the annual conference of the Presbyterian Church. He became increasingly involved with the interdenominational movement and with the YMCA. His arguments on behalf of prohibition were often religious, and his work as Woodrow Wilson's secretary of state often had religious overtones. From 1916, when he left the State Department, until 1925, he wrote more on religious topics than on politics, stressing evangelical revivals, personal piety, and complete abstinence. From 1921 onward, religion had been his overriding passion. Reformation of both the individual and the social order could be achieved, he thought, by action of the Church and the rejection of materialism and commercialism.

Theodore Roosevelt said of him, "By George, he would make the greatest Baptist preacher on earth."

Bryan's theology rested on "man's consciousness of his finiteness in an infinite universe" and man's need to lean "upon the arm that is stronger than his." The linchpin of his faith was a simple and sincere belief in God, and in the Bible as the word of God. He regarded the moral injunctions of the Ten Commandments as the basis of our statute law and the Sermon on the Mount as providing the rules for spiritual growth. The Bible told the story of Jesus, whose gift to the world was a moral code superior to anything it had ever known. The divinity of Christ he never questioned, for he believed Jesus' power was infinite. If that spiritual power were understood and accepted, it would save the world, he was convinced. It was up to those who rejected the Bible as God's word to prove that it was man-made.

Bryan objected to evolutionary theory because he regarded it as poor science. "Did God Use Evolution as His Plan?" asked Bryan in the *New York Times*. He would accept evolution if it could be proved. "If it could be shown that man, instead of having been made in the image of God, is a development of beasts, we would have to accept it, regardless of its effect, for truth is truth and will prevail. But when there is no proof we have a right to consider the effect of the acceptance of an unsupported hypothesis." Evolutionary theory was not wrong because it denied the existence of God, for it did not, but, more dangerously, it put "the creative process so far away that reverence for the creator is likely to be lost." For Bryan, the idea of survival of the fittest was the very antithesis of all Christian values. It put man on a brute basis and ignored spiritual values. It destroyed man's belief in immortality and robbed him of his major stimulus to righteous living and his only source of hope. Teaching evolution meant teaching irreligion. Bryan said of Scopes' prosecution, "Our purpose and our only purpose is to vindicate the right of parents to guard the religion of their children. . . ."

Bryan believed that the clause in the Butler Act providing a penalty for violation was not needed. If teachers gave instruction in evolution, it was only necessary to fire them and remove them from the opportunity to do further damage. Teachers were the hired help of the community, employees paid by the state, and they were under instruction by the state. "A teacher," he said, "is like other employees, subject to the directions given by the employer. No teacher would be permitted to slander superiors and praise kings. . . . Why should a teacher in the public schools be allowed to teach that there is no God or that the Bible is a lie?" Scopes, therefore, was not prosecuted for what he did as an individual. "He was arrested," wrote Bryan,

> for violating a law as a representative of the state and as an employee in a school. As a representative, he has no right to misrepresent; as an employee he is compelled to act under the direction of his employers and has no right to defy instructions and still claim his salary. The right of free speech cannot be stretched so far as Professor Scopes is trying to stretch it. A man cannot demand a salary for saying what his employers do not want said and he cannot require his employers to furnish an audience to talk to, especially an audience of children or young people when he wants to say what the parents do not want him to say.

Fundamentally, the anti-evolution crusade raised the crucial question of who should control the public schools. "The Tennessee anti-evolution law," Bryan wrote, "is based on the theory that the control of the schools is in the hands of the people who created and support them. . . ."

Bryan had no concept of academic freedom, of the freedom of scholars to follow their thinking and develop their understanding and that of their students without restriction. He believed in majority rule in intellectual as well as political matters. The teaching of evolution in public schools was, in Bryan's mind, a challenge to popular democracy. "What right have the evolutionists—a relatively small percentage of the population—to teach at public expense a so-called scientific interpretation of the Bible when orthodox Christians are not permitted to teach an orthodox interpretation of the Bible?" The possibility that majority rule, applied to education, might destroy freedom either did not occur to Bryan or he did not care, so convinced was he of the truth of his position. He viewed teachers as hired hands and not as professionals endowed with the skill and freedom to lead young people to find and know the truth.

What, then, is the proper role of the school and of the teacher? Are they to indoctrinate children with conventional views? Or should they train children to exercise critical judgment? The ideas of the present day may ultimately go out of fashion, but the inquiring mind with a power of analysis is equipped to help build a better society. The Scopes trial involved far more than conflict over the teaching of evolution. It raised a fundamental question about the nature of education.

*   *   *

The trial opened on Friday, July 10, 1925—a day of sweltering heat. Quiet, conventional Dayton, a small southern hill town of 1,800 souls, was transformed overnight. The dusty street to the courthouse was lined with soft drink and sandwich stands along the curb, with vendors hawking religious books and watermelon, calico and notions. Evangelists had hastily built an open-air tabernacle, and the buildings of Dayton were festooned with banners. Monkey jokes, monkey souvenirs, and monkey toys had become the rage. Robinson's drugstore, where the notion for the challenge to the Butler Law had been conceived, featured a "monkey fizz" at the soda fountain, and the local butcher shop carried a sign proclaiming, "We handle all kinds of meat except monkey."

The temperature in the jammed courtroom averaged about 100 degrees. At the defense table sat Clarence Darrow and Arthur Garfield Hays of the American Civil Liberties Union. Hays had a keen legal mind but he was described by Mrs. Bryan unflatteringly as a "Jew . . . who reeks of . . . impertinence." Also there was Dudley Field Malone, an excommunicated Roman Catholic divorce lawyer and member of the international set. And there was John R. Neal, ex-dean of the University of Tennessee Law School. Neal was Scopes' chief counsel and a controversial figure in Tennessee. He had been dismissed as dean when he supported a professor who, two years earlier, had chosen to assign historian-educator James Harvey Robinson's pioneering work, *Mind in the Making* (1921) as a textbook. Neal was eccentric, absent-minded, and somewhat untidy, shaving at irregular intervals and rarely having his hair cut. Neal had run against Austin Peay for governor, making the anti-evolution law the central issue in the campaign, and he had been overwhelmingly beaten.

On the prosecution side, William Jennings Bryan had not actually practiced law for more than thirty years. Bryan's role, except for Darrow's dramatic cross-examination of him, was rather limited. He did little more than lend his presence to the prosecution team while other lawyers did the work. There were Attorney General Thomas Stewart, shrewd and skillful and an orator who could quicken the pulse of his listeners; Bryan's son, William Jennings Bryan, Jr.; and local attorneys.

Judge John Raulston of the Eighteenth Judicial District presided. In addition to his court duties, Raulston served as a lay preacher for the Methodists and had recently led revival meetings. Darrow and the defense team were convinced that Raulston was too close to fundamentalism to give Scopes a fair trial. Moreover, Raulston, a Democrat, planned to run for reelection to the bench in 1927, and it was reported that he would face stiff competition. That was perhaps why Raulston gave the press such easy access to the court, often inviting in photographers to practice their trade.

Darrow expected difficulty in finding suitable jurors, but the jury was impaneled in less than three hours. He was allowed great latitude in questioning prospective jurors, but the method of challenging did not permit his customary choices in getting the kind of jury he wanted. In Illinois (where Darrow was a member of the bar) a lawyer could temporarily accept a venireman onto the jury and drop him later by means of a peremptory challenge. But now Darrow found that he had just three peremptory challenges, and he could exercise them only while questioning a venireman. Once a juror had been accepted, the choice was final. Under this system, Darrow complained, "you never know which one to challenge." Only nineteen veniremen were examined before selections were completed. Darrow consoled himself that since the verdict was pretty much a foregone conclusion, the choice of jurors was less important in this case than in most. The final selection consisted of nine farmers, a farmer–school teacher, a shipping clerk, and the foreman, who was a fruit grower and a onetime United States marshal. All but one were members of evangelical churches. In fact, most of the people of Dayton attended one or another of the town's nine evangelical churches; in the town there were no Catholics, no Episcopalians, and almost no Jews.

When court adjourned for the weekend, Darrow spent his time preparing his case. Bryan occupied himself with haranguing the friendly crowds. On Sunday morning he delivered a lecture at the Methodist Church and that same afternoon spoke to a large crowd assembled on the courthouse lawn.

On Monday morning, July 13, the trial resumed. The case to be made by the prosecution was a simple on: It was not to question the wisdom of the Butler Law, but merely to prove that Scopes had violated it. Moving quickly, on Tuesday and Wednesday the prosecution showed that Scopes had indeed taught evolution to the biology class.

On the defense team there was no agreement among the attorneys. John Neal saw the crucial issue as one that involved the freedom of teaching, "or what is more important, the freedom of learning," not the truth or falsity of evolution. Neal's view was not that of Clarence Darrow and, consequently, he was replaced as senior defense attorney by Darrow himself. Darrow's aim was to focus the nation's attention on the thinking of Bryan and other fundamentalists. His colleague, Arthur Garfield Hays, defined the issue more sharply as "a battle between two types of mind—the rigid, orthodox, accepting, yielding, narrow, conventional mind, and the broad, liberal, critical, cynical, skeptical, and tolerant mind." It was not to be a case of the State of Tennessee against John Scopes, but a battle between the freethinking Darrow and the fundamentalist Bryan.

Under Darrow's direction the defense planned to challenge the constitutionality of the Butler Act as a violation of the First and Fourteenth Amendments. It was unconstitutional, they would assert, because it wrote a religious doctrine into law, and that law was itself unreasonable because it forbade the teaching of a widely accepted scientific theory. To prove the latter, the defense planned to call on leading scientists and theological scholars who volunteered to appear without fee. The first expert was to be Dr. Maynard M. Metcalf of Johns Hopkins University, a zoologist of international renown, an eminent Congregational layman, and a teacher of one of the largest Bible classes in the country. Metcalf had just finished a stint as chief of the Division of Biology and Agriculture of the National Research Commission. He had been president of the American Association for the Advancement of Science. Other experts included Dr. Shailer Matthews, dean of the Divinity School of the University of Chicago, and Dr. Herman Sosenwasser, president emeritus of Hebrew Union College. Matthews was a leading authority on the Bible and was prepared to testify that Genesis contained two contradictory accounts of Creation and therefore could not be used as a scientific text.

Sosenwasser was to testify as an authority on the Old Testament. The defense's plans included many other scholars and scientists—geologists, anthropologists, zoologists, and theologians. But overhanging this strategy was a question of the admissibility of such evidence.

The prosecution argued that such evidence was entirely incompetent. It constituted hearsay, because, according to Judge Raulston, "I don't think you can bring one man to prove what others believe." The prosecution insisted that the only issue before the jury was whether John Scopes had taught in violation of the law. "[W]e maintain that this cannot be the subject of expert testimony. To permit an expert to testify upon this issue would be to substitute trial by experts for trial by jury. . . ."

On the sixth day of the trial, Raulston ruled that the testimony of the experts would not be permitted. The defense was somewhat mollified, however, when agreement was reached that the defense could enter into the record affidavits on the substance of what they expected to prove by such testimony. They could not, however, introduce evidence or examine witnesses. Bryan's desire to rebut the defense's affidavits was turned down because, Raulston ruled, the defense was simply preparing evidence that could be considered by an appellate court. On the basis of the affidavits the appellate court would rule on the correctness of barring such expert testimony.

The court had opened on that Monday, July 13, with the reading of the indictment: "John Thomas Scopes . . . unlawfully did willfully teach in the public schools of Rhea County, Tennessee, which said public schools are supported in part and in whole by the public school fund of the state, a certain theory and theories that deny the story of the divine creation of man as taught in the Bible, and did teach instead that man has descended from a lower order of animals. . . ." The defense moved quickly to quash the indictment. Darrow noted that the Butler Law was a "foolish, mischievous and wicked act." It was, he continued, "as brazen and bold an attempt to destroy liberty as ever was seen in the Middle Ages." Neal became specific, arguing that the Butler Act was in violation of no fewer than six clauses of the Tennessee constitution and of Amendment XIV of the United States Constitution. Among other instances, he pointed out that the act violated that section of Tennessee's constitution which held that "no preference shall be given, by law, to any religious establishment or mode of worship." Judge Raulston took the motion under advisement.

Later in the afternoon, Darrow began, and his opening was aggressive if not bellicose. He started by noting that the state legislature had the right, within limits, to prescribe the course of study in the public schools of Tennessee. It could not, he supposed, prescribe study "under your constitution, if it omitted arithmetic and geography and writing. . . ." He noted also that the constitution said that the people of Tennessee "would always enjoy religious freedom in the broadest terms; so, I assume, that no legislature could fix a course of study which violated that." But, then, could it establish a course that taught that "the Christian religion as unfolded in the Bible, is true, and that every other religion or mode, or system of ethics is false." If so, "the constitution is a lie and a snare and the people have forgotten what liberty means."

Tennessee, he continued, no more had the right to teach the Bible as a divine book "than that the Koran is one, or the Book of Mormon, or the book of Confucius, or the Buddha, or the essays of Emerson, or any one of the 10,000 books to which human souls have gone for consolation and aid in their troubles." Recognizing that the Bible was primarily and essentially a book of religion and morals, a book which had consoled millions in time of need, it was "not a book of science. Never was and was never meant to be. Under it there is nothing prescribed that would tell you how to build a railroad or a steamboat or to make anything that would advance civilization." Even as a book of religion and morals there was no agreement as to its meaning: "There are in America at least five hundred different sects or churches, all of which quarrel with each other [about] . . . the construction of certain passages." This was not merely an American phenomenon, he insisted. In the whole world there were, he said, "at least 500 different Christian sects, all made up of differences. . . ." These differences were not a cause for despair but for congratulation, for there were "no two human machines alike and no two human beings have the same experiences, and their ideas of life and philosophy grow out of their construction of the experiences that we meet on our journey through life."

Tuesday, the third day, was marked by a quarrel over the opening of each session of court with a prayer. Since the trial involved a conflict between science and religion, Darrow pointed out, "there should be no part taken outside of the evidence in this case and no attempt by means of prayer or in any other way to influence the deliberation and consideration of the jury of the facts of this case." Opening the court with a prayer amounted to nothing less than turning "the courtroom into a meeting house."

Attorney General Stewart was aghast at the suggestion. It was not a case that presented a conflict between science and religion, but one "involving the fact as to whether or not a schoolteacher has taught a doctrine prohibited by statute." Therefore, it was not improper "to open the court with a prayer if the Court sees fit to do it." Stewart went on: "Such an idea extended by the agnostic counsel for the Defense is foreign to the thoughts and ideas of the people who do not know anything about infidelity and care less." Judge Raulston ruled in favor of the practice, took note of the exception, and directed that the trial record show each day that the defense had objected to the prayer and that he had overruled the objection.

Having lost on the prayer issue, the defense, in the afternoon session presented a petition from "representatives of various well-known religious organizations, churches and synagogues," asking that the court "select the officiating clergymen from among other than Fundamentalist churches," for there were "many to whom the prayers of the Fundamentalists are not spiritually uplifting and are occasionally offensive." Raulston agreed to refer the petition "to the pastors' association of this town" and to "invite the men named by the association to conduct the prayer each morning." The first minister invited was Charles Potter of New York's West Side Unitarian Church, already present as an expert witness for the defense. Unitarianism was a great distance from fundamentalism, a distance that may have caused some of Dayton's residents even more pain than the absence of prayer altogether.

On the morning of the fourth day, Judge Raulston ruled on the defense motion to quash the indictment. His lengthy opinion followed, point by point, the argument of the state. The Butler Act violated neither religious freedom nor personal liberty; and the state had the right to determine what was taught in the public schools. Thus did the court reject the challenge of the defense.

The state's case rested on the testimony of four witnesses, although two others were also available for further corroboration. The first was Walter White, Rhea County superintendent of schools. Under questioning, White informed the court that Scopes had used the state-approved textbook, that he had taught evolution from it, that he had done so a month after the passage of the Butler Act, and that Scopes had told him that he could not teach biology without teaching evolution. In the Tennessee schools, *Hunter's Civic Biology* had been the officially adopted biology textbook since 1909. On pages 194 and 195 were a brief explanation of Darwinism and a picture of an "evolutionary tree" showing the number of species in each class of animal. There were 518,900 species in all. Of mammals there were 3,500, and man was included in this little circle. White admitted that no textbook had been adopted to replace *Hunter's Civic Biology* after the Butler Act outlawed the teaching of evolution, nor had he warned Scopes or any other instructor about teaching it.

The next two witnesses were fourteen-year-old Howard Morgan and seventeen-year-old Harry Sheldon, both students in Scopes' biology class. Their testimony revealed that Scopes had used those parts of the Hunter text which dealt with evolution and which classified man as one of the various mammals, such as horses, monkeys, and cows. Neither of the boys remembered much about the lesson and both seemed unhurt by the experience.

Q. (Darrow interrogating.) Now, Howard, he said they were all mammals, didn't he?
A. Yes, sir.
Q. Did he tell you what a mammal was, or don't you remember?
A. Well, he just said these animals were mammals and man was a mammal.
Q. But did he tell you what distinguished mammals from other animals?
A. I don't remember.
Q. If he did, you have forgotten it? Didn't he say that mammals were those beings that suckled their young?
A. I don't remember about that.
Q. . . . It has not hurt you any, has it?
A. No, sir.

The interrogation of Harry Sheldon followed the same line of questioning.

> Q. Did you study—did Professor Scopes teach you anything about evolution during that time?
> A. He taught that all forms of life begin with the cell.
> Q. Begin with the cell?
> A. Yes, sir.
> Q. Did anybody ever tell you before?
> A. No, sir.
> Q. That is all you remember that he told you about biology, wasn't it?
> A. Yes, sir.
> Q. Are you a church member?
> A. Yes, sir.
> Q. Do you still belong?
> A. Yes, sir.
> Q. You didn't leave when he told you all forms of life began with a single cell?
> A. No, sir.

The state completed its list of witnesses with F.E. Robinson, druggist and head of the school board, in whose drugstore students obtained their copies of *Hunter's Civic Biology*. Robinson testified that the books came directly from the state textbook depository in Chattanooga.

The first witness for the defense, Dr. Maynard M. Metcalf of Johns Hopkins University, looked to be a typical absent-minded professor, but there was nothing absent-minded about his testimony. Metcalf was the first of the expert witnesses who were to be called to show that the Butler Act was unreasonable and not a proper exercise of Tennessee's legitimate authority over health, safety, morals, welfare—and education. The state took exception, but until Judge Raulston resolved the issue on the sixth day, Metcalf testified, and he asserted without hesitation that there was no important scientist who was not an evolutionist.

The evidence of the men of science and learning, however, was cut short when such testimony was found inadmissible. It was during the arguments over admissibility that Dudley Field Malone delivered for the defense what both friend and foe described as the most eloquent speech of the trial. (Even Bryan rushed over to him and said, "Although we differ, I have never heard a better speech.") Malone, speaking clearly and dramatically, masked biting sarcasm with a veneer of sympathy and understanding. He argued first that the Bible is not an encyclopedia of knowledge but an inspirational and theological work.

> These gentlemen say: "The Bible contains the truth. If the word of science can produce any truth or facts not in the Bible as we understand it, then destroy science but keep the Bible." And we say: "Keep your Bible. Keep it as your consolation, keep it as your guide. But keep it where it belongs, in the world of your own conscience, in the world of your individual judgment."

In response to Judge Raulston's question about whether he believed the theory of evolution to be compatible with the Divine Creation as taught in the Bible, defense attorney Malone replied that he so believed. There was no reason to believe that God could not have created the first single life-cell and then allowed men to evolve "serially." Theistic evolution solved the logical problem, for it restored the role of God as Creator. Malone argued that the defense was seeking the truth, and would admit any evidence that would shed light on it. The capstone of his argument was that if a religious belief like Bryan's was true, it did not need the protection of the law. "Where is the fear?" he asked. "We defy it! We ask Your Honor to admit the evidence [of expert testimony] as a matter of correct law, as a matter of sound procedure, and as a matter of justice to the defense in this case." The applause and cheering were reported to have been even longer and louder than when Bryan spoke.

When scientific testimony was ruled out on the sixth day, the trial seemed over. The defense had built its entire case on the testimony of the fifteen experts brought to Dayton. It appeared that there was no one else to call. The corrosive H.L. Mencken, whose reports of the trial were filled with wit and sarcasm, even packed his bags and left Tennessee. The defense had been careful not to let Scopes take the witness chair and thus open himself to cross-examination. As Scopes later remembered, "Darrow had been afraid for me to go on the stand. Darrow realized that I was not a science teacher and he was afraid that if I were put on the stand I would be asked if I actually taught biology." Darrow had been unwilling to reveal that Scopes' undergraduate major had been law, not science. He had had a course in practice teaching and enough study in mathematics, physics, and chemistry, along with some high school basketball experience, to satisfy Tennessee that he would do for a last-minute replacement in a coaching and teaching job.

It was a surprise not only to the court but to Bryan himself when Arthur Garfield Hays rose and asked that Bryan be called as a witness. Bryan was not eager to testify, but neither was he afraid. He insisted only that Darrow, Malone, and Hays also be put on the witness stand. At the very least, it was most unusual that a counsel for the prosecution be called as a witness for the defense, and even more extraordinary that he should be subjected to questioning so rigorous as to amount to cross-examination by Darrow.

The focal point of the interrogation on the seventh day was a series of questions which Darrow had presented to Bryan two years earlier, but which Bryan had never answered. Darrow was particularly eager to have Bryan respond concerning the literalness to be applied to Biblical analysis. In agreeing to testify, Bryan opened himself to a whole series of debunking questions: Was Jonah really swallowed by a whale? How long was it before the whale spewed him out? Did Joshua make the sun stand still? Is the story of the Flood literally true? When did it occur? Was the earth created in six days?

Darrow's examination of Bryan lasted almost two hours, and the lawyer pursued him relentlessly. Surprisingly, it was Bryan's less than completely fundamentalist views that caused him to lose popularity with the local townspeople.

Q. Do you claim that everything in the Bible should be literally interpreted?
A. I believe everything in the Bible should be accepted as it is given there; some of the Bible is given illustratively. For instance: "Ye are the salt of the earth." I would not insist that man was actually salt, or that he had flesh of salt, but it is used in the sense as saving God's people.

Q. But when you read that Jonah swallowed the whale—or that the whale swallowed Jonah—excuse me please—how do we literally accept that?

A. When I read that a big fish swallowed Jonah—it does not say a whale.

Q. Doesn't it? You sure?

A. That is my recollection of it. A big fish, and I believe it; and I believe in a God who can make a whale and can make a man and make both do what He pleases.

Q. But you believe He made them—that He made such a fish and that it was big enough to swallow Jonah?

A. Yes, sir. Let me add: one miracle is just as easy to believe as another.

Q. Do you believe Joshua made the sun stand still?

A. I believe what the Bible says. I suppose you mean that the earth stood still?

Q. I don't know. I'm talking about the Bible now.

A. I accept the Bible absolutely.

Q. The Bible says Joshua commanded the sun to stand still for the purpose of lengthening the day, doesn't it? And you believe it?

A. I do.

Q. Do you believe at that time the entire sun went around the earth?

A. No, I believe that the earth goes around the sun.

Q. Do you believe that the men who wrote it thought that the day could be lengthened or that the sun could be stopped?

A. I believe that the Bible is inspired, an inspired author, whether one who wrote as he was directed to write understood the things he was writing about, I don't know.

Q. Whoever inspired it? Do you think whoever inspired it believed that the sun went around the earth?

A. I believe it was inspired by the Almighty, and He may have used language that could be understood at the time.

Q. So, it might not; it might have been subject to construction, might it not?

A. It might have been used in language that could be understood then.

Q. That means it is subject to construction?

A. That is your construction. I am answering your question.

Q. Is it your opinion that passage was subject to construction?

A. Well, I think anybody can put his own construction upon it, but I do not mean that necessarily that is a correct construction. I have answered the question.

Q. Don't you believe that in order to lengthen the day it would have been construed that the earth stood still?

A. I would not attempt to say what would have been necessary, but I know this, that I can take a glass of water that would fall to the ground without the strength of my hand and to the extent of the glass of water I can overcome the law of gravitation and lift it up, whereas without my hand it would fall to the ground. If my puny hand can overcome the law of gravitation, the most universally understood, to that extent, I would not set power to the hand of the Almighty God that made the Universe.

Q. I say, you call it interpretation at this time, to say it meant something then?

A. You may use your own language to describe what I have to say, and I will use mine in answering.

Q. Now, Mr. Bryan, have you ever pondered what would have happened to the earth if it had stood still?

A. No.

Q. You have not?

A. No; the God I believe in could have taken care of that, Mr. Darrow.

Q. I see. Have you ever pondered what would naturally happen to the earth if it stood still suddenly?

A. I have been too busy on things that I thought were of more importance than that.

In admitting that he believed the earth moved around the sun, and in describing Joshua as having made the sun stand still, and in accepting that the Bible used language which people of that time, with their limited knowledge, understood, Bryan was hedging on his commitment to literalness. When he admitted that the six days of the Creation as described in the Bible might not have been six days in the literal sense, but periods of time involving eons, Bryan began to lose some followers. His rejection of the theory of evolution had pushed him into a complete acceptance of fundamentalism—a position that he found not quite comfortable, as his testimony revealed. He may have regretted that testimony. But at least in the eyes of some of his former supporters, he had defected from fundamentalism. He had destroyed its authoritative position.

Darrow defeated Bryan that day—some would say ignominiously. For his part, Bryan hoped to put Darrow on the stand after he concluded on the following day, but Attorney General Stewart, who had opposed the examination of Bryan in the first place, decided, as chief counsel, that Bryan should not return to the witness stand. The interrogation had taken the trial outside the limits he had set. Despite Bryan's vociferous protest and demand that he be given the opportunity to rebut Darrow, Stewart's decision held. The next day, Judge Raulston announced that Bryan's further testimony would not be germane to the issue of the trial.

The defense devoted its remaining efforts to preventing the prosecution from rebutting the defense. Realizing that Bryan might try a final address to the jury, the defense pleaded Scopes guilty and waived its rights to a closing speech, thereby depriving the prosecution, under Tennessee law, of the chance to make an address. As Darrow remembered in his autobiography, "By not making a closing argument on our side we could cut [Bryan] down." There was another element as well. It was only after the trial that Scopes revealed to a reporter that he had missed the Darwin lesson. He had been doing something else that day. "Those kids they put on the stand," he said, "couldn't remember what I taught three months ago. They were coached by the lawyers." Scopes had been on trial for something that might never have happened.

With Scopes' plea, the trial ended. The jury found him guilty and Raulston fixed his fine at $100. Scopes was dismissed from his position in the Rhea County public schools. On appeal, the state supreme court ruled that the jury and not the judge should have levied the fine, but it upheld the constitutionality of the Butler Act. Then the attorney general cleverly outflanked Darrow and blocked the road to the Supreme Court of the United States. Scopes, said Tennessee's chief justice, was "no longer in the service of the state. We see nothing to be gained by prolonging the life of this bizarre case." The chief justice was, he made clear, concerned about "the peace and dignity of the state" as he accepted the entry of a *nolle prosequi* by the attorney general that simply nullified the indictment and threw the case out of the courts.

Had the Scopes case gone to the United States Supreme Court, it seems certain that the Butler Act would not have been held unconstitutional. In 1925 neither the Establishment Clause nor the Free Exercise Clause of the First Amendment—which prohibit Congress from establishing religion or interfering with its free exercise—had been incorporated into the Fourteenth Amendment—which restrains the states fron denying "liberty" to any person without due process. It was not until fifteen years later that the Court determined that First Amendment religious liberty is secure from state interference because of the Fourteenth Amendment.

The Scopes case was artificial, set up to test the constitutionality of the Butler Act—a case that had been contrived in a local drugstore. Did the Butler Act get more concern than it deserved? Did the case change minds or simply harden convictions already held? Most commentators agree that the trial pitted fundamentalism against modernism in a way that well reflected the mood of the times but without advancing the cause of either. In the longer term, it put a brake on additional anti-evolution laws, helped bring on the decline of fundamentalism and, most important, encouraged accommodation between religion and science. For John Scopes, the promotion of academic freedom had been the key issue. On that score, the trial was a failure. The teacher's choice of teaching material was at issue and the material did conform to professional standards. Scopes got the sack, nevertheless. The pressures against teaching evolution persisted into the 1930s and beyond. Even today, the language of secondary school biology textbooks is often guarded and evolution is taught in many places only by indirection.

The Butler Law, although not enforced after the Scopes trial, remained on the books until 1967, when it was finally repealed. In 1968 the United States Supreme Court, in *Epperson* v. *Arkansas,* voided that state's anti-evolution law on the ground that it violated the religion clauses of the First Amendment, incorporated into the Fourteenth:

[T]here can be no doubt that Arkansas has sought to prevent its teachers from discussing the theory of evolution. . . . It is clear that fundamentalist sectarian conviction was and is the law's reason for existence. . . . Plainly, the law is contrary to the mandate of the First, and in violation of the Fourteenth Amendment to the Constitution.

In 1981, Arkansas and Louisiana enacted legislation requiring that the creationist account of the origins of life be taught as a viable alternative to the theory of evolution. Taking advantage of the equal rights struggle in other aspects of American life, creationists were demanding equal time for teaching both creation science and evolution science. Where the anti-evolutionists of the 1920s stood four-square on the Bible in opposition to the modernists, the scientific creationists believe that scientific evidence supports the Biblical account of Creation. They have taken their battle to school boards and textbook commissions, to state legislatures and to the courts. In 1982, however, the United States District Court for the Eastern District of Arkansas rejected the Balanced Treatment for Creation Science and Evolution Science Act on the ground that its clear purpose was the advancement of religion.

Victory on this front, however, has not finally put to rest the issue which has persisted since the appearance of Darwin's *On the Origin of Species* in 1859. The creationists are part of a revival of fundamentalism that has been gaining strength since the 1960s. This gain can be seen in the success of radio and television preachers and in a significant increase in political activism among groups that have blocked the Equal Rights Amendment and which strive to reinstate prayer in the schools, prohibit abortion, limit the rights of homosexuals, and achieve a Constitutional Amendment that prohibits burning of the American flag.

As long as the world is beset by problems—and that will be forever—and people feel the need for security and certainty, fundamentalism, in some form, will be part of the fabric of American life. The Bible has served, after all, as a comforting absolute. It has provided stability in times of rapid change as well as security in the face of the unknown.

7

LOEB-LEOPOLD

On Thursday morning, May 22, 1924, the nude and battered body of a 14-year-old boy was found in a concrete drainage culvert near the tracks of the Pennsylvania Railroad just outside Hammond, Indiana. Acid had been poured on his face, abdomen, and genitals. The body was discovered by a night worker walking home in the early morning. He called to two railroad signalmen who brought it to the authorities in a handcar. On June 1, Richard Loeb, age eighteen, confessed to the murder. His partner, Nathan Leopold, nineteen, admitted his guilt a short time later.

The trial of Richard Loeb and Nathan Leopold for the murder of Bobby Franks followed one of the most publicized crimes in American history. The public was aghast at the brutality of the murder, at its seeming senselessness, and at the character and psychology of the perpetrators. Neither young man had the background that the public expected of a criminal.

Nathan F. Leopold was an intellectual prodigy. He had begun walking and talking before he was six months old, and intelligence tests—a relatively new and fascinating psychological tool in the 1920s—gave Leopold scores between 200 and 210. He was fourteen when he entered the University of Chicago and, when he graduated four years later, a member of Phi Beta Kappa, he was among the youngest graduates in the university's history. Leopold then entered the University of Chicago Law School, with plans to transfer later to Harvard. Although he was still in his teens, Leopold had already studied fifteen languages and spoke at least five fluently. He had also developed a strong interest in ornithology and had collected nearly 3000 bird specimens. Leopold read widely in philosophy and religion as well as in science and soon came to reject all religion as superstition. He had studied the German philosopher Friedrich Nietzsche and was particularly attracted to Nietzsche's idea of the *Ubermensch*, or Superman, who achieved his superiority through the power of his intellect. Although governed by no code and impervious to human emotions, the Superman could do no wrong. Leopold determined to become such a being. He crammed his mind with knowledge of every sort and trained himself to repress his emotions, to feel no pity, no sympathy, no remorse for any action.

Physically, Nathan Leopold was not very attractive. He was small in stature, round-shouldered and flat-footed, with bulging eyes—a condition that greatly disturbed him—and a protuberant abdomen. A non-athlete, he avoided sports. Nor did Leopold have a pleasing personality. Shunned by others, he was often thought arrogant as he constantly flaunted his intellectual gifts. He had entered Chicago's Harvard School at age fourteen, a private school that offered prestige and an education of quality. There his classmates made fun of his size and teased him about his precocity, or ridiculed his interest in birds. They called him "the flea" or "Crazy Nathan." The school's yearbook had him saying, "Of course, I am the great Nathan. When I open my lips, let no dogs bark." In college he continued to have difficulty forming friendships. Not only were others put off by his intellectual arrogance and overbearing manner, but he was much younger than his classmates, who often described him as "argumentative," "egocentric," and "conceited."

Nathan F. Leopold, Sr., was a retired box manufacturer and quite wealthy. As a father he had been over-indulgent, giving his son, whom he called "Babe," every material advantage that money could provide. During the first six months of his life, Babe had been cared for by a nurse, only in part because he was sickly. He was raised by a succession of governesses. One of them, Nathan later told his psychiatric examiners, "displaced my mother." His early education consisted of a series of private schools. Then, while he was in college, he received a monthly allowance of $125 and whatever other sums he asked for. Nathan paid for nothing himself, his father taking care of tuition, room and board, books and clothing, personal expenses, and all the costs of maintaining his son's automobile. When Nathan contemplated a vacation in Europe, his father set aside $3,000 for that purpose, at a time when the average annual income of employed wage earners was $1,228.

Leopold's accomplice in the murder of Bobby Franks was Richard Loeb. Eighteen at the time of the crime, he had already graduated from the University of Michigan. Not as gifted as Leopold, Loeb was still far above average in intelligence, with an I.Q. of about 160. His bachelor's degree was completed in only two and a half years, but with no more than average grades. Unlike Leopold, he failed to earn a Phi Beta Kappa key, although he often claimed he had. Indeed, lying came easily to Loeb. Later on, his psychiatric examiners believed that in his fantasies he sometimes saw himself as a master criminal executing the perfect crime—"a murder, nothing less; one which would startle the country and confound the police."

By the time Loeb's association with Leopold began he had become "utterly unscrupulous—a liar, a thief, and a mischief-maker. Conceptions of right and wrong troubled him not at all." Loeb told his psychiatric examiners that after high school his education followed the line of least resistance; that he was lazy and exerted himself only as much as was necessary; and that he had never received any honors. Physically he was quite different from Leopold. Richard Loeb was strong and good-looking. In appearance he had no obvious physical defects save for a barely discernible facial tic. He had overcome stuttering but continued to suffer from spells of fainting. Both he and Leopold were, according to the examiners, physical cowards. Loeb feared injury in a fight, yet could be inexplicably reckless in other ways in regard to personal safety. One of the examiners commented that Leopold "was never able to stand pain or suffering. He says he has always had some fear of physical pain, but that he has never had any fear of death." Socially, Loeb made friends easily, but he also dropped them quickly and frequently.

Like his partner, Richard Loeb had grown up under the care of nurses and governesses. He remembered one governess in particular during his sessions with the psychiatrists: a middle-aged Canadian woman who began to care for him when he was about eleven. She was a strict disciplinarian, governing everything he read, everything he did, and with whom he associated. Breaches of her discipline brought on penalties of extra study or the loss of small privileges. To escape her displeasure Loeb thought up ways to deceive her: She had forbidden the young man to read books or to associate with friends of whom she disapproved. Young Loeb attended the University of Chicago Laboratory School, a preparatory school for the academically able, before he went to college. He had planned to enter the University of Chicago Law School in the fall of 1924.

Albert Loeb, Richard's father, was well known in Chicago as a corporate lawyer. An attorney for Sears, Roebuck & Company, then chief executive, by 1922 he was a multimillionaire. Like the elder Leopold, Albert Loeb indulged his son's every whim. "Dickie" Loeb received an allowance of $250 per month, and there was a standing order from Albert Loeb to the family secretary that "Dickie" was to have any sum at any time without question.

"Dickie" Loeb and "Babe" Leopold had become friends when both were at the University of Chicago. Loeb was fourteen and Leopold a year older. When Loeb transferred to the University of Michigan, Leopold did the same and they became roommates. Many years later, one of Leopold's law school classmates remembered that he had often discussed philosophy with Leopold, particularly Nietzsche. He recalled that Leopold regarded Loeb as the one person who came nearest to being the *Ubermensch*. Leopold was certain, he said, that "Loeb was a superman, that he had a brilliant mind, was handsome and irresistible to women. I tried to tell him that he didn't know what he was talking about, that Loeb was glib, superficial, and lied to impress others. Leopold kept insisting I didn't understand Loeb." To Loeb, the superman, Leopold pictured himself as a slave, not abject and miserable but a powerful slave who "makes Dickie the king, maintains him in his kingdom, like the premier who occupies the principal office over a weakly king."

Leopold's friends did not like Loeb. Loeb's friends did not like Leopold. Soon Leopold left Michigan and returned to the University of Chicago. Nevertheless, despite the physical distance between them, the two saw each other frequently and their relationship deepened. But it was a stormy one. They often quarreled, and sometimes went so far as to threaten each other's life. According to the psychiatric report, Loeb's criminal propensities found scope and assistance in the friendship. The two began cheating at bridge. They threw bricks through windows and automobile windshields "for the thrill of it." They turned in false alarms. In Ann Arbor, Michigan, they set fire to an abandoned building and they burglarized Loeb's fraternity house. Unlike Loeb, Leopold lacked real criminal tendencies, but he needed Loeb, said the psychiatrists, "to complement him and serve as his alter ego."

Loeb and Leopold had planned a kidnapping for a long time. It was to be their perfect crime. They would confirm their own beliefs that they were *Ubermenschen*. They considered a number of victims, rejecting one possibility because his father "was a tightwad" and might not pay the ransom. They also considered kidnapping the grandson of Sears, Roebuck executive Julius Rosenwald. They ended by choosing no specific person but, rather, anyone with the proper qualifications. The victim would have to come from a family wealthy enough to pay a sizable ransom without flinching. The victim should be someone they already knew, since it would be easier to approach an acquaintance and lure him or her into a trap. The fact that they would have to kill the kidnap victim to prevent their being identified gave them no concern. They were not even averse to considering the kidnapping and murder of one of their own fathers, but rejected the idea for the practical reason that they would be under too close a scrutiny. For the same reason, they rejected making Loeb's younger brother the victim.

Loeb and Leopold decided not to select a specific victim but to pick one as opportunity offered. They would, they agreed, cruise around the Harvard School until the right moment, and then grab somebody; they would wait for an easy mark and snatch whoever showed up. The decision would be left until the last minute.

In the meantime, they went about making elaborate preparations to carry out their "perfect crime." The prospective kidnappers drove to a rent-a-car agency to get an automobile. Leopold went in. Loeb drove around the corner to a lunchroom. Introducing himself as Morton D. Ballard, Leopold asked to rent an automobile. He indicated that he was staying at the Morrison Hotel and that he had an account at the Hyde Park State Bank. He gave as references the names of three people in Peoria and one in Chicago, a Louis Mason. He gave the telephone number of the lunchroom around the corner where Loeb was waiting, snacking on raisins and candy and chatting with the proprietor, from whom he had purchased a telephone slug and requested permission to wait for a telephone call. The call came and Mason (Loeb) vouched for Ballard (Leopold): "He'll return the car," said Loeb. "There'll be no problem." The two used the car for several hours. It had served part of its purpose, for now Leopold had an identification card from the Rent-A-Car agency.

In their planning, the two had agreed on the means to be used in killing their victim, on the way to conceal the body, and on the place where it was to be hidden. They had also conceived a plan for obtaining ransom money. They were, they believed, ready to act.

At about eleven in the morning of Wednesday, May 21, 1924, with his classes at the University of Chicago over for the day, Nathan Leopold, as Morton D. Ballard, put down a deposit of $35 to rent a dark blue Willys-Knight touring car. He then picked up Richard Loeb, who was waiting in Leopold's own car, likewise a Willys-Knight but red, and they drove both cars to Leopold's home. When the Leopold family chauffeur came out to meet them, Nathan told him that he would be with Loeb. The brakes on his own car, he said, needed maintenance.

At two-thirty in the afternoon, classes ended at the Harvard School. Loeb and Leopold parked their rented car a block from the school. While Leopold stayed behind the wheel, Loeb walked toward the school building. He met and spoke to several people: his younger brother, a tutor at the school, and Johnny Levinson, the son of a prominent attorney. Johnny did not become the victim, simply because he went off to a nearby lot to play baseball.

Much later in the afternoon Bobby Franks left the grounds of the Harvard School after umpiring a freshman baseball game. He was the son of Jacob Franks, former owner of Franks Collateral Loan Bank— in reality a pawn shop. As Loeb said later, "He just happened along and we got him."

Bobby Franks knew both Loeb and Leopold. He accepted their invitation to go examine a new tennis racket and get a ride home, even though he lived only a few short blocks from the school. But he didn't live long enough to examine the racket, nor did he ever get home. Loeb was sitting in the backseat. As soon as Bobby got into the car through the right front door, Loeb struck him brutally on the head with a chisel, stuffed a cloth soaked with hydrochloric acid into his mouth and, "after the boy became unconscious, wrapped and covered him with the lap robe. He bled profusely." The blood soaked the robe and spilled onto the floor of the car. Earlier, Loeb and Leopold had determined that they would strangle the victim with a rope they purchased. Each would pull on it at the same time so they would share equally in the crime. But that isn't what happened. "We got him into the car," Loeb revealed later. "He was hit over the head with the chisel, dragged . . . onto the back seat from the front seat, gagged, but he was dead, and we didn't need to strangle him."

The two killers had also decided earlier that they would dispose of the body of their victim in a marshy area near Hammond, Indiana; this was in a sparsely settled industrial district, usually deserted after sundown. The marshland was a place to which Leopold sometimes brought his birdwatching group. A large concrete drainage culvert opened alongside a stretch of railroad track. After stopping for some sandwiches in a roadside restaurant, Loeb and Leopold drove on a bit farther. They then stripped the body naked, poured acid over the corpse, and jammed it headfirst into the culvert. The acid was to prevent or at least delay identification. They hid the dead boy's shoes in some brush, threw the bloodstained chisel out of the car, and later burned the rest of Bobby Franks' clothing in the Loeb basement. On the following day they tried to remove the bloodstains from the floor of the rented car before returning it. On the day after, they jettisoned into a lagoon the typewriter on which the ransom note had been written. Before they did so, however, they pulled off the letter keys with a pair of pliers and threw them into the lagoon too. Unable to remove the bloodstains from the lap robe, they saturated it with gasoline and burned it in a vacant lot on the outskirts of Chicago.

Leopold now telephoned the Franks household. He informed Mrs. Franks that Bobby was being held for ransom. The ransom note, already written, was mailed special delivery. Signed by "George Johnson," it directed Mr. Franks to obtain $10,000 by noon of the day of its receipt. The money, in old $20 and $50 bills, was to be placed in a cigar box, ready for delivery according to instructions to be given by telephone. Under no circumstances should there be any appeal for help from the police. If the directions were carefully followed, the note promised, Bobby would be safely returned within six hours after the money was received.

Even before the ransom could be turned over, the Franks family learned that the naked body of a young boy had been found in a swamp, crammed into a concrete drainpipe. Mr. Franks paid no heed for a time. He was certain that the kidnappers would not harm his son. He was doing everything asked of him, and the description given seemed that of a younger, heavier boy. At first Franks refused to send a member of his family to the morgue to look at the body, but he finally agreed to send his brother-in-law who, sadly, identified his nephew.

The early discovery of the Franks boy defeated the murderers' plan to collect a ransom. Nevertheless, Loeb and Leopold remained supremely confident that their crime would not be solved. Loeb, in fact, was so optimistic that he volunteered to help the police.

The discovery of the body within 24 hours of the murder was only the first of many discoveries. Despite their superior intelligence and their months of planning, the crime was far from perfect. It took the police only ten days following the commission of the crime to get to the truth. The most important break in solving the case occurred when a laborer employed in the vicinity found a pair of horn-rimmed glasses near the culvert. At first glance, the glasses seemed to be of a standard pattern, but closer examination revealed that the hinges were not the ordinary kind. Investigators learned that they had been patented by the Bobrow Optical Company of Rochester, New York, and that the firm had only one outlet in Chicago. After checking some 54,000 sales records, the distributor, Almer Coe & Co., discovered it had sold only three pairs of glasses in the city with that type of hinge. One pair had been sold to an elderly woman. A second had been sold to an attorney who had been in Europe for six weeks. The third pair had been sold in November 1923, to Nathan F. Leopold, Jr.

On the basis of this discovery, the state attorney directed that young Leopold be brought in for questioning. To avoid reporters the interrogation took place in a hotel room. When shown the glasses, Leopold admitted without hesitation, "They look like mine. If I didn't know mine were at home, I'd suspect they were." When Nathan failed to find the glasses after searching the house, his older brother, Michael, suggested a possible answer: "This place where they found the body is right where you often go looking for birds. Maybe you dropped them out there without noticing it." It was a plausible explanation. Leopold was teaching ornithology at University High School and he often took his students to the area. He had, in fact, been there on one such birding trip just three days before the murder.

The plausibility of the explanation gave Leopold only a temporary respite, however. The questioning continued. Both boys had anticipated the possibility of being arrested and had made plans to give each other an alibi. If arrested, they would tell a story about picking up two girls and driving out to Lincoln Park with them. Questioned about the details of the story, Leopold said he knew the girls only as Mae and Edna; he did not remember their last names. He described them as "between 19 and 22, rather short." Probing for every detail, the police asked specific questions—and many of them. Where did they pick up the girls? At what time? Where did they take them? Did they have dinner? What did they eat? Drink? Did they kiss the girls? Where did they go in Lincoln Park? Did they see any birds? What were the girls' names again? They never gave their family names? What time did they get back to the Leopold house? Who was home? When was Loeb taken home? How old were the girls?

The questioning was unrelenting, but Nathan Leopold answered each question willingly and without hesitation. It was a dangerous game to be playing, for the alibi was entirely false—and it had a fatal weakness. Loeb and Leopold had failed to decide on the critical timing of the alibi. They had determined when planning the crime that if either of them was arrested within one week, he would tell the story about picking up the girls. But if either was arrested after that, he would say that he had no recollection of what they were doing on the relevant days. They reasoned that the police could not expect them to remember their activities more than a week before, but would be suspicious if they forgot what they were doing after so brief a time.

Shortly after the police arrested Leopold and interrogated him, they arrested Loeb and brought him to the same hotel for questioning, although to a different room. Admitting that he had been with Leopold on the afternoon of the murder, Loeb claimed that he had left Leopold at dinner and that he couldn't recall what happened that night, more than a week after the sequence of criminal actions had begun. But Leopold had spun his tale about "Edna" and "Mae." His timing was based on the fact that it was less than a week since they had completed their efforts to destroy the evidence. It was this discrepancy in their stories that finally did them in. Leopold had stuck to his version, believing that Loeb would corroborate it. Instead, Loeb made a detailed confession. When advised of Loeb's confession, Leopold admitted his part. The two confessions agreed in all substantial particulars except one: Loeb attributed the death blows with the chisel to Leopold. Leopold, on the other hand, blamed Loeb for the killing, pointing out quite reasonably that he drove the car and that Loeb had been sitting in the backseat where the murder was committed.

The confessions notwithstanding, evidence against the two was piling up to such an extent that they probably would have been found guilty without them. Sven Englund, the Leopold family chauffeur, for example, remembered clearly the events of May 21, the day of the crime, and was able to declare positively that Leopold's alibi regarding the car in use that day was false. On the afternoon of May 21, Englund said, Leopold arrived home driving his red Willys-Knight. The brakes were squeaking, Leopold told him; he wanted the squeak corrected. Englund took the car into the garage and began working on it. "Then when you finished, they took the car and left?" he was asked at the trial. "Oh, no," replied the chauffeur. "I worked on the car all day. They used some other machine."

If Englund had been working on the brakes of Leopold's red Willys- Knight, the boys could certainly not have used the car to pick up the two girls. Englund had also been to see a doctor that day. There was neither any mistake about the date on the prescription he received nor, therefore, about the exact date of the events he described. Englund damaged the young men's story even more when he recalled that on May 22, the day following the crime, he saw Leopold and Loeb trying to remove red stains from the carpet of the rented car. It was most unusual, he pointed out, for the boys to do any work at all. They told him that they had spilled wine on the carpet the day before—but they had said earlier it was in Leopold's car that they picked up the girls.

Independently, without benefit of the confessions, the police were able to disprove another element in Leopold's story. He had denied owning a portable Underwood typewriter of the sort used to write the ransom note. But classmates in his law school study group were able to produce carbon copies of notes he had typed on that very machine.

The confessions filled in essential details but they needed corroboration. Police confirmed the rental of the death car. Bank and hotel employees established the identities of Loeb and Leopold as Mason and Ballard. The hardware store, drugstore, and stationery store where the suspects had purchased the chisel, and hydrochloric acid, and the paper used for the ransom note were found. Sales personnel recalled the purchases. Finally, police recovered the battered typewriter from the lagoon in Jackson Park.

It seems strange, given the intelligence of the two young men and the fact that Leopold was a law student, that neither asked for assistance of legal counsel until after they were charged. Had they done so, they would surely have been advised by a lawyer to say nothing. By the time they got that advice it was too late.

After learning of the confessions, the Chicago newspapers clamored for blood. The *Evening American*, one of the two Hearst papers, demanded that the criminals be given the ultimate punishment: "Society requires that there be no slipping in the wheels of justice in this case. It demands that punishment be meted out with the rigorous impartiality of the old law that recognized no new-fangled 'mental psychosis.'" Without a dissent, newspapers reported that public opinion was at "a white heat of indignation" and demanded the death penalty.

The character of the murderers fascinated the American public, and so did the bizarre nature of the crime. It had no apparent motive. It could not be blamed on need, nor on the environment, and certainly not on the lack of intelligence of the murderers. The victim had been selected randomly. What troubled the nation was the apparent inconsistency between what the two young murderers had done and the kind of behavior expected of people in their circumstances. Perhaps intelligence, education, and background did *not* guarantee socially acceptable behavior. Perhaps man's understanding of human nature and human behavior was faulty and needed revising. Perhaps, contrary to some of the central assumptions of American social thought, man was not basically good.

During the 1920s the "new psychology"—a popularization of conceptions of human beings and their motives—was at hand to explain such behavior. Few if any professional psychoanalysts were involved in the movement. Most of it was the work of writers in popular magazines, work generally regarded by specialists as distortions and dilutions of the ideas of Sigmund Freud. Major emphases in the new psychology moved through three phases. The first was characterized by a focus on psychoanalysis. Following psychoanalysis came an emphasis on "glandism," a concentration on the endocrine glands and their role in human behavior. Finally, behaviorism—a mechanistic stimulus–response psychology— became the popular favorite.

The impact of Freud's thinking was pervasive in the 1920s, comparable to that of Charles Darwin in the years following the Civil War. Freud saw the human mind as an elaborate structure seething with conscious and unconscious currents. It was common to explain Freud's ideas with a simplistic "iceberg" metaphor: Because most of the iceberg is below water level, so, too, is it with the mind. Above the water level appears only a small portion, the realm of consciousness and rationality. Freud called this part of the mind the "ego." Below the level of consciousness, below the water line, sits the "id." This larger part carries the sum total of drives, impulses, and passions, the realm of the irrational. Basic to Freud's argument was that "these dark, irrational depths strongly influence thought and behavior." The "libido," which Freud located in the depths of the id, was the province of sexuality.

Central to Freudian psychology was the notion of an eternal struggle between the ego and the id for control of the individual. Because of its size and strength, the odds were on the side of the id. To the aid of the ego came the "superego," the focus of ideals and ethics. The two of them—the ego, or reason, and the superego—attempted to control the destructive energies of the id. The struggle was an unequal one, however, and consequently the ego resorted to trickery. By means of "sublimation" it tried to channel the destructive energies of the id into more beneficial and healthy forms of expression. This was partially successful and, according to Freudian psychology, explained such phenomena as social consciousness and personal responsibility. But to achieve these socially desirable goals required repression of the urges of the "unconscious," the part below the waterline. Too much repression produced mental illnesses, or "neuroses." It was the function of the psychoanalyst, according to Freud, both to discipline the id and still allow expression of hidden desires and anxieties.

The advocates of glandism did not reject Freudian analysis. They incorporated it into their own point of view. Glandism's advocates went beyond the established knowledge that gland dysfunction can cause certain diseases or personality changes. They developed an expanded explanation of the connection between emotion and glandular secretions into a "gland psychology" which suggested that one's entire personality depended on the balance of body chemicals.

In the crisis situation of Richard's arrest, the Loeb family sought the services of Clarence Darrow, one of America's foremost criminal lawyers. Darrow had won a reputation for defending unpopular causes. "Get them a life sentence instead of death," pleaded Albert Loeb. "That's all we ask. We'll pay anything, only for God's sake, don't let them hang."

Darrow had argued for many years "that killing by law is the wrong way to deal with the killer." He was able to use popular fascination with psychological matters as a tool to divert the public's insistence upon quick retribution—the death penalty, for murderers. Calling in such noted psychiatrists as Dr. William Alanson White, president of the American Psychiatric Association and superintendent of St. Elizabeth's Hospital in Washington, DC, and Dr. Bernard Glueck, supervisor of the psychiatric clinic at Sing Sing prison, as well as endocrinologists and other specialists, Darrow succeeded in having the trial focus on the condition of the murderer's minds. Since the crime had been devoid of ordinary human motive, the thrust of Darrow's defense was that Loeb and Leopold were driven by forces beyond their control and that in spite of their great intelligence they committed senseless acts of aggression and destruction.

At the time of the Franks case, Darrow was sixty-seven years old. Suffering from rheumatism and neuralgia, he was intrigued by the facts of the case, however, and not by the size of the fee he could command. Notwithstanding, many newspapers falsely claimed that Darrow was to receive $1 million. Unfounded rumors also reported that he had been called on "to put in the fix." In fact, he took the case because it gave him a chance to strike a blow against capital punishment. In his long career Darrow had helped 102 clients avoid the death penalty. "No client of mine," Darrow later wrote in his autobiography, "had ever been put to death and I felt that it would almost, if not quite, kill me if it should ever happen."

* * *

The murder trial of Richard Loeb and Nathan Leopold began on July 23, 1924. Heading the prosecution team was State Attorney Robert E.

Crowe, among the most powerful Republicans in Illinois. A Yale Law School graduate and an able prosecutor, he was no doubt aware that a successful trial would promote his political ambitions. Crowe was assisted by Joseph Savage, who would receive some of Darrow's harshest words. Joseph Sbarbaro, a onetime medical student, was primed to describe the grisly details of the crime. Thomas Marshall had prepared the prosecution's case on the legal precedents. Milton Smith completed the state's team.

In addition to Clarence Darrow, the defense team consisted of Benjamin and Walter Bachrach, two brothers related to the Loeb family. Benjamin, the elder of the two, had had extensive experience in criminal cases. The presiding judge was John Caverly, Chief Justice of the Criminal Court of Cook County, a kindly and humane judge with whom the death penalty weighed heavily. The trial was to be conducted without a jury. Illinois law permitted the defendants to waive a jury trial, and a jury, given the state of public opinion, was the last thing Darrow wanted.

Quickly Darrow made his first strategic move. He sent the younger Bachrach to Atlantic City, NJ, to attend the American Psychiatric Association's annual meeting. Darrow had a simple purpose: to hire a team of psychiatrists. Counsel for the defense went all the way to Atlantic City because the best known of the Chicago psychiatrists had already been hired by the state. Bachrach was able to persuade Drs. William Alanson White, Bernard Glueck, and William Healy, a pioneer in criminal psychiatry and juvenile delinquency, to examine the two boys; all three men were receptive to the new psychological theories of Sigmund Freud. The defense also employed other psychiatrists, including Dr. Carl M. Bowman of Boston and Dr. Harold S. Hulbert of Chicago, who were brought in to develop a comprehensive psychological history of the defendants. Probably never before in legal history had such attention been devoted to the inner motivation of men who had committed murder. The two physicians examined the boys on thirteen separate occasions in jail. In addition, they interviewed members of the Leopold and Loeb families and even talked to the young men's governesses.

On the other hand, the head doctors on the prosecution's team were traditionalists more concerned with the conscious part of the mind than with the subconscious or the unconscious. "In the vast majority of cases," wrote one of them, "the exhaustive and intricate corkscrewing methods of the Freudians are unnecessary. Sometimes they are harmful."

The day of arraignment had been a harbinger of events to come. Public outrage against the defendants brought the largest crowd ever to come to the Criminal Courts Building a full three hours before the scheduled 7 a.m. hearing time. For the prosecution the issue was clear: It would not really be necessary to produce a host of witnesses. The confessions would provide all that was needed. Nevertheless, the state chose to prove every incident of the crime with consummate thoroughness. By stressing all the grisly details from the conception of the crime to its execution, the prosecution intended to show that each step had been premeditated and carefully calculated in order to insure success and escape detection. Having done that, the prosecution would argue that the ruthlessness of the murderers eliminated any justification for clemency.

On July 21, virtually on the eve of the trial, in a move that was a complete surprise to the Court, Darrow had the defendants change their plea from "not guilty" to "guilty." Nathan Leopold recalled the meeting at which Darrow notified the defendants of the change.

> "Boys," said Mr. Darrow solemnly, "we're going to plead you guilty. I feel that I ought to apologize to you for springing this on you at the last moment, for not telling you earlier. . . . There is only one legal matter, one point of strategy involved. In Illinois there are only two crimes punishable by the death penalty. You were unfortunate to commit both. Mr. Crowe . . . indicted you both for murder and, separately, for kidnapping for ransom. We pleaded not guilty. All right. He'd try you on one charge, say the murder. If he got less than a hanging verdict, he'd turn right around and try you on the other charge. He'd have two chances for the price of one! There is only one way to deprive him of that second chance: to plead guilty to both charges before he realizes what is happening and has the opportunity to withdraw one of them. That's why the element of surprise is absolutely necessary. . . ."

Even though the guilt of the two boys was no longer an issue, State

Attorney Crowe called 102 witnesses. He was determined to impress the Court with the horror and cold-bloodedness of the crime, making use of all the physical evidence available and presenting whatever documentary evidence he had, including the confessions. He proved the facts of the case. The defense stipulated the facts and did not cross-examine. It did not introduce evidence as to the innocence of the defendants. It did not challenge the confessions. For the defense, the only issue was avoiding the death penalty. It soon was ready to call in its expert witnesses.

The first witness, Dr. White, precipitated a storm of argument. It seemed to the prosecution that Darrow was going to seek mitigation of punishment by reason of insanity. The law presumed the defendants sane. They knew right from wrong. They had pleaded guilty. The prosecution objected to any evidence regarding insanity on the grounds that such evidence was inconsistent with the defendants' guilty pleas and, furthermore, under Illinois law such a defense had to be passed on by a jury. Darrow responded:

> We make no claim that the defendants are legally insane. . . . We are not going to introduce evidence of insanity, but we do intend to show that our clients are mentally diseased. We intend to exhibit a condition of mind which does not fall within the legal definition of insanity . . . which has to do with the recognition of right and wrong and the power to choose between them. The mental condition we will exhibit does not constitute a defense but it certainly constitutes evidence which should be heard in mitigation on a plea of guilty, just as testimony regarding youth or the circumstances surrounding the crime may be heard. Youth itself is only relevant because it affects the condition of the mind.

Judge Caverly considered the point—and rejected the objection of the state. He also allowed the comprehensive report of Drs. Hulbert and Bowman to be put into the record, two volumes—one devoted to Loeb and the other to Leopold—that discussed reasons and motivations for the killing of Bobby Franks.

In addition to its psychiatrists, the defense also relied heavily on the testimony of neurologists and other medical specialists. The boys

underwent numerous physical examinations of their vascular and nervous systems and probably every organ, bone, gland, and tissue of the
body that could be explored by visual examination, microscopy, X-
ray, or test. What the physical examinations revealed in the case of
Nathan Leopold was that "there had been a premature involution of
the thymus gland and a premature calcification of the pineal gland in
the skull; that the pituitary gland was overactive; and that the adren-
al glands did not function normally." The significance of these findings, one doctor testified, was that "these abnormalities produced an
early sex development and had a direct relationship to Leopold's
extraordinary precocity and his mental condition."

Richard Loeb, the examinations showed, suffered from conditions
that were equally serious. "His blood pressure was subnormal, the
blood–carbon dioxide content was markedly low, his basal metabo-
lism was minus seventeen." The combined conditions "definitely indicated a disorder of the endocrine glands; he was subject to fainting
spells and suffered a nervous disorder which manifested itself in peri-
odic tremor and twitching of the facial tissues." There was no doubt
in the physician's mind that "such abnormalities" accounted for
Loeb's mental condition.

Nathan Leopold and Richard Loeb were examined by no fewer
than 18 psychiatrists, four on behalf of the state and fourteen on
behalf of the defense. Those working for the state maintained that the
defendants were entirely sane and, with one exception, had no mental
abnormality whatever. Dr. Archibald Church and Dr. Hugh Patrick,
who wrote the prosecution report, conceded that both boys had great
intelligence but had shown no feelings of remorse and were devoid of
human feeling. This was the only mental abnormality acknowledged
by the prosecution.

Darrow used this very point to emphasize that neither of the
defendants was responsible or blameworthy.

I know that they cannot feel what you feel and what I feel, that
they cannot feel the moral shocks which come to men that are
educated and who have not been deprived of an emotional system or emotional feelings. I know it, and every person who has
honestly studied this subject knows it as well. Is "Dickie"
Loeb to blame because out of the infinite forces that conspired

to form him, the infinite forces that were at work producing him ages before he was born, that because out of these infinite combinations he was born without it? If he is, then there should be a new definition for justice.

The prosecution's cross-examination of the defense experts was not fruitful. The state's attorneys did get them to admit, however, that since their findings relied completely on the testimony of Loeb and Leopold—on what the two had told them—they might have been taken in. Loeb was a notorious liar. But the defense experts did not believe they had been fooled. The crime had been carefully and shrewdly planned, but they saw no inconsistency between careful planning and the mental disorders of the defendants.

The prosecution's rebuttal witnesses were no more successful. None of them accepted the findings of "glandular abnormalities." These were, they argued, insignificant. They derided "the tendency of modern science . . . to place altogether too much emphasis on such distortions." Moreover, the state's attorneys had had little opportunity to examine, question, and study the defendants. Darrow's adroitness in changing the plea and in shifting the focus from insanity to mental disorder, together with the rapidity with which the trial followed the arraignment, had given the state little time.

Thomas Marshall and Joseph Savage began the closing arguments for the state. Marshall, scholarly and painstaking, confined himself to presenting dozens of precedents for the execution of convicted murderers between the ages of fourteen and eighteen. When he finished, Savage, mincing no words, restated the case for the prosecution. He did not bother with the medical testimony on which the defense relied. From the testimony of the state's doctors regarding the emotional reaction of the defendants, he stressed those statements that showed they "were caught in the mesh of their lies and contradictions. . . ." Their responses, he argued, were no different from those of ordinary criminals caught in the same situations.

"You have before you," Savage boomed out dramatically and with great passion, "one of the most cold-blooded, cruel, cowardly, dastardly murders that was ever tried in the history of any court. . . . No one would strike a dog the way these murderers had beat the life out of poor little Bobby Franks with a cold chisel. . . . If there was ever a case in history in which the most severe punishment was justified, this is the case." The state's case would end when Robert Crowe gave his summation following those of the defense.

Walter Bachrach led off the summing up for the defense. He was followed by Clarence Darrow, whose final plea began on August 22 before a greater attendance than had appeared in court on any previous day. "The tidal wave of men and women swept over and flattened a skirmish line of bailiffs at the main entrance and poured up the stairs and the elevators, sweeping all obstacles away," one newspaper related. The "setting could not have been bettered—the noisy, milling crowd giving point to [Darrow's] argument that the court was the only thing standing between the boys and the bloodthirsty mob." Before the trial, Darrow's reputation had been well established. After his summation for Loeb and Leopold, his name became a household word.

Darrow was to speak for almost twelve hours over three days. He addressed his opening remarks to the pressure that he and the Court had had to endure from the "almost unheard-of publicity" the case had received. The people of Chicago and throughout the country "have been regaled with stories of all sorts about it, until almost every person has formed an opinion," Darrow said. When the public is aroused it demands punishment, he argued. "It thinks of only one punishment, and that is death." That the boys were the sons of very rich fathers made the pressure even greater, for it had been argued by State Attorney Crowe that the wealth of those families was being used to evade justice.

Neatly reversing the state's argument, Darrow pointed out that "if we fail in this defense, it will not be for the lack of money. It will be on account of money. Money has been the most serious handicap we have met. There are times when poverty is fortunate. . . . Had this been the case of two boys of these defendants' ages, unconnected with families supposed to have great wealth, there is not a State's Attorney in Illinois who would not have consented at once to a plea of guilty and a punishment in the penitentiary for life. . . . We are here with the lives of two boys imperilled, with the public aroused. For what? Because, unfortunately, the parents have money. Nothing else." Despite this reference to a plea bargain, Darrow had never tried to reach an agreement with Crowe. He may have been unwilling to risk a rebuff—not because of his clients' wealth, however, but because of the atrocious nature of the crime.

For the remainder of the first day, Darrow argued for consideration for the defendants because of their ages. "[N]ever had there been a case in Chicago," he cried, "where a human being under the age of twenty-three has been sentenced to death." The judge, Darrow continued, needed to consider not only their youth but their pleas of guilty and the willingness of the defense to accept a life sentence. "We have said to the public and to this Court that neither the parents, nor the friends, nor the attorneys would want these boys released. . . . Those closest to them know perfectly well that they should not be released, and that they should be permanently isolated from society."

Darrow concluded his first day's summation by turning his attention to the closing remarks of Assistant State Attorney Joseph Savage: "[D]id you pick him for his name or his learning?—because my friend Mr. Savage, in as cruel a speech as he knew how to make, said to this Court that we pleaded guilty because we were afraid to do anything else." Darrow did not hesitate in admitting that it was so. "We did plead guilty before Your Honor because we were afraid to submit our case to a jury. . . . Your Honor, if these boys hang, you must do it. . . . Your Honor will never thank me for unloading this responsibility upon you, but you know that I would have been untrue to my clients if I had not concluded to take this chance before a court, instead of submitting it to a poisoned jury in the city of Chicago. . . . I hope, Your Honor, that I have not made a mistake."

Darrow began the second day of his summation by discounting the state's efforts to make the $10,000 ransom the motive for the crime. The defendants needed the money, it was alleged, to pay off gambling debts. Darrow handled the state's claim deftly. He showed that at the time of the crime Loeb had $3,000 in his checking account and three Liberty Bonds, one of which had matured but which he had not troubled to redeem. Leopold received an allowance of $125 each month, and if that was insufficient, "he got money whenever he wanted it." He had $3,000 set aside for a trip to Europe.

Darrow then spent the rest of the day discussing the boys' mental condition. He was intent on showing that the crime was motiveless and thus the product of diseased minds. Critics would wonder, is not the wish for thrill and adventure a motive? Or the desire to commit a perfect crime and prove oneself an *Ubermensch*?

> Who are these two boys? Leopold, with a wonderfully brilliant mind; Loeb with an unusual intelligence. . . . But it takes something besides brains to make a human being, who can adjust himself to life. . . . The emotions are the urge that makes us live; the urge that makes us work or play, or move among the pathways of life. . . . Whatever our action is, it comes from the emotions, and nobody is balanced without them. . . .
>
> [Nietzsche's] very doctrine is a species of insanity! Here is a man, a wise man—perhaps not wise, but brilliant—a thoughtful man who has made his impress upon the world. . . . His own doctrines made him a maniac. And here is a young man, in his adolescent age, harassed by everything that harasses children, who takes this philosophy and believes it literally. . . . Do you think this mad act could have been done by him in any other way? . . .

Darrow, a great civil libertarian, came close to advocating censorship to protect young people from the corruption of Nietzsche. "The publishers of the book—and Nietzsche's books are published by one of the biggest publishers in the world—are more to blame than he," Darrow said. Nathan Leopold was brilliant. If his powerful intelligence could be warped by such books, the danger to less able minds was so much greater.

Finally, Darrow came to the subject closest to his heart: ". . . the inhumanity, futility, and evil consequences of capital punishment." He had debated the question throughout the country and had appeared before state legislatures and legislative committees urging the repeal of death penalty statutes. Now he spoke passionately and at great length.

> The more men study, the more men doubt the effect of severe punishment on crime. And yet Mr. Savage tells the Court that if these boys are hanged, there will be no more murder. Mr. Savage is an optimist. He says that if the defendants are hanged, there will be no more boys like these.. . .
>
> What did they find in England? That as they got rid of these barbarous statutes, crimes decreased instead of in-creased; as

the criminal law was modified and humanized there was less crime instead of more. . . . [Y]ou can scarcely find a single book . . . that has not made the statement over and over again that as the penal code was made less terrible, crimes grew less frequent.

If these two boys die on the scaffold . . . what influence will it have upon the millions? . . . Would it help them, Your Honor, if you should do what the State begs you to do? What influence would it have upon the infinite numbers of children who will devour its details as Dickie Loeb has enjoyed reading detective stories? Would it make them better or would it make them worse? . . . What influence . . . will it have for the unborn babies still sleeping in their mothers' wombs? And what influence will it have on the psychology of the fathers and mothers yet to come? Do I need to argue to Your Honor, that cruelty only breeds cruelty?—that hatred only causes hatred; that if there is any way to soften the human heart . . . it is not through evil and hatred and cruelty; it is through charity and love and understanding.

As Darrow ended, many in the audience were crying. One newspaper reported: "There was scarcely any telling where his voice had finished and where silence had begun. Silence lasted a minute, two minutes. His own eyes, dimmed by years of serving the accused, the weak, were not the only ones that held tears." Following Darrow's tour de force, Benjamin Bachrach closed the case for the defense with a few brief words: ". . . frankly begging and pleading, Your Honor, to let these boys live and not bring upon the suffering that death upon the gallows to these boys must necessarily bring."

The state was not yet finished, however. Prosecutor Crowe presented the final message for almost two full days. He was "unrestrained, sarcastic, vituperative." The *Chicago Daily News* reported that Crowe

spoke in a frenzy. He shouted and stomped and waved his arms. . . . Into the faces of the two defendants he hurled epithet after epithet, his eyes blazing and his voice screaming anger. The boys were ruthless killers, he shouted. They were dangerous to society. Quoting statistics of Great Britain and the American federal courts, he contended that severe punishment did in fact deter others. Coming to the report of Hulbert and Bowman and their conclusions about the lack of emotion in the defendants, he said that, as for the murderers, if it was their fate to pay the full penalty, you will find these cowardly perverts will have to be carried to the gallows.

Crowe's choicest remarks were left for Darrow. The real defense in the case, he contended, was Darrow's philosophy of life, a dangerous softness. Ultimately, the crime itself could not cause as much harm as a decision that for some reason "you ought not to hang when the law says you should. . . ." Such a decision would strike "a greater blow . . . to our institutions" than a thousand murders.

Judge Caverly took the case under advisement until September 10. When he then arrived at the courthouse at the appointed hour, a reporter from the *Chicage Tribune* noted that he was visibly nervous, that he looked pale and weary. Illinois law required only that he pronounce sentence. He was not required to explain his decision, but he chose to do so.

The guilty plea, Judge Caverly began, did not create a special situation that favored the defendants. If it did, anyone accused of an especially heinous crime would always be able to avoid the death penalty by pleading guilty. Caverly then pointed out that the defendants were no more abnormal than many criminals, and even if they were, they should not be excused from the death penalty. He declared that he was satisfied "that neither in the act itself, nor in the lack of motive, nor in the antecedents of the defendants" could he find any mitigating circumstances.

Caverly seemed about to pronounce the death sentence, but then suddenly there came a shift. The easiest solution, the judge continued, the line of least resistance, would be to impose the death penalty. But he did not like to impose the ultimate penalty on teenagers, on persons not of full age. He read on: "This determination appears to be in accordance with the progress of the criminal law all over the world and with the dictates of enlightened humanity. More than that, it seems to be in accordance with the precedents hitherto observed in this state. The records of Illinois show only two cases of minors who were put to death by legal process—to which number the court does not feel inclined to make an addition."

He proceeded to pass formal sentence on each of the defendants: "For the crime of murder, confinement at the penitentiary for the term of their natural lives. For the crime of kidnapping for ransom, similar confinement for the term of ninety-nine years." And he recommended that Loeb and Leopold never be paroled. "[I]f this course is preserved in the punishment of these defendants it will both satisfy the ends of justice and safeguard the interests of society."

The trial was over and sentence pronounced.

Loeb and Leopold were sent to Joliet penitentiary, thirty miles from Chicago. Only rarely thereafter did newspapers carry stories about them. After a time, the two were transferred, first Leopold, then Loeb, to a new prison facility at Statesville. Leopold reorganized the prison library there. In 1932, both prisoners were instrumental in improving the educational facilities at the penitentiary and they opened a correspondence school.

On January 28, 1936, inmate James E. Day slashed Richard Loeb to death. Seven doctors were unable to halt his loss of blood. According to Day, he acted in self-defense. Loeb attacked him, he said, with a razor after he had spurned Loeb's homosexual advances. But Loeb, a physical coward, had almost sixty deep cuts. Day had none; and Loeb's throat had been slashed from the rear. Whatever the reason, Richard Loeb died that day in 1936.

On March 13, 1958, Nathan Leopold stepped through the gates of the penitentiary at Statesville, a free man. He had served 33 years in prison, where he had reclassified the prison library, spent three years gathering statistics on parole prediction, and established, with Loeb, the correspondence school. But most important was Leopold's participation in a project directed by University of Chicago scientists. In the summer of 1945 he was one of a number of convicts to volunteer for innoculation with malaria and receive treatment with experimental sera. Leopold devoted long hours to working with the program, and scientists were able to identify SN-13276, known as pentaquine, as an effective cure. Leopold was one of the first human beings ever cured of malaria by a safe and usable drug.

Despite Judge Caverly's strong recommendation, he had had no power to prevent parole. That power was discretionary with the parole board. In February 1947, the governor asked the state parole board to review the cases of the malaria project volunteers. Leopold had still not served the minimum term required for eligibility; even after he gained eligibility, action on his case was deferred. While he waited, Leopold wrote his autobiography. In 1958 the parole board reconsidered, and two weeks later Nathan Leopold again breathed free air. It is no exaggeration to say that Leopold had been rehabilitated. On the day after his release he flew to Puerto Rico to work as an X-ray technician in Castaner, a village about three hours from San Juan. He stayed there for two years and then went on to the University of Puerto Rico to earn a master's degree in social service. He remained to teach, and then turned to research in the social service program of the island's Department of Health. He also did additional research on leprosy at the university's School of Medicine. Leopold soon published another book, this time on his favorite subject, birds. In 1961 he married a former social worker from Baltimore and his wife was with him when he died on August 30, 1971, "a quiet, natural death."

The crime of Richard Loeb and Nathan Leopold had horrified the nation. The murder of Bobby Franks by the children of over-indulgent parents became a classic in the annals of criminal behavior. The trial of the two murderers excited widespread public interest at a time in the 1920s when the "new psychology" was much in the public eye. This psychology was one of two major emphases in the defense presented by the era's best-known attorney, Clarence Darrow. Unconscious impulses spur human behavior, Darrow believed, impulses that can lead to acts of unspeakable evil, and all of us are vulnerable. Judgment of evil must be tempered by understanding.

The appeal to understanding can be seen in the second major emphasis in the Darrow defense: its rejection of capital punishment. In the years since 1924, the proponents of capital punishment have continued to lose ground. The trial of Leopold and Loeb provided a major forum for debate on the issue and, as the *Chicago Sun-Times* editorialized on the day after his death, Leopold's was

> . . . a clear case of rehabilitation. And clearly it argues against the death penalty even for heinous crimes, for no one can reasonably say that Society would have benefited more by Leopold's execution. . . . Three lives were lost in that long-ago

moment of youthful madness. Justice was served. And the only saving feature was that one of the killers was able, in a small way, to prove that redemption is sometimes possible.

8

TEAPOT DOME

Above all else, announced presidential candidate Warren G. Harding in 1920—coining a term—the country needed a return to "normalcy." His election signified a new order, a pro-business administration of the kind that had been absent from the White House since the days of William McKinley. Only a handful of western Republicans and western and southern Democrats still struggled to keep alive the legacy of progressivism. The decade ahead would be free from troublesome muckrakers—those busybodies who had done so much in the past to annoy businessmen. The decade would be given over to business.

Harding's administration is best remembered for a series of scandals, the most famous and perhaps the most important of which came to light only after Harding had passed from the scene. "Teapot Dome," featuring an unholy mixture of oil and politics, became a symbol of the political chicanery of the 1920s. The story has its roots in the past, in the quarrels concerning the conservation of natural resources that developed prior to the First World War. The conservation movement, part of the larger progressive movement championed by Republican Party leaders like Theodore Roosevelt and Gifford Pinchot, sought to preserve what resources were left in the national domain. Up to that time, national policy had been one of simply distributing public land and other national riches as rapidly and as cheaply as possible to anyone willing to exploit them. It was commonly believed in the nineteenth century that rapid exploitation would benefit both private individuals and the nation. Conservation-

ists, on the other hand, saw a need for government safeguards to preserve irreplaceable resources—such as oil.

Although progressivism was in sharp decline during the 1920s, the
Teapot Dome controversy reveals that its spark was still alive. Since
1909 the key issue had been whether or under what terms government
should lease natural oil reserves to private interests. Businessmen
wanted to tap the reserves and they had the support of some influential politicians. Conservationists fought to keep them out. The clash
between the oil leasing policy of President Harding's Secretary of the
Interior, Albert B. Fall, and conservationist policy was a continuation
of a struggle that had begun a decade earlier.

By the 1920s, the world's industries and the world's navies had
begun to turn from coal to oil. Because geologists mistakenly predicted that there would be insufficient oil for the United States Navy's
needs unless its resources were safeguarded, President William
Howard Taft withdrew, by executive order, public oil-bearing lands in
Wyoming and California from possible private exploitation. In 1912
U.S. Naval Oil Reserves No. 1 and No. 2, totaling about a hundred
square miles, were created in Elk Hills and Buena Vista Hills,
California. In 1915 President Wilson, at the suggestion of Secretary of
the Navy Josephus Daniels, created Reserve No. 3, Teapot Dome, in
Natrona County, Wyoming—so named for an eroded sandstone rock
formation shaped something like a teapot that sat over an oil dome.

The election of Harding pleased some of the leading old progressives and conservationists who were concerned about the country's oil
supply. The Republican ticket was acceptable to Gifford Pinchot
because both Harding and vice presidential candidate Calvin Coolidge
had affirmed conservation in their acceptance speeches. Conservationist apprehensions were then aroused, however, by the
appointment of Albert Fall as Secretary of the Interior, for his ideas
were well known. As early as 1912, Fall announced that he looked
forward to the day when the Interior Department would be abolished.
The best place for public lands, he said, was in private hands. As a senator from New Mexico, Fall had fought against Wilson's conservation
program.

When Fall was appointed to the Harding cabinet, Pinchot wrote,
"On the record it would have been possible to pick a worse man for
Secretary of the Interior, but not altogether easy." Another conserva-

tionist regarded him as "absolutely unfit for such a post by every detail of his record in the Senate. He had been an exploiter and a friend of exploiters. He had always opposed the conservation movement." To Harry A. Slattery, onetime secretary to Pinchot and onetime secretary of the National Conservation Association, and esteemed in the 1920s as the spokesman of the conservation movement in America, it was not merely Fall's appointment that caused great concern. Slattery was dismayed by the appointments of Edwin Denby as Secretary of the Navy and of several assistant secretaries with suspect conservation records in other cabinet departments. No sooner had Fall taken up his post than Slattery reported hearing that he was moving out of the Department of the Interior "many trained and zealous public servants" and filling the department with personal friends, resulting in a "lowering tone . . . going down through the whole Department."

Wilson's Secretary of the Navy, Josephus Daniels, concerned about the naval oil reserves, had arranged to place them under his department's authority. A special amendment to the 1920 naval appropriations bill directed the Secretary of the Navy to acquire possession of the oil reserves and "to serve, develop, use and operate the same in his discretion, directly or by contract, lease or otherwise." With the change of administration, Edwin Denby took over as Navy Secretary. Not very long after, Harry Slattery heard a rumor that Secretary of the Interior Fall had convinced President Harding to transfer the naval oil reserves from the Navy Department to the Interior. For such a watchdog conservationist as Slattery this was ominous. His apprehension grew when he read in the April 16 release of the Navy Department's information sheet, "Navy News," that Denby had determined to lease drilling rights in one of the California naval oil reserves to private companies. The reason for doing so, Denby explained, was that the government was losing oil to private companies which had drilled wells on the rim of the reserve areas. The government would thus benefit by allowing the leasing. Admiral Robert S. Griffin, former chief of the Naval Bureau of Engineering, protested to Denby that if the Interior Department took over the administration of the reserves "we might just as well say good-bye to our oil."

Harding approved the transfer by executive order, seeing Fall's request as a simple matter of proper departmental jurisdiction. Once

Fall assumed control, drilling rights were granted to the Pan-American Petroleum and Transport Company, the corporate name of Edward L. Doheny, multimillionaire and longtime friend and mining partner of Albert Fall. Doheny won the lease with an offer to make royalty payments in the form of storage tanks, docks, wharves, and other facilities to be constructed at Pearl Harbor for the fueling of the Pacific Fleet. Doheny's bid was the only one received since, by the terms of the transfer to Interior, Fall was not required to hold competitive bidding for the leases. Doheny also won the right to preferential consideration in any future California leases.

Not long afterward, Fall leased the entire Teapot Dome reserve to Harry Sinclair, head of the Sinclair Consolidated Oil Company. To handle the lease and development of Teapot Dome, Sinclair created the Mammoth Oil Company. The lease was to run for 25 years and "so long thereafter as oil or gas is produced in paying quantities from said lands." The contract called for the United States government to receive royalties of 12.5 to 50 percent on the production of the wells with payment in "oil certificates." These could be exchanged for fuel oil and various petroleum products, could be redeemed in cash, or could be exchanged for oil storage tanks—all such exchanges to be with the Mammoth Oil Company.

Neither the public nor the Congress had been informed that administration of the oil reserves had been moved from Navy to Interior, but after Slattery heard rumors of the transfer and even before the leases had been contracted, he went into action. Expecting a sympathetic ear from the son of one of the nation's leading conservationists, he sought an audience with Theodore Roosevelt, Jr., Assistant Secretary of the Navy, to protest Fall's actions. Roosevelt assured him there was nothing to worry about. Fall, Roosevelt reminded him, had fought with the Rough Riders and was "a good friend." Unconvinced, Slattery next went to see Senator Robert La Follette of Wisconsin, who became committed to a Senate investigation when he learned that there had been no competitive bidding on the Sinclair lease. La Follette also discovered that there was no basis for the rationale given by the Interior Department that naval preparedness and national security were involved. Why, he asked, was there so much secrecy surrounding the Sinclair lease? Why had there been no public announcement? For what reasons had a lease been granted for the entire reserve when earlier leases had been justified only to stop drainage along the reserve's rim?

La Follette moved for an official inquiry into all the leases on the naval reserves. He considered that the leases, which had followed so quickly the transfer from the Navy Department to the Interior Department, "came as a great shock to the country." The American people had a right to know "who were the real organizers of the Mammoth Oil Company who were to be favored by the Government with a special privilege in value beyond the dreams of Croesus?" When he requested the Senate hearing, La Follette believed that evidence of corruption would be forthcoming. "I am going as far as I can in the charges I make. . . . I can't prove that there has been corruption but if we get this investigation I am confident it will be shown."

When the Senate approved the inquiry, responsibility for carrying it out went to the Committee on Public Lands; La Follette did not trust the Naval Affairs Committee, loaded as it was with administration supporters. The Committee on Public Lands counted among its members important Republican insurgents and strong conservationist Democrats.

La Follette badgered Democratic Senator Thomas Walsh of Montana into accepting leadership of the committee's investigation. Already burdened by more committee assignments than any other man in the Senate, Walsh accepted reluctantly only when he became convinced that most Republican members of the committee, led by Reed Smoot of Utah, were opposed to the probe. His acceptance would insure an honest and thorough inquiry. Although Walsh's law practice had been largely in the field of mineral rights, and he was hardly a conservationist, he lived by the conviction that honorable public service was the highest good. He was personally incorruptible and a relentless prosecutor.

La Follette turned over to Walsh all the evidence he had gathered—a small amount compared to the truckload of materials sent to the committee by Fall himself in June of 1922. Fall apparently did not expect the committee to be able to analyze so many items. He had first made a full report to the president regarding his handling of the naval oil reserve issue. Harding accepted Fall's account and endorsed it. The Interior Department materials came to the Senate committee with a letter of transmittal from President Harding that affirmed his faith in both Secretary Fall and Secretary Denby.

Senator Walsh had no reason to doubt the president's affirmation of faith at the time he began sifting through the avalanche of materials. But as he plodded through an intricate maze of details relating to oil drainage, leasing, and private contracts, several developments occurred which seemed oddly coincidental, if not suspicious. Senator La Follette's office was rifled not long after the resolution establishing the investigation had been passed. Walsh himself suspected that his phone was being tapped and his mail opened, and that his own past in Montana was being investigated. Something seemed to be going on behind the scenes.

Senator Walsh worked carefully and methodically for eighteen months to study the leases and the history of leasing. He was then ready to begin committee hearings and call for testimony, but by that time Warren Harding had died and Calvin Coolidge had assumed the presidency. The leases to Sinclair and Doheny had been completed and the lessees had taken over the properties, built storage facilities, drilled wells, and started extracting the oil. By then, too, Albert Fall had resigned as Secretary of the Interior, citing his desire to devote more time to his own business affairs in the Southwest. When he left the Interior Department, Fall's public character was still untainted, although conservationist Harry Slattery believed that "the threat of the coming . . . investigation . . . drove Fall out." But Fall had earlier had serious financial problems and he also fretted over his loss of influence in New Mexico politics, where he had long been a powerful figure. In 1923, Fall became associated with Sinclair's oil company and that same spring accompanied Sinclair to the Soviet Union, where they negotiated for oil concessions on the northern Pacific island of Sakhalin.

*   *   *

The hearings before the Senate Committee on Public Lands opened on October 25, 1923, with a report from two geologists. Teapot Dome, they testified, originally had held an estimated 135 million barrels of oil. Because of drainage into adjacent areas, it now held less than 70 percent of that amount. There were, they reported, only three ways to alleviate this problem: the government could employ structures known as offset wells to limit the drainage; the government could drill wells and extract and store the oil; or the government could lease its lands to private companies for drilling and operation in return for a royalty payable in oil to be stored for future use. In Utah Senator Smoot's mind, the testimony justified Fall's actions: "If the reports of the experts are accepted, the theory that the government made a mistake in leasing this . . . reserve has been exploded. The action of the government has been entirely justified." Senator Walsh remained skeptical.

On the following day, Albert Fall himself appeared to testify. Many years before, Fall had entered politics as a Democrat and held a number of local and territorial New Mexico posts. He earned a reputation as one of the ablest criminal lawyers in the Southwest, and President Cleveland appointed him to a territorial judgeship in 1893. When New Mexico became a state in 1912, Fall had already shifted his politics and was elected as a Republican to the United States Senate, where he served until his appointment as Secretary of the Interior in 1921. Fall's anti-conservationist view seems not to have played a part in Harding's decision to appoint him; further, he was popular with his Senate cronies and had no trouble with confirmation. After a time in the Department of the Interior, Harding told him, he would fill the first vacancy on the Supreme Court.

Fall, who had hurried back from Europe in August 1923, two months before, to attend Harding's funeral, testified for two days. Belligerently, he defended the leasing policy and the secret contracts, and he took full responsibility for the execution of the leases. The drainage was serious, he said, and had to be dealt with. He had not asked for competitive bids because he was certain he could get a better price through private negotiations. He insisted that secrecy had been necessary for reasons of national security. He had acted in what he regarded as a military matter under the supervision of the president of the United States and he did not propose to call international attention to the fact that contracts were being made for storage of enormous quantities of oil for use in a possible future crisis. When Walsh asked whether he had received any compensation from Doheny and Sinclair, Fall replied that he had never suggested compensation and had never received any. Since his resignation, however, he stated that he had made a business trip to Russia for Sinclair and Sinclair had paid his expenses—$10,000.

Secretary of the Navy Edwin Denby followed Fall. He gave a pathetic performance, for he had simply turned over complete control of the situation to Secretary Fall, and now revealed his ignorance of any specifics. Denby could not even remember whether he had signed any of the contracts or leases with the Sinclair and Doheny companies, and his general knowledge of governmental policy with respect to the conservation of oil for navy use was practically nil.

Denby was followed by a flood of witnesses—mining and geological experts—from the navy and other government departments to ascertain whether Reserves 1, 2, and 3 were in imminent danger from drainage by outside wells. Their testimony revealed a sharp and irreconcilable conflict over the evidence, and even conflict among the naval officers as to the merits of a reserve policy. Commanders Harry A. Stuart and John Shafroth, Jr., testified that they had protested vigorously to their superiors against the government's relinquishing control and leasing to private interests and, they added, they had been punished for their opposition. Each had been detached from his assignment. The first hearing of the Senate committee thus ended indecisively and, for the most part, unproductively.

The committee resumed its hearings on December 3, 1923, with testimony by Edward Doheny and Harry Sinclair. Doheny indicated that his company expected to get as many as 250 million barrels from its leases and to make as much as $100 million in profit. Both witnesses declared with righteous indignation that Fall had not received "any benefits or profits, directly or indirectly, in any manner whatsoever" from their connection with the leases. At this point, the investigation seemed to have reached a dead end and Walsh appeared to be swamped in trivia, finding nothing. Politicians and political commentators believed that he had gone as far as he could go.

Very shortly, however, prospects for the investigation improved. Evidence concerning Albert Fall's ranch began to arrive from New Mexico. The ranch had been started at the turn of the century, when the owner of a small piece of property had failed to meet his tax bill and Fall bought the judgment. He continued to add to his holdings, buying more land at every opportunity until the spread, known as Three Rivers, covered 700,000 acres scattered in tracts of various sizes over a distance of 55 miles. The ranch was next door to an Apache Indian reservation, between the villages of Tularosa and Oscuro, and miles away from the nearest railroad station. Fall spent thousands on irrigation ditches, installing tanks and pumping plants to carry water from the San Andreas Mountains. When he took office, Three Rivers Ranch was the largest in the state. Only one major piece in the land pattern was missing, that of the neighboring Harris ranch, which controlled the headwaters in the Three Rivers canyon. Fall's ranch raised range and thoroughbred cattle, hogs, horses, sheep, and hunting dogs; he stocked his streams with fish, and grew alfalfa, corn, wheat, fruit, and nuts. All this naturally required a tremendous monetary outlay. In 1921, when he became Secretary of the Interior, Fall owed $140,000 and had not paid taxes for eight years.

The testimony of a newspaperman from Albuquerque revealed that Fall, early in 1923, had begun making costly improvements on his New Mexico ranch, at about the same time he had leased Teapot Dome. Carl Magee, editor of the *New Mexico State Tribune* and one of Fall's oldest and bitterest enemies, swore before the Senate committee that in 1920, before his appointment to the Department of the Interior, Fall had complained that he was dead broke and deeply in debt. Then, in 1922, there was a noticeable and remarkable change in Fall's financial condition. He paid all his tax arrears. He made improvements on his ranch which Magee estimated at $40,000. He purchased a neighboring ranch for $91,500 and additional land for $33,000. Soon after, Fall built an irrigation reservoir and hydroelectric plant at a cost of $40,000. J.T. Johnson, Fall's manager at Three Rivers, revealed that Harry Sinclair had visited the ranch around Christmas in 1921, and soon afterward blooded stock—cattle, horses, and a racehorse from Sinclair's estate in Ramapo Hills, New Jersey— appeared in Fall's herds.

An unexpected witness then came forth. Archibald B. Roosevelt, younger brother of the Assistant Secretary of the Navy, volunteered to testify. He had just resigned as vice president of one of Sinclair's oil companies. Roosevelt revealed that G.D. Wahlberg, Sinclair's confidential secretary, had hinted that someone might have loaned Fall $68,000 in a payment made to Fall's ranch foreman. Other events also seemed suspicious to Roosevelt: a sudden and apparently unnecessary trip by Sinclair; the departure for Europe of several people who had been involved in the naval oil leases. Roosevelt believed the $68,000 payment was a bribe. He felt he had no alternative but to resign.

Wahlberg's testimony the next day was disingenuous. He had indeed spoken with Roosevelt and they had spoken about Fall's ranch. But Roosevelt, Wahlberg insisted, was mistaken about the $68,000. He had said no such thing. He had probably said that Sinclair had sent "six or eight cows" to Fall's ranch. "Six or eight cows" might easily have been taken for "sixty-eight thous." A simple misundersanding.

No matter how Wahlberg explained it, Walsh and the committee had gotten hold of something really solid, however. Fall, in 1922, had come into possession of a large sum of money. Explanation was needed and the committee requested that Fall make another appearance. This time, Fall claimed to be too ill to come in. He would submit a written statement regarding his finances that would end all further inquiry.

Fall's statement bristled with indignation. But it was not given under oath. He had gotten the money, the statement said, from Edward B. McLean, publisher of the *Washington Post*. Fall vigorously denied that he had received any money from either Doheny or Sinclair. Never "have I ever received from either of said parties one cent on account of any oil lease, or upon any other account whatsoever."

Not wasting any time, Walsh summoned McLean from his vacation in Florida to appear before the committee. As Fall had done, McLean pleaded ill health; because of "bad sinuses" and the poor health of his wife, McLean asked to be excused from an appearance. He did, however, corroborate Fall's explanation in a statement of his own which, like Fall's, was not sworn. Himself a sinus sufferer, Walsh did not believe McLean was suffering from "a dangerous malady," and he decided to go to Palm Beach personally, as a subcommittee of one, to take testimony. Walsh left on January 9, 1924, found that McLean was well enough to talk, put him through a relentless probing, and brought forth a new and remarkable story.

What McLean said dumbfounded Walsh. In November 1921, Fall had asked for a loan to buy the neighboring Harris ranch. McLean drew three checks totaling $100,000 from his personal bank accounts and gave them to Fall. Several days later, Fall returned the checks to McLean, explaining that he was getting the money from another source. When McLean appeared before the committee later the same month—this time under oath—he justified his earlier failure to explain that Fall had returned the money. Fall had asked him to tell Walsh and the committee that he, McLean, was the one who had made the loan. It had "nothing to do with Harry Sinclair or Teapot Dome," Fall had told him. "They are barking up the wrong tree." McLean had been willing to lie for his friend when not under oath, but would not do so at risk of indictment for perjury.

On the day after McLean's testimony, Senator Walsh received a startling letter from Albert Fall. It read, in part:

> I desire to advise you that I have carefully read the testimony which Mr. McLean gave today, and that I will endorse the accuracy of the same. I will also say that before giving his testimony, Mr. McLean had a conference with me, and I told him that so far as I was concerned, it was my wish that he answer freely; and in this connection I will say that it is absolutely true that I did not finally use the money from Mr. McLean which he expressed himself willing to give me because I found that I could readily obtain it from other sources. I wish it thoroughly understood that the source from which I obtained the money which I used was in no way connected with Mr. Sinclair or in any way involved in the concession regarding the Teapot Dome or any other oil concession.

What Fall hoped to gain by writing this letter is difficult to determine. He admitted to a lie—the money had not come from McLean. There was no way that Walsh would or could back off from pressing him to tell the committee where he did get the money. Fall had now put Doheny and Sinclair on the spot, and they would have to face the committee again and subject themselves to a renewed and more intense probing.

Doheny was the first to act. After consulting with one of his attorneys, Doheny returned to Washington to try to convince Fall to tell the whole story. If Fall did not see fit to talk, Doheny would appear before the committee as a voluntary witness. When Fall seemed incapable of making up his mind about what to do, Doheny appeared before the Senate committee for a second time and read a prepared statement.

I wish to state to the committee and the public the following facts. . . . I regret that when I was before your committee I did not tell you what I am now telling you. When asked by your chairman whether Mr. Fall had profited by the contract, directly or indirectly, I answered in the negative. That answer I now reiterate.

I wish to inform the committee that on the thirtieth of November, 1921, I loaned to Mr. Fall $100,000 upon his promissory note, to enable him to purchase a ranch in New Mexico. This sum was loaned to Mr. Fall by me personally. It was my money and did not belong in whole or in part to any oil company with which I am connected. In connection with this loan there was no discussion between Mr. Fall and myself as to any contract whatever. It was a personal loan to a life-long friend. We have been friends for thirty years. Mr. Fall had invested his savings for those years in his home ranch in New Mexico, which I understand was all that remained after the failure of mining investments in Mexico and nine years of pub-lic service in Washington, during which he could not properly attend to the management of his ranch. His troubles had been increased in 1918 by the death of his daughter and his son, who up to then, had taken his place in the management of his ranch. In our frequent talks it was clear that the acqui-sition of a neighborhood property controlling the water that flows through his home ranch was a hope of his amounting to an obsession. His failure to raise the necessary funds by real-izing on his extensive and once valuable mine holdings had made him feel that he was a victim of an untoward fate. In one of these talks, I indicated to him that I would be willing to make him the loan and this seemed to relieve his mind greatly. In the autumn of 1921 he told me that the purchase had become possible, that the time had arrived when he was ready to take advantage of my offer to make the loan.

Doheny said that his son, Edward Jr., delivered the $100,000 to Fall in a little black satchel. This was, noted Walsh, "a strange way of transmitting money," wasn't it? Doheny replied,

I don't know about that. I will say that I think I have remitted more than a million dollars in that way in the last five years. . . . In making the decision to lend this money to Mr. Fall I was greatly affected by his extreme pecuniary circumstances, which resulted, of course, from a long period, a lifetime of futile efforts. I realized that the amount of money I was loaning him was a bagatelle to me, that it was no more than $25 or $50, perhaps to the ordinary individual. Certainly a loan of $25 or $50 from one individual to another would not be considered at all extraordinary, and a loan of $100,000 from me to Mr. Fall is no more extraordinary.

Doheny was not able to produce the note that Fall was supposed to have given him. Six days later he located the note, but the signature had been torn from it. Doheny gave a strangely involved explanation. He had torn it from the note himself since, if he should die before Fall could repay the loan, Fall might be pressed for repayment to the Doheny estate at an inconvenient time. He gave the signature to *Mrs.* Doheny, so that the two together still held Fall's entire note. Edward Jr. knew of the arrangement, and in case his father and mother should both die, he could get a new note from Mr. Fall simply by asking.

A few hours after Doheny's testimony, Fall returned to Washington, where he was immediately served with a subpoena. For the next few days, while Fall remained incommunicado, Harry Sinclair testified that he, too, had provided Fall with a considerable sum of money, not in cash but in Liberty bonds.

The committee turned again to Doheny. Obviously nettled by what he regarded as an effort by the Democrats to make political capital out of the situation, Doheny dropped a few political bombshells. He announced defiantly that over the years he had contributed as heavily to the Democratic Party as to the Republican, and he named members of Wilson's cabinet who had been on his payroll at one time or another. He named Franklin K. Lane, former Secretary of the Interior; Thomas W. Gregory, former Attorney General; and, most important of all, William G. McAdoo, son-in-law of ex-President Wilson and Secretary of the Treasury in the Wilson cabinet. "I paid them for their influence," Doheny told the committee. In the case of

McAdoo, Doheny had retained him as counsel at an annual fee of $25,000 to assist in his Mexican interests. These were in no way connected with the oil leases, but McAdoo's reputation was tainted by the injection of his name into a proliferating scandal. At the moment, McAdoo was one of the top contenders for the 1924 Democratic presidential nomination and was strongly supported by Walsh. Even though his employment by Doheny was legitimate—he had had no contact with Doheny or any of his companies while he held office— the connection was harmful. He missed the nomination by a small margin.

While these disclosures were impacting on the country, Albert Fall finally reappeared before the committee on February 2. His appearance was very brief. Once ruddy and robust, the former Interior Secretary had lost over forty pounds. He seemed weak and gaunt, trembling as he came forward to testify in the jammed Senate caucus room. Even before the chairman had the opportunity to ask a single question, Fall read from a small piece of paper. "I decline to answer any questions on the ground that it may tend to incriminate me." Taking the arm of his lawyer, Fall left the room, never looking up at his former Senate colleagues.

Chairman Walsh recalled Harry Sinclair. A comparatively young man, Sinclair had become one of the world's richest oilmen, with extensive holdings in North and South America, Europe, Asia, and Africa. In this second appearance before the committee, Sinclair refused to answer any further questions. Unlike Fall, however, Sinclair did not base his refusal on the Fifth Amendment privilege against self-incrimination.

> I do not decline to answer any questions on the ground that my answers may tend to incriminate me, because there is nothing in any of the facts or circumstances of the lease on Teapot Dome which does or can incriminate me. . . . I shall reserve any evidence I may be able to give for [future consideration in a court of law] and shall respectfully decline to answer any question propounded by your committee.

When Sinclair then refused to answer a series of questions put to him by Senator Walsh, the chairman reported his refusals to the

Senate. He was declared in contempt of the Senate and indicted immediately. After giving the required bail, Sinclair was released pending
trial.

Fall's refusal to answer led, the same afternoon, to a Senate resolution authorizing the president to institute a suit for cancellation of
the leases because they had been executed "under circumstances indicating fraud and corruption" and were therefore contrary to law and
the settled policy of the United States government. The resolution also
called for appointment of a "special counsel," who would be independent of the Justice Department, for the purpose of prosecuting any
civil or criminal actions warranted by the facts. President Coolidge
selected two prominent attorneys: Owen J. Roberts and Atlee W.
Pomerene. Roberts' work in the Teapot Dome cases won him a national reputation and in 1930 President Hoover appointed him to the
Supreme Court, where he served until 1945. Pomerene had served as
a senator from Ohio from 1911 to 1923 and President Hoover
appointed him chairman of the Reconstruction Finance Corporation
in 1932. Roberts was a Republican and Pomerene a Democrat.
Coolidge's bipartisan appointments were intended to forestall any
possibility that he would be charged with playing politics.

The Democrats were looking hopefully to the 1924 presidential
election, seeking to gain some benefit from the shadow of scandal
enveloping the Harding administration. As the *Boston Transcript* put
it, the Democrats expected Teapot Dome to show "government by
favoritism and friendship which the American people have always
resented." Senator Thad Caraway of Arkansas, one of the Democratic
"jeer leaders," showed how the Democrats planned to go after the
Harding administration. Harding, he said, had been responsible for
issuing an illegal executive order, and Secretary Fall, more infamous
than Benedict Arnold—who wanted only to sell "a rocky fortress on
the Hudson River"—willingly gave away "the last gallon of American
naval reserves fuel." Senator Walsh joined in and called for Denby's
resignation. Denby resisted attacks for several weeks, but in February
1924 he left office, boldly protesting his innocence.

With Denby out of office, the heat now turned on Attorney
General Harry Daugherty. Burton K. Wheeler, Democratic freshman
senator from Walsh's state, Montana, led the attack. He told the committee that Daugherty was a friend of McLean, Sinclair, Doheny, and

other "grafters." More important, the Justice Department under his direction was not performing its duties satisfactorily. It had not turned up "one scintilla of evidence" for the Committee on Public Lands during its investigation. It had failed to prosecute large corporations as illegal monopolies despite the recommendation of the Federal Trade Commission. Daugherty had allowed illegal sales of liquor permits to bootleggers and he had connived in the illegal distribution of films of the Dempsey–Carpentier fight. No Republican came to his defense, and Daugherty was left to fend for himself; only one senator opposed a resolution authorizing an investigation of the attorney general. The nation later learned it was Daugherty who was responsible for having Walsh's office ransacked twice, tapping his phone, sending anonymous threatening letters, and for a crude attempt to frame Burton Wheeler with a woman in a hotel room.

President Coolidge was under severe pressure to force Daugherty's resignation, but he hesitated until late March. Having finally made up his mind, he had his secretary send Daugherty a blunt note. The president, the note read, "directs me to notify you that he expects your resignation at once." Daugherty complied.

The Democrats had been encouraged by the 1922 congressional elections and they were optimistic about their chances in the 1924 presidential election, believing that the perfidy of the Harding administration would carry them to victory. Unexpected developments diminished their confidence. Harding's sudden death created sympathy for the incompetent president who was also seen as a scapegoat for scandals, of which Teapot Dome was only one. Moreover, Coolidge's personal characteristics redounded to his advantage. He was the very image of puritanical rectitude, a "Mr. Clean," and this image helped to dissociate scandal and Republicanism. Even more important, the disclosures had shown that the corrupt interests had been, as they usually are, bipartisan in seeking political favors. Oilman Edward Doheny, despite his close friendship with Albert Fall, ranked high in Democratic circles. His relationship with McAdoo discomfited many Democrats, as did his business ties with other leading Democrats. Even Senator Walsh confessed to a long friendship with Doheny.

The election on which the Democrats had earlier placed such high hopes turned into a rout. Coolidge received almost 55 percent of the popular vote. John W. Davis, the compromise Democratic candidate, received less than 30 percent. Apparently, a scandal needs to be fed a constant diet of new revelations. When none appeared, the public's interest began to abate. In April and May of 1924, newspaper reports and magazine articles detailing developments about Teapot Dome diminished in number. Public attendance at the committee hearings shrank away until finally not a single spectator showed up. On May 24 the committee adjourned. To the relief of the party in power, the storm was abating.

Despite the Republican label on so many of the scandals of the 1920s, Coolidge was not personally associated with them. Although charges persisted, throughout the early months of Teapot Dome, that he had been present at cabinet meetings where the leases were discussed, Coolidge emerged unscathed. Voters cast their ballots for him because they liked him. They installed a puritan in the White House in an era of luxury and pleasure and seemed to feel that the self-indulgence of so much of the nation was balanced by the frugality and rectitude of its leader. They enjoyed the contrast between the flamboyance of the good life that so many Americans were pursuing and the serious and reserved demeanor of the chief executive. As for the two major parties, both seem to have suffered from Teapot Dome. If there was any victor at all, it was the conservation movement, which received a great deal of sympathetic attention in a decade of exploitation.

*　*　*

On February 19, 1924, special counsels Owen Roberts and Atlee Pomerene began their work. They soon uncarthed evidence that Doheny's loan of $100,000 had been made concurrently with Secretary Fall's decision to lease the Elk Hills reserve to him. A number of other secret leases had been granted in addition. They uncovered deposits of some $200,000 in Liberty bonds made by Harry Sinclair to either Fall's account or that of his son-in-law in several western and southwestern banks. All together, Fall had received over $400,000 in one way or another from Sinclair and Doheny.

The government prepared to institute legal procedures to set aside the contract and the leases to Doheny's Pan-American Petroleum and Transport Company. A civil trial, without a jury, opened on October 21, 1924, in the United States District Court for the Southern District of California. The government presented no freshly gathered evidence. It relied entirely on evidence and testimony initiated by Walsh's Senate investigating committee. Although neither Fall nor Denby took the stand, their statements made before the Senate committee were received in evidence.

After an extended hearing, the court ruled that Doheny's $100,000 loan to Fall constituted a bribe that had induced Fall to grant the leases. Both Fall and Doheny were guilty of fraud and conspiracy. President Harding had exceeded his authority in allowing transfer of the oil reserves. Denby, because his role on the transaction, was "passive," did not share the guilt of the other two. The court's decision meant that the contract between the United States and Pan-American Petroleum was nullified. Furthermore, Pan-American would have to pay for oil it had already extracted, although the government was to reimburse Doheny for work completed by his company on storage tanks at Pearl Harbor.

Both the U.S. Court of Appeals in southern California and the United States Supreme Court affirmed the judgment of the district court. In fact, the court of appeals also held that the company had been trespassing illegally on the land and was not entitled to recover any money it had already laid out. The Supreme Court simply, but unanimously, affirmed the lower court's rulings.

The United States District Court for Wyoming ruled against the government in a companion case. The court held the contracts to be of real value to the government. "It is not only possible, but very probable, that . . . if the contracts are fairly and honestly carried out, [they] will actually conserve oil which would otherwise have been lost."

Prompt action by the government led to reversal by the circuit court of appeals in St. Louis. The court ordered cancellation of the lease and subsequent contracts as fraudulent; it enjoined the oil company from further trespassing on the leased land; and it called for a complete accounting of oil taken from the reserve in consequence of the lease and contracts. The United States Supreme Court followed the precedent set in the earlier Pan-American Petroleum case. The government's victory was complete.

During these trials Owen Roberts and Atlee Pomerene had made some new and sensational revelations. Doheny, as the Senate investigating committee had discovered, was able to bribe Fall with cash that he had on hand. Sinclair's approach to bribery was different. He decided to raise the necessary money, and a great deal more, through a short-lived Canadian corporation. On November 17, 1921, a group of wealthy oilmen met in a New York City hotel room, a group that in combination held an interest in a major portion of the western hemisphere's oil. They created a dummy corporation, the Continental Trading Company. The newly formed company then contracted to buy crude oil from one of the conspirators, Colonel A.E. Humphreys of the Humphreys Mexia and Humphreys Texas Oil Companies. The oil was to be immediately resold at a higher price to the companies of Harry Sinclair and James E. O'Neill, two other members of the group. Continental Trading collected more than $3 million in profits and, acting through its Toronto attorney, purchased $3 million worth of United States Liberty bonds. This turned out to be a serious blunder. The bonds and their coupons were numbered and could be traced after they had been cashed.

No sooner had the company exhausted its capital by purchase of the bonds than the Senate investigators got hot on its trail. Abruptly, with no assets, save for Liberty bonds with traceable numbers, the company liquidated itself and destroyed all its records. Of the illicit profits, Sinclair took about $750,000. The remainder was divided among three of the other members of the cabal. Only Humphreys got no cut, because he had made a substantial profit from the sale of the oil. None of the four who shared the booty told the directors of their respective companies what they had done. Sinclair took his share, but Roberts and Pomerene were able to prove that $25,000 in Liberty bonds had made their way to Fall's bank account in El Paso, Texas, and $230,000 of the bonds had been turned over by someone to Fall's son-in-law, M.T. Everhart. Government counsel were able to prove from the serial numbers that, without a doubt, they had been included among the bonds purchased for the Continental Trading Company. The government's efforts to get to all of the parties involved in this operation, however, were unsuccessful.

The civil cases had ended with a complete victory for the United States. The criminal prosecutions that followed were a different matter. Legal maneuverings and trials went on for almost six years, beginning on June 4, 1924. There were four indictments: one in which Fall and Sinclair were to be tried jointly for conspiracy to defraud the United States; one against Fall, charging him with bribery; one against Fall and Doheny, charging them with conspiracy to defraud; and one against Doheny and his son, charging them with bribery. Of the four cases, the first—*United States* v. *Edward L. Doheny and Albert B. Fall*—was the most protracted and the most significant.

Owen Roberts, along with Atlee Pomerene, carried the burden of the government's case. On the other side, Edward Doheny relied on the legal skill of Frank J. Hogan of Washington and on the legal staff of the Pan-American Petroleum and Transport Company. One of the great criminal lawyers in the country, Hogan's fee was rumored to be $1 million. A small, slight man, a dandy in dress with an ingratiating manner and a quick temper, Hogan had a face, said a reporter for the *Brooklyn Eagle*, that reminded him of the newspaper's name. Albert Fall's chief lawyer was Wilton J. Lambert. He lacked Hogan's prestige, but he was knowledgeable, feisty, and not a little cocky.

For its part, the government, seeking to prove conspiracy to defraud, called more than fifty witnesses in the Doheny–Fall trial. Some were summoned to provide background for the record; others appeared to give their opinions regarding the threat to the reserves by drainage. A number of oil company representatives reported that Fall had ignored their requests to be considered bidders and that he had adopted a policy of preferential treatment. Edward McLean described Fall's request for the $100,000 loan, his failure to cash the checks because he had made other arrangements for a loan and, finally, Fall's asking him, "Would you mind saying that you loaned me that money in cash? Some of my political enemies are deviling me, and it would be a great assistance to me." McLean did not hesitate in answering, "Certainly." The government then showed from whom and in what manner Fall had received the money. Little that was new was disclosed by the government's witnesses.

Defense witnesses testified as to the seriousness of the drainage problem and the legality of the contracts. Admiral John K. Robison, retired chief of the Naval Bureau of Engineering, defended preferential treatment of bidders as being in the national interest. He said that secrecy was in accordance with the Navy's declared policy. The appearance of ex-Secretary of the Navy Denby brought a crowd of spectators. His performance before the Senate committee had been an embarrassment and the crowd probably expected the same confusion. This time, however, his testimony was prompt and forthright: He explained how and why the transfer to Interior had taken place and that he had never met Doheny until after the contract with Pan-American Petroleum had been signed. Under Roberts' rigorous cross-examination he held up well. How was it, Roberts asked, that "at the time of the Senate hearings, when the events were recent," Denby had been unable to recall any of the details connected with the Elk Hills contract? Denby explained that he had then recently been released from the hospital following a painful illness and had not had the time to refresh his memory with documents and correspondence that related to the matter.

The testimony of Mrs. Doheny cleared up the mystery of the signature missing from Fall's note for the $100,000 loan. When asked what had become of the signature, Mrs. Doheny said that she had put it in her bank safe deposit box. Although she had forgotten where it was when the Senate hearings were taking place, she now produced the torn piece of the note and identified Fall's signature on it. The piece fit perfectly into the main portion of the note, which the government had previously offered in evidence. Neither Roberts nor Pomerene chose to cross-examine Mrs. Doheny, nor did they do so after Edward L. Doheny, Jr., testified as to the role he had played in delivering the $100,000 in cash to Fall at his Wardman Park Hotel apartment.

The senior Doheny testified in his own defense. After indicating that he and Fall had been friends since the 1880s, when they had both been prospectors, Doheny explained that he had been approached by Admiral Robison about the need to construct huge fuel oil facilities at Pearl Harbor. The admiral had warned of the warlike intentions of Japan and the possible destruction of the fleet and even an invasion of the United States' West Coast. The fuel oil facilities would help the United States to ward off the Japanese. Robison, he continued, appealed to him to do his patriotic duty and bid on the project. In this way his company had gotten involved. Doheny concluded his testimony by denying absolutely that he had bribed Fall. The $100,000 loan to Fall, five months before the contract was given to Pan-American, was completely unrelated to any contract. The thought of influencing

Fall had never even entered his mind.

Roberts was shrewd in his cross-examination. He questioned Doheny mildly, not using the slashing tones he had brought to bear on Denby and others. Doheny was now an old and feeble man, and he had responded in an apparently forthright manner on direct examination. Aggressive cross-examination might offend the jury. Nevertheless, Roberts questioned every detail, especially the "unusual" and "extraordinary" features of the loan transaction. Why had Doheny obtained the money from his son's and not his own bank accounts? Why was the loan made in cash and not with a cashier's check? Why did he send his own son to deliver it?

There was nothing sinister in these events, Doheny countered. At the time of the request he had only about $10,000 in his account. His son had more than $100,000 on deposit with a New York banking firm. Fall, he reminded the prosecutor, had indicated that he wanted the money in cash. The younger Doheny delivered the money personally, not as a way of covering up the transaction, but because he had been in on it from the start. All in all, Doheny made an excellent witness for himself.

Albert Fall chose not to take the stand.

Roberts began the summation for the government. He characterized Doheny as a man "conscious of and obsessed with the power of money" and Fall as "an impecunious cabinet officer" looking for the main chance and not overly scrupulous about how he got it. The action of President Harding, in office less than three months, to allow transfer of the oil reserves was made with little regard for the public good. It was, however, against the loan and everything about it that Roberts directed his sharpest comments. Why didn't Fall want a check? Why did he want cash? Because otherwise the bank would have a record of it. And why was this enormous amount of cash delivered by Doheny's son? Because "no other human being was to know of the transaction but his own blood," and if Doheny sent his son to the Wardman Park Hotel, where Fall lived and where the Dohenys had also lived and were well known, no one would notice the visit.

> Now, Gentlemen, why was all that secrecy observed? Do I need to argue to you? Do I need to labor that kind of question with you intelligent men? It was concealed because if it had

become public these men knew they would be ruined.

Why did [Doheny] take a demand note? If Fall could not pay for a long while, if it were a reasonable and proper transaction, why not a year note or a two year note? But no, Gentlemen, with a demand note he held the whip over Fall.

And what can be said about the part the defendant Fall played? Albert B. Fall knew that the $100,000 business was a dirty business. He knew it would bring down the condemnation of every right thinking American citizen who heard of or knew of it. When the Senate committee heard of Secretary Fall's sudden wealth, of his going down and buying this ranch for $100,000, what happened? Fall knew that some explanation was required. . . . What did he do? He sent for Edward B. McLean, a man who was his friend.

There could be no reasonable doubt, concluded Roberts, that "Doheny realized and knew that that $100,000 would tend to make Mr. Fall favorable with regard to Government contracts," or that Doheny, by his own words, expected to make a million dollars in profits from the contract.

Frank Hogan began his summation for the defense by deriding the notion that the $100,000 constituted a bribe. It was simply a loan to an old friend. There was nothing, he insisted, that was sinister in the tearing of the promissory note. If there had been, Mrs. Doheny would have been cross-examined. Since the nation's president had approved what Denby and Fall had done with the oil reserves, the chief executive had been "a silent witness" for the defense. The documentary evidence and the testimony of witnesses made clear, Hogan went on, that the idea of fuel storage at Pearl Harbor and the concomitant exchange of crude oil for fuel oil had originated with the Navy.

Mark Thompson, another of Fall's attorneys, continued the summation. Fall's purchase of the Harris ranch, he said, was a clean and open transaction. It was a direct purchase, openly made. It would surely not have been, if the money had been tainted. Fall certainly lied, he admitted, to the Senate committee as to the source of the money. He did so because the "so-called committee" had no legal or moral right to exact from these men anything respecting their personal transactions.

Pomerene's summation closed the government case. He attacked the notion of "war peril." Admiral Robison, the source of the idea, had informed no one else of it and had not reported it to Congress. Only Doheny was given the information. "Who believes that stuff?" Pomerene asked. The actions of the U.S. government belied the whole notion. "[O]n March 24, 1924, a month before the execution of the Pearl Harbor contract, the United States Senate ratified a treaty among this country, Japan, France, and Great Britain for the drastic limitation of naval armaments."

On December 15, 1926, Judge Hoehling made a brief charge to the jury on the presumed innocence of the defendants, on the necessity to prove beyond a reasonable doubt, and on the law of evidence applicable to the charge of criminal conspiracy. After nineteen hours of deliberation, the jury found both defendants "not guilty." Fall, suffering from tuberculosis, went back to New Mexico to await his second trial. Doheny, returning to California, was given a hero's welcome and a huge testimonial dinner. While California applauded, editorial comment around the nation indicated widespread disagreement with the verdict. A discouraged public correctly assumed that the case against Fall and Sinclair would probably end the same way.

* * *

Ten months later, the Fall–Sinclair case opened on October 17, 1927, in federal court in the District of Columbia, with Roberts and Pomerene and their staffs again arguing the case for the government. Thompson and Lambert, who had appeared successfully for Fall in the earlier case, also represented him in the second trial. Martin W. Littleton and members of the legal staffs of various Sinclair companies appeared for Sinclair.

The government's case turned on the evidence that had been presented in the civil case three years earlier, when the Teapot Dome contract and leases had been set aside. The government had almost finished presenting its case when the trial was halted by a sensational development. Pomerene suddenly moved for a mistrial, charging a "close, intimate, objectionable and improper surveillance" of the jury by operatives of the well-known W.J. Burns International Detective Agency. The agency had been hired by Sinclair, and such surveillance,

Pomerene argued, amounted to obstruction of justice and contempt of court. Judge Frederick L. Siddons allowed the motion and discharged the jury.

Sinclair did not deny that he had engaged the detectives to "shadow" the jury. According to his sworn statement, he did so because he had reason to believe that "the veniremen had been under surveillance by representatives of the Department of Justice" and he feared that "efforts would be made unlawfully to influence them." The Burns agency plan called for eleven of the jurors to be followed from early morning until late at night. Even though there was no evidence that any of the operatives had approached a juror, or that any juror actually knew that he or she was being followed, the trial judge found Sinclair and the Burns operatives in contempt. Surely this was obstruction of justice, in the opinion of the judge. Sinclair was sentenced to six months' imprisonment. This was to be added to three months already meted out for contempt of the Senate.

A new trial for conspiracy got underway early in April 1928. Too ill to travel to Washington, Fall did not stand trial. He was able only to give a deposition from his bed in New Mexico as a witness for Sinclair. The government's case against Sinclair was stronger than the one made against Doheny, but again the jury returned a verdict of not guilty. The acquittal, many believed, was astonishing, given the weight of evidence. Roberts and Pomerene reacted as though struck by lightning. To Senator Gerald P. Nye of North Dakota the verdict confirmed the obvious truth that "You can't convict a million dollars in the United States." Senator George W. Norris of Nebraska agreed, and upped the ante. It is, he said, "very difficult, if not impossible, to convict one hundred million dollars."

But the Teapot Dome trials had not yet ended. Despite his illness, the government opened its case against Albert Fall on the charge of accepting a bribe from Doheny. This was quite different from conspiracy to defraud. To defend themselves against that charge Fall, Doheny, and Sinclair had been able to present plausible evidence that drainage threatened the naval oil reserves, that the new government policy adopted by President Harding was desirable, and that the leases that had been granted were fair, reasonable, and beneficial to the United States. In a case of bribery it is immaterial whether the bribery is beneficial or harmful in its effects. Fall stood accused of taking a bribe while he was an officer of the United States, acting in his official capacity. If the accused should "ask, accept, or receive any money . . . with intent to have his decision or action upon any question . . . which may at any time be pending before him in his official capacity . . . influenced thereby . . ." the crime of taking a bribe had been committed.

Arguments followed the pattern of the Doheny–Fall conspiracy trial. Frank Hogan, Fall's attorney, argued as he had done earlier the innocent nature of the loan and its complete independence of any negotiations that had taken place between Fall and Doheny. He concluded with a plea for fair treatment for "a faithful servant," now a "tragic figure . . . shattered and broken . . . an old man tottering on the brink of the grave." No one in the courtroom was unmoved. Nevertheless, on October 25, 1929, the jury found Fall guilty; it recommended mercy. In consideration of his physical condition he was sentenced to prison for only a year, although the penalty could have been as high as three, and fined $100,000. The court of appeals of the District of Columbia upheld the sentence and the Supreme Court refused to review.

There was another matter still unresolved. While Fall's appeal was pending, an indictment against Doheny for bribing Fall was called to trial. Considering evidence that was practically the same as that offered in the Fall case, the jury found Doheny not guilty. On its face, the verdict seems to substantiate the statements of Senators Nye and Norris following Sinclair's trial. Doheny was a millionaire, the businessman-as-hero image of the 1920s. But the trial took place five months after the stock market crash of 1929, when that image was a trifle tarnished. Moreover, under the United States criminal code the offer of a bribe is a separate and distinct offense from the acceptance of one. In each case, the defendant's intention and perception of what is happening determines or establishes guilt. Doheny took the stand at his trial, denied his guilt, and made a good witness for himself. Fall, in his own trial, did not testify at all. Doheny went free. Fall, because he was suffering from tuberculosis, was allowed to serve his sentence in the agreeable climate of New Mexico.

And so ended the story of Teapot Dome. Its legal character was established by the verdicts in the Fall and Doheny cases. The scandal, while one of many, was certainly the most famous of the Harding era.

How significant was it in its larger implications? For one thing, it was a victory for the American people. It resulted in restoring to the United States Navy the fabulously rich oil reserves of Teapot Dome and Elk Hills. In addition, the pipelines, storage facilities, and refined oil available to the Navy on the West Coast and at Pearl Harbor after December 7, 1941, were at least partly a result of the Fall oil leases.

Teapot Dome also offers some insight into the political culture of the decade. Revelation of a scandal, it turned out, was an ineffective political weapon. The momentum of prosperity was simply too strong—when combined with Coolidge rectitude—for mere corruption to unseat the governing party. At the same time, despite the public's affection for Republican "normalcy" and its almost fawning adulation of businessmen, there persisted a strong strain of progressivism, a strain that would reemerge and flourish in the coming decade of the Great Depression.

9

THE CASE OF SAMUEL INSULL

America's eight years from 1921 to 1928 were exceptionally prosperous. Gross national product rose from $88.9 billion in 1920 to $104.4 billion in 1929, and annual per capita income zoomed to $716 from $522. Car registrations almost tripled between 1920 and 1929, and the effect of the motor car on the national economy was remarkable. Steel and all the industries that produced what was needed for automobiles and motor travel were galvanized as total output increased by more than 60 percent during the decade. The rush to urbanization meant new streets, highways, and bridges for cars and trucks as well as buildings of all kinds -- industrial, commercial, and residential. More and more private homes were built, along with public housing, hospitals, hotels, schools, post offices, stores and office buildings, factories and skyscrapers. The estimated value of construction rose from over $12 billion in 1919 to a peak of more than $17 billion in 1928.

Between 1922 and 1930 the capacity of electricity generating stations almost doubled, from 22 million kilowatt hours to 43 million. Technological improvements made possible a reduction in the cost of generating electric power and made practical the transmission of power over long distances. This led in turn to interconnections among power companies that served local regions; pools of power-generating capacity were created so that peak loads could be carried by drawing on the surplus capacity available in a large area, rather than by adding to the capacity of individual generating stations. In this way large economies could be realized. The most effective means of organizing a great regional electric power system was through centralized control, and the device that made such control possible was the holding company. The best known, and perhaps the most notorious, of the holding company magnates in the electric power industry was Samuel Insull.

Insull's supremacy coincided with the great bull market—the rip-roaring, ever-expanding stock market that flourished as the greatest illusion of the period. At the same time a strain of progressivism persisted in America, and it was an element in the struggle between private and public interests over control of electric power. On one side stood men like Gifford Pinchot and Harold Ickes and Donald Richberg, who advocated greater public control, and Senator George Norris of Nebraska, who would have had all power publicly owned. On the other stood Samuel Insull, the advocate of ever-widening private monopoly.

In an era that had a full array of heroes and heroines, Samuel Insull was to the business world what Babe Ruth became to the world of sports. As ordinary folk flocked to the ballpark or listened to the radio to applaud the doings of the mighty Ruth, so did they lavish their admiration on Insull, affirming it by investing in all his stocks. Even the titans of Wall Street viewed him with awe. Insull became a super-titan, symbolizing his age as Rockefeller and Carnegie had symbolized theirs. He was rich, he was powerful, he was self-made—a man ruthless in dealing with his adversaries but kind and generous in dealing with the weak. He reflected America's image of itself.

Insull was born in England in 1859 to a lower-middle-class family. When he was not yet 20 years old, he answered an advertisement by an American banker, Colonel George E. Gouraud, who was seeking a secretary; Gouraud was also the European representative for Thomas A. Edison. On becoming secretary, Insull showed himself to be ambitious, bright, and hardworking. He kept a sharp eye open and carefully studied all the documents concerning Edison that came within his reach. By the fall of 1879 Insull had a thorough knowledge of the office, and when Edison's chief engineer, Edward Johnson, came to London on some business for his employer, he found that young Insull knew more about Edison's business affairs in Europe than perhaps the inventor himself did. Less than two years later, when Edison's secretary suddenly resigned, Johnson cabled Insull to come to the United

States to take up the role of private secretary to Edison himself.

Over the next twelve years, Insull became indispensable to his employer. He was Edison's unofficial manager and most trusted advisor, with exceptionally varied responsibilities. He worked out cost analyses involving conversion from gaslight to electric light; he was involved in developing the financing of Edison enterprises; he bought his employer's clothes; and he held Edison's power of attorney, signed his checks, and answered his mail. And Insull kept learning. He thoroughly understood the electric power business.

In the late fall of 1886 Edison decided to move his Electric Tube Company and his Edison Machine Works to Schenectady, New York. He instructed Insull to go there to "run the whole thing," not specifying what Insull was to do but simply commanding him to "Do it big, Sammy. Make it either a big success or a big failure." Within six years, the Edison labor force grew from 200 to 6,000. With the backing of railroad magnate Henry Villard and the financial underwriting of J.P. Morgan, Edison General Electric Company was organized in January 1889. Three years later, the new $50-million corporation became known simply as the General Electric Company. Insull accepted the second vice presidency— but only temporarily. He had no intention of staying with the company, for his analysis of the power industry had convinced him that production of electricity—the creation of the power itself rather than the manufacture of equipment—was where the greatest opportunity would lie.

In 1892 Samuel Insull left Schenectady for Chicago, where he assumed the presidency of the Chicago Edison Company. Although he took a large salary cut, from $36,000 to $12,000, he would be running the business himself, and he would be able to develop the enterprise as befitted his talents. It was a propitious time for a man in Insull's position, for it was just a year before the great Columbian Exposition, Chicago's world fair of 1893. The exposition provided a great opportunity for an electric company to stage an enormous and dazzling display of electric lighting and equipment. Insull seized the chance, expanded his production and his operations, and made the Chicago fair blaze with light. When the exposition closed a year later, Insull's power company was the world's largest. For forty years longer, Insull remained the leader in electric power.

In those early years in Chicago, prior to the First World War, Insull created a massive organization of three great operating companies. Commonwealth Edison, a $400-million company, was built from a merger of Commonwealth Electric with Chicago Edison. In 1907, Commonwealth Edison obtained an exclusive franchise to provide electricity for the city of Chicago for forty years. Four years later, Insull acquired control of the Public Service Company of Northern Illinois to supply gas and electricity to over 300 rural communities, some of them with fewer than 400 inhabitants. Within fifteen years, the Public Service Company became a $200-million enterprise. The third company, Peoples Gas Light & Coke, a $175-million utility providing gas for Chicago, became Insull's in 1913. Peoples Gas had sought out Insull in a frantic search for a capable manager to steer the company through a turbulent period. Insull regarded this acquisition as the most spectacular achievement of his career, because he took over a moribund company, "within about two jumps of the sheriff," as he later said, and turned it into a flourishing utility.

Until 1912 Insull concerned himself primarily with the production and distribution of gas and electric power. In that year he created the Middle West Utilities Company, a holding company, and started on the road that made him the ruler of an empire that had, at its peak in 1926, combined assets of $3 billion. By the mid-1920s almost four-fifths of the country's electricity was either in the hands of various holding companies or was passing into their control. Insull was in the forefront of the movement toward the super-holding company, with its pyramids of holding companies, sub-holding companies, and subsidiaries heaped one upon another in a fashion known nowhere else in the world. Insull's empire was so complicated that no one, including the boss himself, could completely disentangle it.

Some explanation of the elements is needed for clarity. A holding company controls a majority or at least a portion of another company's stock large enough to control its policies. Ownership of more than 50 percent of voting stock needs no explanation, but when the stock of a corporation is widely dispersed, as it is with corporate giants, effective control can be obtained through ownership of a smaller percentage of its stock; owning the right kind of stock makes control even easier. In the 1920s, corporations issued principally two kinds of stock: common and preferred. Preferred stock received a fixed dividend but no voting rights. Holders of common stock received dividends irregularly, as profits permitted. By using a technique known as pyramiding and applying proceeds from sales of bonds, preferred stock, and non-voting common stock, the first holding company might pyramid atop another, its subsidiary company. Some holding companies were six layers deep, but there was no reason in theory why pyramiding might not go on indefinitely. By the end of the decade, just ten holding companies controlled about three-fourths of the electric power generated in the United States.

In Insull's case, the structure was marvelously complex. Consider the example of the Georgia Power Company, one of the companies at the bottom of Insull's empire. Georgia Power was an operating company producing electric power and light. It sold power to manufacturing and commercial enterprises and to homes, it employed workers and managers, and it paid wages and salaries. Its assets consisted of the land it occupied, the buildings in which it was housed, the machinery and equipment it used, and the goodwill it had gained. Control of just over half the voting stock of the Georgia Power Company would give control of the entirety of Georgia Power's assets to any person or group able to obtain the stock. The Seaboard Public Service Corporation gained such control. Seaboard had or did nothing else— no machinery, no equipment, no production. It consisted of one small office from which its directors bought and sold securities. And just as Seaboard could control all of Georgia Power by controlling half its stock, so the National Public Service Corporation could control both Seaboard and Georgia Power by controlling enough of Seaboard's voting stock. National Public Service was also no more than an office, and was in turn controlled by the National Electric Power Company. National Electric Power controlled National Public Service, which controlled Seaboard, which controlled the only operating company, Georgia Electric Power.

The ceiling had not yet been reached, however, for still higher up was the Middle West Utilities Company, a giant corporation in respect to its assets, but no more than an office in physical terms. It held stock in many other holding and operating companies, including the National Electric Power Company. Through National Electric Power, Middle West Utilities controlled Georgia Power and all the layers above it. But there was still more. Higher yet was Insull Utilities Investments, Inc., formed in 1928 to control not only the Middle West

Utilities Company but three other corporate giants: the Public Service Company of Northern Illinois, the Commonwealth Edison Company, and Peoples Gas Light & Coke Company. And beyond even Middle West was the Corporation Securities Company of Chicago, whose holdings were so intricate as to defy intelligent unraveling. It was truly a super-holding company.

Corporation Securities—known as the "Corp"—and Insull Utilities controlled each other. The former owned almost 20 percent of the latter's stock, while the latter held nearly 30 percent of the Corp's stock, a controlling interest. The nature of the holding company pyramid focused the power of an investment the way a magnifying glass focuses the power of the sun. A single dollar invested in the voting stock of Insull Utility Investments, Inc., controlled $1,750 of the assets of the Georgia Power Company. What an opportunity for a skillful promoter!

Samuel Insull is best remembered as the genius of the holding company. And it was what wrecked him. Few remember that he pioneered turbine generators, high transmission lines, and other technological innovations in the generation and distribution of power. He was one of the great builders of America, bringing electricity to areas that other utilities companies ignored. In Chicago for many years he was "Aladdin reincarnated." Chicagoans remember him, too, for his passion for grand opera and as the builder of the still flourishing Chicago Civic Opera, now known as the Lyric Opera.

Insull began his drive for empire by organizing the Middle West Utilities Company as a holding company to control scattered properties in southern Indiana and elsewhere outside Chicago. Within a short time, the Insull organization boasted five major components. There were the three operating companies: Commonwealth Edison, Public Service of Northern Illinois, and Peoples Gas; and there were the holding companies: Middle West Utilities and Midland Utilities, an Indiana company whose subsidiaries represented, in 1926, an investment of $300 million and provided gas and electricity for 700 communities. Also by 1926, Middle West Utilities had several hundred subsidiaries grouped into a half dozen major divisions and representing an investment of $1.2 billion that provided gas and electricity for 5,000 communities in 32 states. There were, in addition, Chicago's miles of elevated railways and three interurban lines connecting Chicago with its suburbs. The North American Light and Power Company helped organize Insull's properties around St. Louis that were held by the similarly named North American Company. And there were the investment trusts, a relatively new type of organization in the 1920s. Small investors who did not have enough money to buy a variety of stocks and who knew little of the value of securities could buy a few shares in an investment trust which, with its accumulated funds, could perform these functions. Individual investors wanting to be secure against loss could diversify their holdings and rely on experienced knowledge concerning what to buy and sell and when to do so. The Insull investment trusts managed four hundred millions of dollars in 1930.

At its peak the Insull empire had about 600,000 stockholders and about half a million bondholders. It served more than 400,000 customers and produced about one-eighth of the gas and electricity consumed in the United States. Its companies appeared to be well run and soundly financed, models of good business in the 1920s. Or so it seemed. Only later was it learned that profit statements were sometimes padded. At the time, it seemed to hundreds of thousands that Insull had found the key to wealth. Operating from his headquarters in Chicago, Insull dominated that city in a way that Henry Ford never dominated Detroit. In addition to economic strength, his political dominance was achieved by the judicious placing of bribes and a general encouragement of corruption. In 1926 he passed out $238,000 to the political campaigns of both parties. Many observers believed that he actually ran Chicago while Mayor "Big Bill" Thompson made a circus out of city hall and threatened to "bust King George in the snoot." What's more, Insull's power extended even beyond Chicago, pushing into no less than thirteen other states.

In both public and private affairs Insull was driven by a ruthless determination to have his own way, to have it without challenge, and to have it all the time. Marquis Childs, writing in the *New Republic* in 1932, characterized Insull as believing in his own infallibility, "armored with self-righteousness"; and, "holding the mass in contempt as he did, it was not difficult for him to confuse the welfare of Samuel Insull with the welfare of the public."

Insull was responsible for shaping the National Electric Light Association—the public relations, or propaganda, agency of the industry. The N.E.L.A. distributed its literature to newspapers, libraries, schools, and other organizations. It lobbied unceasingly. It secretly employed college students to inject the proper ideas into the classroom and it paid off professors, lecturers, and editors to carry the message as well. Textbooks that revealed truthfully how utilities were financed were opposed until others took their place. The right message, in the view of the N.E.L.A., was a relentless attack on the idea of public ownership of utilities. It was un-American, it was unthinkable, it was bolshevik. The propaganda campaign was intense and it was powerful.

* * *

In the depths of the Great Depression, in April 1932, the Insull empire of pyramided holding companies went into receivership—up to that time the greatest single crash in American business history. Almost a billion dollars was lost by thousands of individuals. For them, it made no difference that Insull's own fortune went under at the same time. Nor did it matter that he was forced from the directorships of more than sixty corporations. Insull had seen his personal fortune increase from about $5 million in 1926 to $150 million in 1929. By mid-1932 it had fallen below zero. He was "too broke," as one banker put it, "to be bankrupt." But Samuel Insull's personal troubles were no solace to those who had invested in his gigantic financing efforts. His very name became anathema. The Midas of the '20s came to be pilloried as a charlatan, a crook, an embezzler. He became the scapegoat for the business collapse.

Insull's troubles did not end with the collapse of his empire. Indicted for mail fraud in 1933, he fled to Greece. He tried to stave off extradition but was returned to the United States for trial. Even acquittal on all charges, however, did not lead to his vindication. Why did the great Insull empire disintegrate, not during the great crash of 1929, or even shortly afterward, but in 1932? Was it the result of a scheme to defraud that went awry? Was it caused by honest mistakes and bad judgment? Perhaps it was due to something inherent in the structure of the empire itself, or in the decay of the American business environment. How is it that Samuel Insull gained acquittal—a man who was once a business hero but, by 1934, a business villain, one of the now reviled high rollers of the previous decade?

In 1926 Insull was sixty-seven years old. The empire he had built was an impressive success and he could look back with a great deal of satisfaction on a full and worthwhile life. With a personal fortune of $5 million—not nearly as much as both friends and enemies thought— he seriously considered retirement. He also considered an offer he had received from British Prime Minister Stanley Baldwin, who urged him to return to his native land and lead a commission planning to build a unified, government-operated power system for England. Insull was tempted by both possibilities but he chose to remain in Chicago, to consolidate and strengthen his interests and to prepare his son as imperial heir apparent. His motive was ambition, but only in part. He was also prepared to meet danger in the form of outsiders seeking to muscle in, to wrest control of his holding company world.

Insull turned increasingly to pyramiding as the way to protect his interests. In late 1928 he created Insull Utilities Investments, Inc., an investment holding company. IUI was controlled through direct ownership by Insull, his brother, his son, and a circle of friends. They exchanged all their own utilities holdings for IUI stock and through IUI sought to buy enough voting stock in the utilities companies to assure that Insull and his group would retain control. Managerial authority was not enough for Insull, however. In exchange for their utilities stocks, which had a market value of almost $10 million, they received 764,000 shares of the common and 40,000 shares of the IUI preferred stock. A price of $12 per common share was set, with the usual list of insiders taken care of in the initial flotation.

On the first day, IUI stock opened at $25 and closed at $30. The great bull market was under way. Two IUI constituents, Commonwealth Edison and Middle West Utilities, rose from $202 and $169 to $450 and $529, respectively. On August 2, 1929, IUI reached an all-time high of $147 per share. During that month, Insull securities were appreciating at a phenomenal rate and reached a total of more than a half billion dollars. Insull's own (paper) fortune rose to almost $150 million.

Insull had taken advantage of leverage in the expansion of his operations, primarily to manipulate securities earnings and to extend control. Leverage acted on per-share earnings of a company's common stock when a portion of the earnings was paid out in bond interest and preferred stock dividends before the common stock was entitled to its share. Leverage may be advantageous for common stock when earnings are good, but may work in the opposite direction when earnings decline. For example: Company X has issued 1,000,000 shares of common stock. No bonds or preferred stock are outstanding. Earnings decline from $1,000,000 to $800,000 or from $1 to 80 cents a share—a drop of 20 percent. Company Y also has 1,000,000 shares of common stock, but must pay $500,000 in bond interest each year. It, too, has earnings of $1,000,000. Bond interest consumes $500,000, and another $500,000—50 cents a share—is available for the common stock. If earnings decline to $800,000, only $300,000—30 cents a share—is available for the common stock. Common stock owners suffer a drop of 40 percent.

On the other hand, suppose earnings of Company X increase from $1,000,000 to $1,500,000. Earnings per share then rise from $1 to $1.50, an increase of 50 percent. But if the year's earnings of the company which pays $500,000 in bond interest increase that much, earnings per share of common stock jump from 50 cents to $1 a share, a leap of 100 percent. There is no leverage when a company issues only common stock because all earnings are available for the common shareholders. As earnings rise, so does the price of a company's securities, making borrowing still easier. By the late 1920s some large companies were observing that the more they borrowed, the higher were their earnings. And the higher their earnings, the more they could borrow. But if the market went down . . .

The mania of the 1920s stock market had an additional impact on Insull Utilities Investments, Inc. By overinflating the prices that IUI had to pay for Insull stocks, its initial purpose was negated. Further action was needed. And because an outside group might still seize control of IUI, Insull believed that formation of a second investment trust was necessary. Corporation Securities Company of Chicago was organized on the same basis as IUI, but with a significant innovation: Corporation Securities ("the Corp") and Insull Utilities Investments partially owned each other. By means of a complex system of cross-financing, the Corp owned 19.7 percent of IUI while IUI owned 28.8 percent of the Corp, and control of the latter was assured by means of a voting trust. These two related investment trusts became the twin thrones of the Insull empire.

Taking advantage of the bull market, Insull refinanced the Middle West Utilities Company. Because its common stock had become so high priced, Insull's long-held hope for widely based popular ownership was in danger of disappearing. Middle West also had outstanding debts bearing high interest. In a major refinancing operation the debt was retired, the stock was split ten-for-one, and dividends were to be paid in common stock rather than cash. It was, said Insull, the largest undertaking in his experience, completed in September 1929, just weeks before the Great Crash. Astute as he was, Insull could not foresee that the crash presaged a general business collapse; in this respect he was not different from most business and government leaders. Nor did Insull recognize that holding company pyramiding and investment trusts were a source of weakness rather than strength. As long as the earnings of the company at the bottom of the pyramid remained secure, all would be well. But the companies up above issued bonds or, sometimes, preferred stock based on the earnings of the companies below. Once those earnings stopped, the bonds would go into default or the preferred stock would take over. The pyramid would collapse; trust would erode; confidence would evaporate; investment would be suspended; regular procedures of the operating companies would be interrupted; and spending by the ordinary public would diminish.

After the 1929 crash, Insull needed to maintain confidence and the flow of investment. He took three steps which ultimately weakened his position. First, he proceeded with expansion plans as if nothing had happened. It was necessary, he believed, to expand the electric companies, especially the Middle West system, to keep generating and distributing capacity ahead of maximum demand.

In order to finance this expansion, Insull relied on the sale of bonds and debentures, promissory notes backed solely by general credit and reputation and not secured by a mortgage or lien on any specific property. Stocks, following the crash, had become very unstable. Insull increased bonded indebtedness by more than $200 million. This meant, of course, that reverse leverage would operate if stock prices started to tumble. Third, Insull purchased 160,000 shares of Commonwealth Edison, Peoples Gas, and Public Service of Northern Illinois, hoping finally to make himself invulnerable to outside raiders and particularly Wall Street bankers. He paid $56 million, and to finance the purchase was forced to turn to those very Wall Street bankers when Continental Bank of Chicago, on which he had relied, was not able to fulfill its promise of financing the entire purchase. The indebtedness of IUI and Corporation Securities was increased by $48 million, of which $20 million was owed to New York bankers. For collateral these took $30 million in the voting stock of the three major operating companies.

By 1930, expansion of facilities, new stock acquisitions, and major refinancings such as that of Middle West Utilities had created a tremendous floating debt. A major portion of the income of the "twin thrones" of the Insull empire was in stocks of the Insull utilities. Any reduction in the market value of the stock would immediately reduce the earning power of IUI and the Corp and would prevent the retirement or permanent financing of their floating debts. They would have to depend on bank credit. Moreover, each drop in the market would force the investment trusts to put up more collateral against their bank loans. Conceivably, there might be no end until the bankers held the entire portfolios of IUI and Corp. The banks would control the whole Insull empire.

By the late fall of 1931, the economic picture had become worse. The depression was spreading worldwide. Economic conditions in all the European countries were bad and still deteriorating. The drain on the Bank of England for gold had forced Britain off the gold standard—an event that shook the business world. The New York Stock Exchange reacted with hysteria. During the week of September 9 the stocks of IUI, the Corp, Commonwealth Edison, and Middle West Utilities dropped by $150 million and were still heading downward.

As the market went down, IUI and the Corp put up increasing amounts of security as collateral against loans. Insull borrowed $5 million from the National City Bank of New York on his personal signature, putting up as collateral securities loaned to him from the portfolio of the Corporation Securities Company. In December he borrowed another million from General Electric on his personal note and secured it with $1.25 million in securities from the same source. Although Insull had left General Electric many years before, his relations with G.E. had remained cordial; the loan was simply a business transaction. By the middle of December the portfolios of IUI and the Corp were in the hands of bank creditors. Worse, there was no rise in the market at the beginning of 1932 as there had been in 1930 and again in 1931. Conditions actually worsened and stocks plunged again. Such blue chip stocks as General Electric, General Motors, and United States Steel sold for one-tenth of their 1929 highs.

By all signs it was a hopeless struggle, but Insull continued until April 1932. He exhausted his resources and his credit. First, Middle West Utilities and then the Corp and IUI went into receivership. He avoided personal bankruptcy by turning over to his creditors everything he had—a remnant of securities, a million-dollar life insurance policy against which he had borrowed half, and his 4,000-acre estate in Libertyville, Illinois. (The estate had a bathtub which had been coated in gold leaf at a cost of $30,000. Visitors on its terrace could observe swans and goldfish swimming in its clear lagoons.) Mrs. Insull signed away her dower rights as well, rights that would have given her, should she become a widow, some claim on her deceased husband's property. Insull resigned from the chairmanships which he held in some sixty-odd companies.

Samuel Insull was dethroned. He was broke and badly defeated, exhausted and anxious to get away from hounding and prying by newspapermen. As he had done on other occasions when he needed to get away, Insull decided on Europe. Going by way of Canada would be slower and more relaxing than sailing from New York. He and Mrs. Insull took a train bearing them north to Quebec, and on June 14, 1932, the Insulls sailed out through the Gulf of St. Lawrence, bound for Cherbourg and the wished-for European relaxation.

With no plans except rest, the Insulls spent an idle and untroubled summer, living quietly and inexpensively in Paris. Then Insull learned of investigations being planned and of efforts to indict him. At his son's suggestion the couple left Paris for northern Italy, then decided on Greece when Insull learned that the United States did not have an extradition treaty with that country. Insull believed that a trial in which he was the defendant would be a political trial, and that he would be crucified.

Insull had by then already become a political issue in Chicago politics. John Swanson, Republican state's attorney for Illinois' Cook County and a longtime friend of Insull's, faced overwhelming odds in his bid for reelection. In an unguarded conversation Swanson revealed that he was about to launch an investigation into scandals alleged in the collapse of the Insull empire. "You know," said Swanson, "Sam Insull is the greatest man I've ever known. No one has ever done more for Chicago, and I know he has never taken a dishonest dollar. But Insull knows politics, and he will understand. But I've got to do it."

Swanson was responding to the widespread hue and cry against Insull that was growing out of the public's search for someone to blame for shattering the dream of an economic utopia.

Insull's empire was one of the big three of the nation's utility groups. United Corporations was a super-holding company controlled by the House of Morgan. There was also Electric Bond and Share, led by Sidney Z. Mitchell. Both were larger than Insull's financial and industrial structure, but their capitalization was simpler and less responsive to sudden fluctuations; and both were intimately connected with Wall Street. Of the three, only the Insull empire collapsed, and Insull became the focus of public outrage.

The Swanson investigation began looking for violations of the Illinois "Blue Sky" law regulating the issue and sale of stocks, bonds, and other securities within the state. Such laws in a number of states were supposed to protect investors from fraudulent schemes that had no more foundation than "the blue sky" above. Investigation revealed that there were secret lists of insiders who had been allowed to buy into the initial offering of Insull Utlities Investments Company common stock at $12 a share. The insiders got 250,000 shares, and when IUI stock climbed to $30 at the end of the first day of trading, Insull's friends, both social and political, might have cleared millions within a few hours.

When this information became public, the U.S. attorney for the northern district of Illinois, Dwight H. Green, announced on September 25, 1932, that the federal Department of Justice had commenced a full-scale investigation into the affairs of the Insull companies. Less than ten days later, a Cook County grand jury returned indictments against Insull and his brother, Martin, charging them with embezzlement from Middle West Utilities.

There was more to come. On February 27, 1933, a federal grand jury returned an indictment against Insull and 16 others, charging them with violation of a section of the U.S. criminal code forbidding use of the mails to further a scheme to defraud. A second indictment came down several months later, charging Insull, his son, and Harold Stuart, a banker, with having illegally transferred property of Corporation Securities. They were alleged to have intended to defeat the purpose of the National Bankruptcy Act in giving preference to selected creditors by distributing assets in anticipation of bankruptcy.

The government's most immediate problem was how to get hold of Insull and bring him to trial under the various indictments. In November of 1932 the United States Senate finally ratified an extradition treaty with Greece. Under its terms no person could be extradited without presentation of substantial evidence at a hearing before a panel of five Greek judges, evidence that might prove the accused guilty of a crime under Greek law. Embezzlement, for which Insull had been indicted in Illinois, was a crime under Greek law, but the judges were not convinced by the evidence. Moreover, the federal crime of using the mails to defraud was not a crime at all under Greek law. The judges refused to order extradition.

Frustrated in its legal efforts, the Roosevelt administration resorted to extralegal means to force the Greek government to surrender. The State Department approached the membership of the Greek-American Merchants Association, many of whom regularly sent money to relatives in Greece. The merchants were told that unless they put pressure on the Greek government and forced it to yield Insull to the federal authorities, the United States would prohibit further exportation of money to Greece. Despite pressure from the association, the Greek government still refused to extradite, but it did order Insull to leave the country. He was given until midnight on March 15, 1933.

Borrowing money from friends, Insull chartered a Greek vessel and prepared to depart Greece. For two weeks he sailed the Mediterranean. Meanwhile, he mulled over an invitation to come to Romania to head its Ministry of Electric Power. Believing that he might travel to another country or even seek refuge somewhere in the Middle East, the United States would not permit Insull to get away and was quite willing to use its muscle to send a signal to every nation. At the urgent request of the State Department, Congress authorized the arrest of Insull in any country in which the United States had extraterritorial rights established by treaty.

When the S.S. *Maiotis* put into Istanbul for provisions, the United States ambassador, acting on orders from the State Department, requested the Turkish government to arrest Insull without delay, even though no extradition treaty or provision of international law covered such action. After a hearing that lasted less than twenty minutes, Insull's extradition was ordered. Neither the United States nor the Turkish officials were deterred by the absence of a legal extradition process. Insull was simply handed over. He was placed on a vessel of the American Export Line, S.S. *Exilona*, bound for New York. In a brief press statement made after his arrival, Insull foreshadowed his defense against the acculmulated charges:

> I have erred but my greatest error was in underestimating the effects of the financial panic on American securities and particularly on the companies I was trying to build. I worked with all of my energies to save those companies. I made mistakes, but they were honest mistakes. They were errors of judgement and not dishonest manipulations.

The case of the *United States* v. *Samuel Insull et al.,* charging use of the mails to defraud, was set for October 1933. This was the first charge brought to trial and the case on which the prosecution would concentrate its energies. The government would argue that formation of the Corporation Securities Company had been a scheme concocted in 1929 and carried out in 1930 and 1931 to use the mails and other means to unload worthless securities on an unsuspecting public. The schemers, it would be alleged, carried out a nationwide sales campaign through the medium of circulars, letters, telegrams, booklets, bulletins, and oral representations.

Appearing for the defendants was Floyd W. Thompson, a former justice of the supreme court of Illinois. He had served on the bench for nine years, after which he retired to private practice, specializing in trial work and acquiring a reputation as a brilliant trial lawyer. The prosecution team was led by Dwight H. Green, U.S. attorney for the northern district of Illinois. Not satisfied with the dozens of skilled investigators sent from Washington, Green called for additional help and the Justice Department sent Forrest Harness, its ablest special prosecutor in the Midwest. A week before the trial, Green prevailed upon U.S. Attorney General Homer Cummings for still more help, and Cummings sent the brilliant and flashy special prosecutor Leslie E. Salter from the Department of Justice. The government was prepared to open with one of the most thoroughly prepared cases it had ever put together.

The twelve people selected for the jury, along with two alternates, came from Cook County and the remainder of Illinois' northern fed-

eral district. Of the 14, five were salesmen, two were retail grain dealers, one was a grocer, one a farmer, one the proprietor of a garage, one
a bookbinder, one a heating engineer, and two were unemployed.
None was familiar with the world of high finance and monetary
manipulation.

In an opening that went on for two hours, U.S. Attorney Green
quoted at length from the 50-page, 25-count indictment. All the
counts were similar, differing only in regard to the specific matter that
was mailed to the specific recipients. The core of the government's case
was that Middle West Utilities had been in considerable trouble before
1929 and had been able to remain solvent only through dishonest
bookkeeping. In 1929 the defendants had schemed to solve their problems by running up the price of the stock and refinancing the operation. They bought $13 million of the stock on the open market by
August and then organized the Corporation Securities Company to
take the Middle West stock off their hands. They put together a high-
pressure, nationwide selling campaign, made false statements about
the Corp, and juggled its books to create the illusion that it was a prosperous company. Within a year following its organization, the Corp,
needing money, offered and sold a variety of commercial paper: common and preferred stock, notes, and interest-bearing bonds in the
amount of $110 million. The sale of this paper, the government con-
tended, was accomplished by fraudulent representations and concealment of the true condition of Corporation Securities Company.

Shunning Wall Street brokerage houses, Insull had turned to
Halsey, Stuart & Company, a Chicago-based securities firm. Halsey,
Stuart placed the sale of Corp stock in the hands of its salesmen, who
immediately contacted potential customers to whom offering literature had already been sent, somewhat in the manner of a military
assault following an initial barrage. The offering literature, contended
the government, was filled with cleverly worded misrepresentations.
Government witnesses pointed to the statement that the company
would start its business with $80 million in assets—$30 million in
cash and $50 million in marketable investments. At that time, they
alleged, the Corp had nothing but some 304,000 shares of IUI that
had cost $7 million, and a liability of $3.5 million on outstanding
bank loans.

The government claimed that oral representations made by

Halsey, Stuart salesmen—and the company, not the salesmen, were responsible— were palpably false; an investment in such offerings was not "good," "safe," "sound," and "interest-paying." How could it be, when the Corp's outstanding preferred stock required an annual cash outlay of more than $2 million to pay its dividend, and its portfolio was heavily loaded and was to be even more heavily loaded with Middle West Utilities common stock paying no cash dividends? Corporation Securities Company's common stock was not a worthwhile investment and the officers knew it. As a result of their deception, Insull and his circle were enriched, and thousands of investors lost their life savings.

The government built its case in three steps, beginning by introducing all corporate records that could bear on the allegations charged in the indictment. Account books, minutes of meetings, correspondence among company officials and with outside persons, stock transfer records, accounting data, annual reports, promotional literature— all were carefully identified and entered into the record. Next, the government brought in its witnesses, honest citizens who testified that they had been hoodwinked into purchasing in good faith securities that soon turned sour. They read unsolicited mail advertising, they listened to high-pressure salesmen, they invested, and they lost their money. Finally, the government provided a painstaking, step-by-step analysis of the company's records, using the testimony of former employees, independent accountants, government agents, experts, and college professors—all to show how Insull's companies "cooked" their books.

Oh, how tedious was the testimony, hour after hour! There were 83 witnesses, the greater part of them employees of the several companies or of receivers, called to testify, verify, and authenticate the records. They then interpreted those records to demonstrate the guilt of the defendants. The government's case proceeded quietly and methodically. There were no major quarrels over the validity of the documents. Rather, accuracy and reliablity were at issue—and, most especially, interpretation. Among the members of the jury a different idea was developing than that intended by the prosecution. One juror was a former sheriff with many years of experience in law enforcement. He revealed this new idea when he commented that in all his years of dealing with lawbreakers, he had "never heard of a band of crooks who thought up a scheme, wrote it all down, and kept an honest and careful record of everything they did." The crooks in his experience "kept no records, falsified them, or destroyed them."

Interpreting the records was central to the case. The conflict between the government and the defendants was over the construction to be placed on those records. The circular or prospectus sent out to prospective investors was a critical piece of evidence. Government witnesses pointed to the claim that the Corp would begin operating with assets of $80 million in cash and securities. This was shameful fraud and deception, according to the prosecution, because all the Corp had when it commenced business was the 304,000 shares of IUI stock purchased for $7 million and the bank obligations that cut its total assets in half. The company made up the difference, the government said, by juggling its books. The $80 million figure was created by such devices as writing up the 304,000 IUI shares at $30.4 million and adding 557,000 shares of Middle West Utilities stock at $23 million. All that existed at the time was a contract to purchase the shares at $13 million. Moreover, said the government, investors were not told that most of the Middle West shares would pay only a stock dividend, not cash.

Van Lamont, a former controller for Halsey, Stuart, brought out some facts that seriously weakened the government's allegations: Under prevailing commercial practice, when corporations made new stock offerings the circulars sent to prospective investors represented the financial status of the offering company as of the date that proposed financing was to be completed. The Corp, after the shares had been sold, did in fact have even more than $30 million in cash and $50 million in securities figured at market value. As if to underline the weakness in the prosecution's case, the officers of Halsey, Stuart & Company had been so certain that the Corp was a sound investment that all of them had made large and voluntary purchases of the securities at their offered price, held them to the end, and took big losses.

Skillful cross-examination also discredited the testimony of several additional government witnesses. One had given damaging testimony as to the stock manipulations of the Insulls, focusing on fictitious transactions. Under cross-examination he was forced to admit that his only training as an accountant had come through a correspondence course, that his only experience had been with a small firm in Wyoming, and that he had never seen a brokerage account before the government's investigations began. Worst of all, he had been told what to find. A second witness had testified as to the proper treatment of stock dividends in the company's accounting procedure. Under cross-examination he admitted that there was disagreement as to proper accounting methods and that reputable accountants were divided on the matter.

As had been the case with testimony on the offering circular and the proper treatment of stock dividends, the testimony of government witnesses on the treatment of "organization expense" was shaken by adept cross-examination. Here, too, expert opinion on accounting procedures was divided. There were recognized authorities who considered organization expense an intangible asset, one that was of possibly significant value. Insull's accountants treated it that way and, far from seeking to conceal or deceive, they were following a procedure accepted in some quarters. Even the federal government, for income tax purposes, treated organization expense as a permanent asset.

Insull was the principal defendant and he did not hesitate to appear as a witness on his own behalf and for everyone indicted with him. He had to convince the jury that he was not a crook. His empire had not collapsed and caught in its downfall thousands of people as the result of wicked schemes devised by him to defraud them. His testimony was intended to convince the jury that he, too, like so many others, was a victim. He had not been spared by the economic disaster that had engulfed them all.

Judging from newspaper coverage of the trial, Samuel Insull was the one the world most wanted to hear. Defense counsel Thompson took him skillfully, step by step, through his story. Much of it was autobiographical. He described his childhood in England, his first job and his fortunate connection with Edison, his early Chicago years, and his acquisition of utilities properties. He told of his operating problems, and the education and preparation of his son to carry on the enterprises he had created. He explained the creation of IUI and the reorganization of Middle West Utilities. There was not, he said, anything sinister either in its formation or in the formation of the Corp. He declared that the tremendous and unexpected break in the stock market in 1929 was regarded as nothing more than a temporary setback. His departure for Paris, he said, occurred before he was aware of any investigation into his conduct, and he only read about it in the

Paris edition of the *Chicago Tribune*. He left the United States because he was "sick and tired." He did not return when he was asked because he believed that politicians were trying to make political capital out of his misfortunes. There was no secrecy about his movements.

It was clear to both sides that Insull was a superb witness. The jury was entranced by his testimony. Prosecuting attorney Salter discovered the jurors glowering at him every time he made an objection. During cross-examination, Insull's responses were prompt, confidently stated, and gave fully the impression of an honest man much beset by unfair adversaries. Salter, for example, used tax returns to show that Insull's salary for the five years before the collapse totaled half a million dollars each year. Here was the rich and greedy Insull squeezing money from his investors. But the point came quicky to naught when the same returns showed that Insull's charitable contributions amounted in some years to more than his entire salary. Indeed, seventy-five-year-old Samuel Insull was a remarkable witness. The prosecution might have been better off with no cross-examination at all. After Insull's, some additional testimony was heard and on Friday, November 16, 1932, the defense rested.

The prosecution's final summation consisted of a carefully prepared review of government evidence and a plea by Salter to enforce the mail fraud statutes because "you are passing upon a state of facts here based upon the most wonderful act of Congress that has ever been passed for the protection of the public, the protection of investors from exploitation. This is a wonderful statute. . . . It is the only statute in all the statute books of federal law that would in any way fit the facts of this case." The weakness of the government's case stood revealed by the sentimental appeal for admiration of a "wonderful statute."

Floyd Thompson summarized for the defense. He began by reviewing Insull's career, from his humble beginnings in London to leadership of an industrial and financial structure of breathtaking scope. He spoke glowingly of Insull's charitable and civic contributions. Warming up, he directed the jurors to the concept of crime. If a crime had been committed, he said, it had to consist of two elements: the first was the act itself; the second, the intent with which the act was done. Whoever heard, Thompson asked, of a scheme to defraud in which the schemers had made no effort to fill their pockets? For, he reminded the jury, there was no evidence that any of the defendants profited personally even "to the extent of a dollar." Whoever heard, he asked, of a scheme where the schemers had not tried to cover up their tracks? On the contrary, the Insulls had turned over to the government without hesitation every book, every letter, every scrap of paper that had been requested during its two-year investigation.

For forty years, declared Thompson, Insull had used his energy, his knowledge, and his skill to build up, strengthen, and increase the Chicago and Middle West properties. In all those years thousands of investors had put millions of dollars to work building the utilities industry. In all those years there had never been a default on a single obligation. In all those years there had never been a hint of wrongdoing or irregularity. Was this, asked Thompson, the record of a schemer and a crook?

Then why had the United States government brought charges gainst Insull and the other defendants? For Thompson the answer lay in Insull himself. His very name had become the symbol of an age of wild speculation. Millions of dollars had been risked and lost. The failure of the Insull companies raised more dust and created more anguish because of their size. Someone needed to be blamed. Samuel Insull and 16 of his associates were chosen. "I say we are trying that age [of speculation excess]. The test is whether or not these men shall be made a horrible example, whether they shall be convicted because of a situation in which they lived. . . ."

Insull expected and predicted his acquittal. Two hours after the jury began its deliberations, it found all the defendants innocent of all charges. Actually, it took the jury only five minutes to reach a verdict. But given the importance of the case, the great sums spent on investigation and prosecution, and the worldwide publicity generated, five minutes of deliberation seemed quite inadequate. Besides, the former sheriff pointed out, might not so quick a verdict give rise to suspicions of bribery? So the jurors made small talk and marked time while the world waited. Two hours seemed long enough.

The ordeal had not yet ended, however. The defendants still had to face other charges, state indictments for embezzlement, and a federal indictment for violation of the National Bankruptcy Act. On March 12, 1935, a jury in the criminal court of Cook County returned a verdict of not guilty on the charge that Insull and others had embezzled $66,000 from Middle West Utilities. Three months later Judge John C. Knox of the U.S. District Court for the southern district of New York, having listened carefully to full argument as Insull and the others were being tried on charges arising from the federal bankruptcy law, turned to the members of the jury. He advised them that ". . . the proof offered by the government is not of a quality which would, if the case were submitted to you, enable you to find the defendants guilty beyond a reasonable doubt." He directed a verdict of not guilty.

The government had prepared its prosecution of Samuel Insull very carefully, but the trials that took place revealed essential weaknesses in the cases. Why were the trials held at all, when the charges were so poorly substantiated? Why did the government take such great pains and then proceed despite the weakness of what had been prepared? The answer can only be that attorney Floyd Thompson was correct, that the trials were far, far more political than they were criminal. What was on trial was the entire era, with its loose business practices, its lack of regulation, its lust for a quick buck. Much of the information in the government's cases had come from a five-year investigation of the utilities industry by the Federal Trade Commission. Begun in 1928 with President Coolidge's blessing, its conclusions stimulated a scathing denunciation of business practices in the industry. Donald Richberg, one of Insull's oldest enemies, voiced what became a popular evaluation: "The true significance of the career of Samuel Insull lies in the fact that his sins were not exceptional save in the sweep of his ambitions and the extent of the injuries he inflicted."

But Insull's acquittal did not bring vindication. It was not, argued many in the business community who became his harshest critics, the system that was at fault, but men like Insull who gave the system a bad name. For academic critics like economist John R. Commons, Insull was the symbol of decadent laissez-faire capitalism. And many Americans were, despite the acquittals, convinced that Insull was a perpetrator and not a victim. The anti-Insull bias of the reform legislation of the New Deal reflects the public perception of Insull's role.

This bias against Insull and more generally against holding companies led Franklin Roosevelt in his Commonwealth Club speech in September 1932 to denounce the "Ishmaels and the Insulls." Senator George W. Norris, who was to lead such a gallant fight for public power in the Tennessee Valley, had spent much of his time during the

72nd Congress denouncing holding companies, ". . . one of the great evils connected with the power question . . . which is something comparatively new in our industrial development." They were, he said, parasitical and had little valid reason for existence. Congress, in direct response to Insull's wrongdoings, real or alleged, enacted some of the most far-reaching legislation in the nation's history. The laws creating the Tennessee Valley Authority and the Rural Electrification Authority were responses to the utilities industry's doings. During the long fight over the dam and power station at Muscle Shoals in the Tennessee River valley, revelations concerning propaganda disseminated by the utilities companies tarnished Insull's image further.

The Securities Act of 1933 and the Securities and Exchange Act of 1934 aimed to prevent insider manipulation of the securities market by placing trading practices under federal regulation. The latter act sought to end misrepresentation by requiring registration and full disclosure of information on all securities traded on the exchanges. The Public Utilities Holding Company Act of 1935 destroyed some of the utilities pyramids, dissolved all utilities holding companies that were more than twice removed from their operating companies, and increased the regulatory power of the SEC over them. Where financial decisions emanating from Wall Street once determined all activity on the securities markets, where Wall Street brokers once controlled all the decisions to make or to break, now Washington took on a new and dramatically more important role. The actions of federal agencies now loomed so important that they were carefully watched throughout the nation and the world. It is no exaggeration to see in the legislative innovations of the New Deal a phoenix arising from the ashes of the Insull empire.

10

THE COURT MARTIAL OF BILLY MITCHELL

Charles A. Lindbergh, the Lone Eagle, was America's aviator hero of the 1920s, a pilot who celebrated the values of rugged individualism and machine technology and who focused public attention on the wonders of interoceanic flight. Less well known to the public, but at least as important in his impact on military aviation, was General William Mitchell of the United States Army.

Six years before Lindbergh's flight, brash, outspoken "Billy" Mitchell had wheedled the U.S. Navy into allowing him to demonstrate that a bomber force he had assembled could sink battleships. That, Mitchell believed, spelled the end of the battleship's role as defender of America's coastlines. But despite Mitchell's show, the army and navy high command were unpersuaded.

Billy Mitchell's temperament did not tolerate rejection. He went on to challenge the Establishment, disregarding such cherished traditions as chain of command, ignoring official censorship, and thumbing his nose at the idea of proper deportment for an officer. He was a maverick, contemptuous of protocol, a ranker who had not gone to West Point and who lacked any hint of elite military background. Mitchell's zealous advocacy of air power and a unified air force—a distinct service separate from the Army and the Navy—angered the brass of both those establishments. His blunt and corrosive criticisms of the policies then pursued by the War and Navy Departments brought on his court-martial for insubordination and for "conduct prejudicial to good order and military discipline."

William Mitchell was born to well-to-do parents on the French

Riviera in 1879, the first of ten children. His father, a Democrat, served in both the United States House of Representatives and the Senate, representing Wisconsin. The senior Mitchell acquired a reputation for being wildly visionary and for supporting such outrageous schemes as the income tax and the eight-hour day. Critics used the same uncomplimentary words to describe both father and son.

When war broke out with Spain in 1898, Billy, then in college in Washington, enlisted in the infantry. In doing so he proved to be his father's son, a maverick within his own family, for John Mitchell, a pacifist, was one of the most outspoken Senate opponents of the war. The elder Mitchell had declared that "no soldier should be mustered in for the purpose of shooting our ideas of liberty and justice into an alien people." But he did nothing to dissuade his son, and Billy Mitchell began his 28-year career in the United States Army. Within a week he had become a second lieutenant, the youngest officer in the service. After the war he volunteered for duty in Alaska, where he was instrumental in directing the construction of a considerable section of the Alaska telegraph line. Soon he was the youngest captain in the Army, aware of the immense strategic importance of Alaska and of the subarctic territory in general.

When the United States entered World War I in 1917, Mitchell transferred from the Signal Corps to the Air Service. He had learned to fly in 1916, and he persuaded his superiors to send him to France with a team directed to observe the manufacture and development of aircraft and to report on French methods in combat, training, and organization of airmen. He also got a firsthand look at the carnage of trench warfare. This experience helped develop his theories on the importance of the airplane as an efficient and swift weapon of war.

> One flight over the lines gave me a much clearer impression of how armies were laid out than any amount of traveling around on the ground. A very significant thing to me was that we could cross the lines of these contending armies in a few minutes in our airplane, whereas the armies had been locked in the struggle, immovable, powerless to advance, for three years. . . . It looked as though the war would keep up indefinitely until either the airplanes brought an end to the war or the contending nations dropped from sheer exhaustion.

By 1918, some 69 million men had been mobilized into the armies fighting the Great War. Almost 9 million had been killed and 22 million had been wounded. For Mitchell there seemed no alternative to the brutality of the Western Front except Civil War General William T. Sherman's strategy of carrying the war to the enemy's economic structure and civilian population. As Mitchell put it, "The advent of air power, which can go straight to the vital centers and either neutralize or destroy them, has put a completely new complexion on the old system of making war. It is now realized that the hostile army in the field is a false objective, and the real objectives are the vital centers." It was not necessary, he argued, "that these cities be destroyed. . . . It will be sufficient to have the civilian population driven out so that they cannot carry on their usual vocations. . . ." The mere threat "of bombing a town by an air force will cause it to be evacuated, and all work in factories to be stopped. To gain a lasting victory in war, the hostile nation's power to make war must be destroyed."

Although it was not air power but Germany's exhaustion that ended the war, the technological and tactical advancement of the airplane was enough to encourage Mitchell. At St. Mihiel in the war's waning months Mitchell, commanding the First Army Air Service, led the largest aggregation of aircraft ever assembled for an offensive operation—almost 1,500 planes. His force effectively harassed the enemy, attacked communications and lines of retreat, and tactically supported the advance of American ground forces. Had the war continued, Mitchell planned a parachute drop behind German lines. After receiving the congratulations of General Pershing, commander of the American Expeditionary Force, Mitchell wrote to his mother about the event and added, "I have been recommended to be made a general at once, to be decorated with our Military Cross and the Legion of Merit."

Some of Mitchell's ideas on the use of air power had probably been influenced by British General Hugh Trenchard. At St. Mihiel, Mitchell had the cooperation of Trenchard and the newly established Royal Air Force. Trenchard advocated tactical bombing in support of ground troops and was a strong champion of a unified and independent air service. Mitchell was also acquainted with the air power theories of Giulio Douhet, the head of Italy's Central Aeronautical

Bureau. Douhet had grasped the concept of total war and he argued that air power ought to be used to carry war to vital locations in enemy territory, to attack not only military installations behind the lines, but industries and cities. Under the destruction and terror of unremitting bombardment from the air, he held, the morale and will to fight of an enemy people could not survive.

During the postwar decade, Mitchell developed and articulated his ideas at the very time that reaction against the war led to a drive for arms limitation. Most Americans had no desire for large peacetime military forces and wanted them reduced to the lowest point consistent with national safety. Congress acted speedily to bring about demobilization, cutting back the massive wartime army to a small peacetime cadre of professionals. Congress refused to authorize new naval vessels and it even threatened to cut out those that had been authorized in 1916. The press and the public enthusiastically endorsed the efforts of Senator William Borah of Idaho in 1920 to bring about discussions among the United States, Great Britain, and Japan to reduce their projected naval armaments for the next five years. Congress responded accordingly: the Senate approved Borah's resolution unanimously and opponents in the House could muster no more than four dissenting votes. The Five Power Treaty of 1922, including also France and Italy, was the result—a product of both an idealistic reaction against the war and a concern for the American taxpayer. The signatories would not only limit projected naval armament but scrap existing tonnage as well.

In the summer of 1921 Mitchell himself bolstered the cause of naval disarmament. As the Navy Department debated and argued about which ships to scrap, Mitchell bluntly asserted that no naval vessel could withstand an attack by bomber aircraft and that battleships were "as obsolete as knights in armor after the invention of gunpowder." To prove his point, Mitchell began a whirlwind campaign to bring about what one commentator described as a "gladiatorial match between Army bombers and a battleship." Congressman Bascom Slemp of Virginia pointed out that it would be most difficult to demonstrate Mitchell's claim "with certainty." "Give us the target ships," Mitchell told the House Naval Affairs Committee, "and come out and watch the show."

After much haggling between Mitchell, now assistant chief of the

Air Service, and Navy Secretary Josephus Daniels, they agreed on joint tests near the entrance to Chesapeake Bay. Daniels grudgingly furnished some target vessels, elements of the Imperial German Fleet that were now merely surplus junk. The main attraction would be the battleship *Ostfriesland*, a 27,000-ton veteran of the Battle of Jutland, a ship which Admiral Alfred von Tirpitz had declared to be unsinkable; it had survived no fewer than eighteen direct hits and a tremendous mine explosion. Despite such awesome punishment, the *Ostfriesland* had been able to return home under its own steam.

The bombing group began with the sinking of a submarine. It followed with successful attacks on a destroyer and a cruiser. Finally, and dramatically, the bombers demolished the "unsinkable" *Ostfriesland*. Twenty-one minutes after the army bombers began their run against the battleship, the old warrior raised its bow toward heaven, rolled to port, and slipped under the waves stern first. Mitchell had proved that aircraft could sink a battleship.

The controversy over the relative merits of the battleship and the bomber gave Americans their first sustained look at military aviation, and they saw in it the postwar New Era virtues of efficiency, economy, and technological innovation. Air power took on special appeal in light of widespread sentiment to reduce federal expenditures after the orgy of wartime spending. Mitchell had testified before a House committee in 1920 and told members that not only were battleships "almost worthless" but that the cost of a single battleship could pay for "as much as a thousand bombers" and that it would take only a "few fliers to destroy the most powerful fleet."

The use of air power responded also to postwar disillusionment over involvement in European wars: a self-reliant America could defend its shores without venturing abroad. Mitchell created a comforting notion of the bomber's defense role, a picture of American planes roaming maritime approaches to the continent and smashing any sea or air armada that approached its shores. And Mitchell preached the humanity of aerial attacks on an enemy's "vital centers." Aerial bombardment would democratize the horrors of war and inflict them quickly. All of a country's inhabitants would be indiscriminately subject to sudden destruction so that "either a state will hesitate to go to war, or, having engaged in war, [air power] will make the context sharper, more decisive, and more quickly finished."

This "quick way of deciding a war" would be, Mitchell added, "really much more humane than the present methods of blowing up people to bits by cannon projectiles or butchering them with bayonets." In bombing attacks many, of course, would die, but success would be gained less by killing than by disrupting the economy and provoking terror. Because terror brought rapid demoralization and quick results, the war of air power would be more humane than bloody, indecisive ground campaigns.

Although one may doubt that much was proved by repeated runs over vessels that could not take evasive action and that lacked both anti-aircraft guns and fire control crews, Mitchell claimed that there was great significance in the test results. In his official confidential report Mitchell declared that "aircraft now in existence or in development, acting from shore bases, can find and destroy all classes of seacraft under war conditions, with a negligible loss to the aircraft." Because other nations knew of the tests and would act accordingly, the principal threat to the United States would no longer come from hostile navies but from hostile air forces. "It is now necessary," he concluded, "to provide an air organization and a method of defending not only our coast cities, but our interior cities, against the attack of hostile air forces." Further, Mitchell rejected the idea of a multipurpose warplane. He believed in an air force of fighter and bomber aircraft. Good pursuit planes combined with adequate reconnaisance patrolling, he believed, could blunt an attacking force.

Mitchell also argued that the airplane had become indispensable for the defense of America's overseas possessions. If air power could nullify the offensive capability of foreign navies approaching American shores, foreign planes could do the same to ships of the United States. The U.S. Navy could no longer be the principal means for the protection of American military installations overseas and for the defense of American insular possessions.

Mitchell, like many Americans after the defeat of Germany, came to believe that the most probable enemy in the next war would be Japan. Against Japan, American sea power would be vulnerable to air attack and the strategic position of the United States in the Pacific weakened. Any American naval expedition crossing that ocean to defend the Philippines or to attack Japan would have to sail into the teeth of Japan's land-based air power. Defending the Philippines would become increasingly difficult. Defending Hawaii would be virtually impossible, for Mitchell had little faith in the potential of the aircraft carrier. "Aircraft acting from suitable floating airdromes can destroy any class of surface craft on the high seas," but the carrier itself would be "more vulnerable than the battleship to enemy attack." Rather than turn to the aircraft carrier, Mitchell put his hopes for the protection of American interests in the Pacific in Alaska. Establishing bases there would make it possible for long-range bombers to threaten Japanese sea power in the northern and central Pacific and in the Japanese home islands themselves. Alaska became strategically important in Mitchell's thinking because it was the meeting place of Japanese, Russian, and American spheres of power.

Mitchell showed remarkable prescience. He prophesied the attack with which Japan would launch the war in 1941. He was right both as to time and geography, and also that the battle line of the U.S. Pacific fleet could be knocked out by a single blow from the air. Command of the air proved, of course, to be the most critical element in every Pacific campaign during World War II. No island could be attacked or defended without it.

Despite the apparent success of Billy Mitchell's bombing demonstrations, interpretations of their significance differed. Some people accepted Mitchell's conclusions completely; others were skeptical; still others rejected them. The navy brass, excepting a few heretics, with their own interests and traditions at stake, belittled the significance of what had been demonstrated. They pointed out that the *Ostfriesland* had been easy to hit. It was a ship at anchor, a sitting duck. Had it been steaming at full speed and zigzagging, the case would have been very different. Because the ship was not defending itself, having no rapid-fire anti-aircraft batteries, the tests proved nothing.

Supporters of the Navy's position in the legislative and executive branches of government added their voices. Senator Miles Poindexter, chairman of the Senate Naval Affairs Committee, responded to the tests with outright denial: "[T]he sinking of the *Ostfriesland* was a matter of coast defense" at best, he opined, but the "primal purpose of a navy is to carry the power of the nation onto the high seas and into foreign waters if necessary." The Assistant Secretary of the Navy, Theodore Roosevelt, Jr., found a relevant parallel for criticism in an African safari: "I once saw a man kill a lion with a 30-30 caliber rifle under certain conditions, but that doesn't mean that a 30-30 rifle is a lion gun."

Argument on the other side was equally vigorous. For airplane designer Glenn Martin, the tests signalled a change in the course of world events because, "[n]o fleet afloat is safe if it loses control of the air . . . an enemy by gaining control of the air can now carry his own peace terms into the heart of any country. The sinking of the *Ostfriesland* will be epoch-making." General C.C. Williams, chief of Army Ordnance, regarded the sinking as a "bomb that will be heard around the world." And even among some naval officers there was recognition of the significance of the tests. Admiral William A. Moffet, head of the Bureau of Naval Aeronautics, was a strong advocate of air power. He disagreed with Mitchell on two important issues: the usefulness of the aircraft carrier and navy control of its own air arm. "The lesson," he said, "is that we must put planes on battleships and get aircraft carriers quickly." More strongly supportive of Mitchell was retired Admiral William Fullam, long an advocate of modernizing the Navy. Following the demonstrations, he sent congratulations to Mitchell, saluting ". . . the greatest of all revolutions in warfare aloft and ashore. Forts are gone and no nation that has good sense will lay the keel to another battleship of the present type. Indeed it is difficult to outline the general features of future battleships that resist air and submarine attack. It seems impossible."

Among the most impressed by the demonstrations were Japanese observers. Although Captain Osami Nogano (later chief of the Japanese Naval General Staff) was present, no report is available of his reaction. Nogano played a major role in the attack on Pearl Harbor, twenty years in the future. In 1921 the *Hartford Courant* reported the comments of two other Japanese observers. One declared, "Our people will cheer your Mitchell and study his experiments. . . . It would be gravely embarrassing to the American people if the ideas of your General Mitchell were more appreciated in Japan than in the United States."

The official verdict on the bombing demonstrations, written by a joint board of army and navy officers headed by General John Pershing, was negative. It concluded: "The battleship is still the backbone of the fleet and the bulwark of the nation's sea defense and will so remain as long as safe navigation of the sea for purposes of trade and transportation is vital to success in war."

Mitchell was shocked by the report and infuriated by official refusal to accept what he believed to be the overwhelming evidence of the bombing tests. His determination to get his truth to the public led to a serious defiance of orders. He now moved to file his own evaluation of the tests in a confidential report, not to be made public without official permission. When excerpts of the confidential report leaked out mysteriously, the *New York Times* carried the story and said, "A sensational chapter has been added to the aircraft vs. capital ship discussion. . . . General Mitchell in this report flatly contradicts the reports submitted to congressional committees that witnessed the bombing tests."

Upon assuming that Mitchell had deliberately leaked the information, the Adjutant General wrote to him: "It is now desired that you state if you showed or otherwise communicated your report . . . to any person outside the military service, and if so, to whom." Mitchell answered that he had not authorized the leaking of any part of the report. The matter was dropped, but Mitchell remained under a cloud. He could not publish anything without War Department permission. At this point his enemies in the armed services stood ready to pounce. They did so as Mitchell's domestic life began to come apart. When his wife charged that his conduct had become "erratic," Secretary of War John W. Weeks was informed that Mitchell was "unstable." He was ordered to report to Walter Reed Hospital for a mental examination. His enemies gloated, although their pleasure was brief; a battery of psychiatrists declared him entirely sane and "fit for duty."

From 1921 to 1924, Mitchell faithfully obeyed the injunction against publishing anything without prior permission. When the editor of the *Saturday Evening Post* asked him in October 1924 to write a series of articles on his favorite topics—aircraft bombings and a unified air command—he agreed to do so provided he could get permission from the president. In this way he would circumvent the orders of Secretary Weeks. President Coolidge granted only conditional approval: "Confirming my conversation with you this morning, I do not know of any objections to your preparing some articles so far as I am concerned, but of course I cannot speak for your superior officers. The matter should be taken up with them and their decision in relation to the articles followed." Weeks knew nothing of this as Mitchell sought and received permission from General Mason Patrick, head of the Air Service. Later, when Secretary Weeks asked Patrick to explain the publication, the general insisted that he had been deceived by Mitchell. He had not been shown the presidential letter. "If I had known the President's permission . . . was contingent upon the approval of his 'superior officers' . . . I should certainly have taken the matter up with the War Department . . . and required General Mitchell to submit copies of the articles to me."

The articles appeared at a time when Mitchell and the Navy were quarreling over another bombing test against a battleship. The target of this test was the unfinished battleship *Washington*, scheduled to be scrapped in accordance with the naval limitations treaty. The *Washington* was the only modern ship to be sacrificed in the test, an all-navy show with no army planes involved in the bombing runs. Billy Mitchell, however, obtained a box seat as an observer.

Following the test, navy inspectors insisted that the demonstration proved that the *Washington* had withstood bombs and depth charges, and had to be sunk with naval gunfire. Had it been equipped with pumps and anti-aircraft guns, it would have remained substantially secure. Mitchell was enraged. Summoned to appear before a House committee chaired by Representative Julian Lampert of Michigan, Mitchell testified that not a single bomb had been dropped on the *Washington*. The Navy, he said, had used blank projectiles. The test had been a subterfuge.

The articles in the *Saturday Evening Post* were far from sensational. They did little more than advocate greater use of air power, and there was no effort to expose the *Washington* findings. Nevertheless, Mitchell by now had committed a number of sins. Because of his statements before the Lampert Committee, and because he told the committee that many air-minded officers were silenced by their superiors and were afraid to speak out, and because he went over Weeks' head in seeking President Coolidge's permission to publish, the Secretary of War asked the president to allow him to remove Mitchell from his post as assistant chief of the Air Service. There was no other choice, Weeks insisted, for Mitchell was continuing a course "so lawless, so contrary to the building up of an efficient organization, so lacking in reasonable teamwork, so indicative of a personal desire for publicity at the expense of everyone with whom he is associated, that his actions render him unfit for a high administrative post."

President Coolidge approved the request. General Mitchell was demoted to colonel and exiled to an army post in San Antonio, Texas. For the *New York Times*, not always a defender of Mitchell, this was "a scandalous misuse of authority." No other officer in either the Army or the Navy, "has done more by example and initiative to advance military aviation," the *Times* reported. The *Cleveland Press* warned, "We may wait a hundred years for another display of such courage." Humorist Will Rogers remarked that ". . . it does seem a strange way to repay a man who has fought for us through a war, and who has fought harder for us in peace, to be reprimanded for telling the truth."

Mitchell's demotion and exile did not silence him. In August 1925, he continued his crusade in an article which appeared in *Liberty* magazine. In "Exploding Disarmament Bunk" he asked, "Why Have Treaties About Battleships, When Airplanes Can Destroy Them?" He provided an answer: why permit continuation of expensive battleships, he charged, "largely preventing open and free discussion of their uses, are the propaganda policies maintained by navies. . . ." In his book, *Winged Defense*, which appeared in the late summer of 1925, Colonel Mitchell ignored the War Department ban on public mention of the bombing tests. He was clearly spoiling for a fight. "The truth of our deplorable situation is going to be put before the American people, come what may. If the War Department wants to start something, so much the better."

The stridency of Mitchell's criticism of armed services leadership mounted as a result of two naval air mishaps in September of the same year. Three navy PN-9 flying boats were being made ready for a flight from California to Hawaii. When Mitchell learned that the pilots who were to fly the planes had been trained only on Chesapeake Bay, he was disturbed. When he learned that the planes would refuel at sea from station ships positioned at two-hundred-mile "strides" from point of departure to point of arrival, and that the project had been designed by men who had never flown a plane, he was beside himself. Later, when he learned that the leading plane had gone down somewhere in the Pacific within a few hours' flight of Hawaii, he was furious. Still, he did not berate the Navy publicly, at least not yet.

Just a few days later, the navy dirigible *Shenandoah* crashed in a thunderstorm in Ohio en route to a fairground exhibition. The disaster killed fourteen, including Commander Zachary Lansdowne. When some of the details of the tragedy were made public, Mitchell seethed with anger. The Navy had egregiously misused both the crew and the aircraft. Prior to takeoff, Lansdowne had quarreled heatedly with the Chief of Naval Operations. Lansdowne wanted to scrub the flight, which he considered a non-military mission, because the craft lacked some safety valves and there were ominous weather reports. Heavy storms were raging in the Great Lakes area. Nevertheless, Lansdowne had been ordered to proceed as planned. Not only Mitchell but the nation's press bristled with indignation.

Afterward, Mitchell distributed copies of a prepared statement to a swarm of reporters. The full document ran to 6,080 words. It was replete with incendiary comments written, Mitchell declared, only "after mature deliberation." The frightful disasters, he said, were a "result of the incompetency, the criminal negligence, and the almost treasonable negligence of our national defense by the Navy and War Departments." He charged the heads of both the Army and Navy with making every effort to prevent a separate air force. He accused them of distorting facts and "openly telling falsehoods about aviation." Flyers, he charged, were "bluffed and bulldozed" until they dared not tell the truth lest they be banished, as he had been, to an American Siberia. He listed other offenses. What business, he asked in regard to the *Shenandoah* flight, "has the navy over mountains, anyway?" He charged navy headquarters with launching the Hawaii flight with "primitive, good for nothing, big lumbering flying boats."

> The impression is given to the public at large that the *Shenandoah* was a modern ship, properly constructed, properly operated and completely equipped. This is not the case. It shakes the faith of the people in airship transportation because they are not given the exact facts on the subject. . . . This is a demand for the facts of the case, so that we will not be hindered in the commercial development of this splendid aircraft on account of the accident due to the incompetence of the Navy Department and the criminal negligence in ordering this trip.

Mitchell had already gone far enough to assure his own court-martial, but he concluded with these words: "We may all make mistakes but the criminal mistakes made by armies and navies, whenever they have been allowed to handle aeronautics, show their incompetence. . . . This, then, is what I have to say on the subject, and I hope that every American will hear."

It was only a matter of time before official action would be taken against Mitchell. He had, in the words of *Aviation* magazine, uttered the "most daring indictment of the War and Navy Departments ever made by an officer." Five days after Mitchell made his statement, President Coolidge appointed his old friend, banker Dwight Morrow, to head an aeronautical board to investigate aviation in the United States, an eight-member blue-ribbon panel of high-ranking military and political figures. Even before Mitchell appeared to face the board, however, a decision to bring court-martial proceedings had been taken.

The American press and the American public overwhelmingly supported Mitchell, although hostile comments were not hard to find. The brother of the *Shenandoah*'s navigator, in a letter to the *Houston Chronicle*, said to Mitchell, "You have no place in the service of your country when you have so little respect for its authority." Similarly hostile was the *New York World*: "Permit this violent outburst to go unpunished and every private in the Army and enlisted man in the Navy will feel at liberty to denounce superior officers. Armies and navies are not made that way."

More typical was the comment of the *Los Angeles Record*: "And what did President Coolidge say when he heard of the disaster? 'It is God's will.' God's will! Pious fiddlesticks! Sanctimonious drivel! We suggest rather than a court-martial we might rather try our distinguished fellow townsman, the Secretary of the Navy, for criminal stupidity." And appearing before an American Legion convention, the colorful mayor of Boston, James Michael Curley, excoriated the administration for its policies: "There is one man that is not lacking in courage. While other nations are gaining supremacy of the air with the finest planes and decent appropriations we are sending the bravest and best of our sons in rotten planes into the air."

Mitchell did not make a strong case in his testimony before the Morrow Board. He read many pages of now familiar charges against the War and Navy departments from his book, *Winged Defense*. Often his selections contained broad generalities, ambiguous strategic estimates, and predictions of events in the unforeseeable future. Much of what he said was lacking in solid data or concrete proof. His criticisms of the Navy and War secretaries and of the force commanders verged on libel. Significantly, the Morrow Board ended its hearings just before the date set for the court-martial. Its final report discounted the danger of future air wars, rejected Mitchell's proposals for a buildup of air power, and recommended instead a less ambitious and less expensive program. The most striking passage in the report took issue with Mitchell's key concept of "vital centers." "The next war may well start in the air," the report said, "but in all probability it will wind up as the last one did, in the mud." The timing of the board's final report may have been chosen in the hope of detracting from the defense's case.

The court-martial of Billy Mitchell began on October 28, 1925, in Washington, DC. No such high-ranking military tribunal had been assembled since the trial of Major John Andre, Benedict Arnold's associate in their famous conspiracy. The court consisted of eleven generals and one colonel. The last was the "law man," a legal expert from the judge advocate's department. Mitchell had known many of the panel for more than twenty years and one of them, Douglas MacArthur, later supreme commander in the Pacific theater, was a boyhood friend from Wisconsin. The generals were from the cavalry, the artillery, and the infantry—not a single flyer among them. This provoked a young congressman from New York, Fiorello LaGuardia, to charge that "Billy Mitchell is not being tried by a board of his peers but by a pack of beribboned dog robbers of the General Staff."

Mitchell's chief civilian counsel, Congressman Frank Reid of Illinois, challenged the right of Brigadier General Albert L. Bowley to sit on the court. Bowley was unacceptable, he said, for reasons of "prejudice, hostility and animosity." The charge was based on elements in a speech Bowley had made just a week before the trial. "A single air service?" Bowley had raged. "Do we want this? The backbone of every army is the infantry. . . . There is no more reason for a single air service than there is for a single medical corps, or a single ordnance department."

Bowley was excused. So was General Charles P. Summerall, commander at Governors Island. Summerall was known to the men under him as "Oliver Cromwell in khaki." Like Bowley, he was challenged for prejudice. After Mitchell had visited the Hawaiian Islands and inspected the defenses under Summerall's command, he was sharply critical of what he had seen. Hawaii's defense was, Mitchell stated, "inefficiently handled, badly organized, and ignorance of its application manifested by [Summerall] and his staff.

This . . . would lead to certain defeat in case of war." Summerall called the criticisms "superficial impressions," "academic discussions," and "unfair." At another time Summerall had said, "Aviation is a new arm. We will admire it. It is spectacular . . . but the public is being misled by the fanciful and irresponsible talk emanating from a source either without experience or whose experience in war is limited to the very narrow field of aviation."

Upon being challenged, Summerall withdrew, declaring, "In view of the bitter personal hostility toward me by Colonel Mitchell, I couldn't consent to sit as a member of this board and I shall ask the court to excuse me." He felt deeply hurt and told the press, "Only ten minutes before court convened I shook hands with him. Now it's all over. We're enemies, Mitchell and I." A third member of the tribunal, General Fred W. Sladen, was also excused. Unlike Summerall, who was furious at having been challenged, Sladen welcomed the chance to get off the court. The number of sitting judges was reduced from twelve to nine, but only six were legally required for a general court-martial. The court convened with General Robert L. Howze, reputed to be "the best cavalryman who ever rode a horse," as president.

Joining Congressman Reid as assistant defense counsel was Clayton Bissell, an expert on aviation matters and at one time Colonel Mitchell's aide and a member of the circle of air power advocates. Although Frank Reid was only a freshman in Congress, he had been a member of the Lampert Committee, where he had openly sided with Mitchell. Mitchell turned down the suggestion that he hire Clarence Darrow as counsel because Reid, having practiced with Darrow, had, he judged, acquired the necessary skill.

Mitchell was charged under the 96th Article of War for "conduct of a nature to bring discredit upon the military service" and tried on eight specifications. The first was that in his statement of September 5, 1925, having accused both the Army and Navy of incompetence and criminal negligence, he had conducted himself "to the prejudice of good order and military discipline." Specifications two and three held that his statement was "insubordinate" and "highly contemptuous and disrespectful," and was meant to discredit the War Department. The fourth specification was similar, but directed at the Navy Department. The last four repeated the same accusations in regard to a statement made four days later, on September 9. This second statement was considered even more inflammatory than the earlier one. Mitchell wrote:

> What I have said about the conditions in our national defense hurts the bureaucrats in Washington. It ought to hurt them, because it's the truth. . . . Let every American know absolutely that we are going to better our national defense, and that we are on the war path and we are going to stay there until conditions are remedied. The barking of little dogs that follow the main pack should not delude any thinking person as to the subject of our case.

Mitchell did not deny being insubordinate. "Discipline is a difficult thing to define. Some people call it the unhesitating obedience of a junior to a superior officer," he said, but when superiors were negligent and incompetent, they needed to be criticized for the nation's good. His trial, he demanded, should be before the American people, a public trial that would present "all the evidence." The tribunal "should be composed of representative Americans instead of members of the Army and Navy bureaucracy. Let its members be from the east and west, north and south, men from the fields and factories as well as from the counting houses. Then and only then will we begin to get at the actual facts involved and remove it from the petty politics and bureaucratic supression." As far as he was personally concerned, he averred, the outcome was less important than was the edification and enlightenment of the broad public. ". . . [I]t does not matter to me whether I am in the Army or not. If the bureaucracies wish to throw me out they probably have the machinery for doing it, and it will be only one more evidence of the condition into which our national defense has drifted."

Because the prosecution based its entire case on what Mitchell had said, Reid and his staff conceded their client's guilt as charged. The case for the defense, then, was Mitchell's right to freedom of speech. After all, said Reid, President Coolidge had recently told graduates of the Naval Academy that the "officers of the Navy are given the fullest latitude in expressing their views before their fellow citizens. . . . It seems to me perfectly proper for anyone upon any suitable occasion to advocate the maintenance of the Navy in keeping with the greatness and dignity of our country." Did the same right apply in the Army? The prosecution was basing its case on what Mitchell had said; the defense was basing its case on the truth of what Mitchell had said, working from the great principle of the eighteenth-century case of John Peter Zenger: truth dispels libel.

Congressman Reid prepared 66 accusations against the War and Navy departments. They included:

> That the *Shenandoah* was designed for the use of hydrogen as a lifting gas and that when helium was substituted without changing the structure her safety factor was reduced.
>
> That the *Shenandoah*, lost during a "publicity stunt," was flown under the protest of its commander, had been overweight and unsafe and had been ordered to fly by men who knew nothing of aviation.
>
> That Mitchell was demoted and transferred because he told the truth before the Lampert Committee.
>
> That the War Department had spent a great deal of effort in trying to make the American people believe that anti-aircraft guns and machine guns were effective in air defense.

Reid would prove, he claimed, "that Colonel Mitchell, after exhausting every usual means to safeguard the aerial defense of the United States without result, took the only way possible that would cause a study of true conditions of national defense to be made." Reid intended to present a string of witnesses to prove the truth of Mitchell's charges.

Since Mitchell never denied his two statements, the prosecution had only to show that, in violation of the 96th Article of War, Mitchell had discredited the armed services and was guilty, regardless of his motives, his loyalty, or his overriding concern for the defense and security of his country. There was great surprise, therefore, when the tribunal permitted "the defense to present evidence of the proof of these statements and establish the truth of the defendant's accusations against the War and Navy Departments' air administrations."

Heading the prosecution team was Trial Judge Advocate Sherman Moreland, a man in his early sixties, bespectacled and gruff-voiced. Major Allen W. Gullion joined him. Gullion was arrogant and loud and had a reputation as a courtroom bully, heckling witnesses and playing on the emotions of the crowd.

Since the tribunal had given the defense permission to prove the truth of its accusations, the defense became in effect the prosecution. The courtroom would be a forum for Mitchell to present his arguments to the country. For this purpose Reid planned to subpoena 73 witnesses.

One of the first was Major Carl Spaatz, a young Air Service tactical chief, later known during World War II as "Tooey" Spaatz, commander of the United States Strategic Air Forces in Europe and the Pacific. The bulk of the Air Service, he testified in 1925, "is either obsolescent or obsolete." Did he think, asked Reid, that the War Department had impeded the development of aviation? When he replied affirmatively, over the prosecution's objection, the crowd applauded. At another point, Reid asked Spaatz if the fliers were trained sufficiently in gunnery to be ready for war. He replied negatively. Did he believe someone was responsible for this shortcoming? Spaatz's reply stunned the court: "Well, in the case of the First Pursuit Group, the commander of the Sixth Corps Area has charge of it." The commander of the Sixth Corps Area was General William S. Graves, a member of the court-martial.

General Graves interrupted to ask whether the air squadron had ever been denied help when such was requested. Spaatz's reply rocked the room with laughter. He had once, he said, tried to obtain a field for gunnery practice. The people of the small town of Oscoda, Michigan, had offered one for a nominal fee, but, Spaatz declared, he had trouble getting the War Department to pay the sum required. The price that Oscoda wanted was a dollar a year.

Major "Hap" Arnold testified forthrightly. Arnold, who would command the United States Army Air Force during World War II, said that American air strength was about half that of France or England. He described the obsolete De Havilland training planes used by the

Army as "flaming coffins." He produced records showing that 517 Air Service officers and men had been killed in crashes over the preceding six years.

America's "ace of aces" during World War I, Captain Eddie Rickenbacker, was also a witness for the defense. Rickenbacker had accounted for the greatest number of enemy aircraft shot down by any American pilot: 26 airplanes and barrage balloons. His testimony confirmed much of what had already been said. "The graveyards throughout the United States" revealed that most army equipment was antiquated. Moreover, it was "suicide" to fly without a parachute—an opinion that supported Mitchell's charge that the Navy had been criminally negligent for not providing the *Shenandoah* crew with parachutes. Fiery Fiorello LaGuardia was one of Mitchell's strongest congressional advocates. He welcomed an invitation to testify, and he relished the opportunity to expose old "fogeyism" in the services and publicize Mitchell's ideas. To illustrate the ineffectiveness of ground defenses against air attacks, LaGuardia actually acted out at the trial an anti-aircraft test he had observed at Fort Tilden, Brooklyn, waving his arms in the air to show the bombers flying overhead. He imitated the artillery officers scrambling to mount a defense and mocked their radio messages intended to draw the planes within firing range.

Any chance to nail Mitchell with accusations of libel vanished with the sensational testimony of Commander Lansdowne's widow. Soon after her appearance before the navy board investigating the *Shenandoah* disaster, she revealed to Mitchell that a naval officer had tried to persuade her to give false evidence. She now began her testimony before the court-martial by recounting what had happened just before the hearing by the navy board.

> Q. Was there a communication delivered to you purporting to come from Captain Foley, the Judge Advocate of the *Shenandoah* Court of Inquiry?
> A. It was delivered to me the day before the court.
> Q. Have you a copy of the communication?
> A. I have not. . . . I tore it up.

Then, describing the statement she was asked to sign, Mrs. Lansdowne continued, "It began with the remark that when I first accepted the invitation to appear at the *Shenandoah* court and testify in my husband's behalf, I had done so with the idea that my husband was in need of defense," but, Mrs. Lansdowne was supposed to say, "my opinion has been changed. . . . I thought the court was absolutely capable of handling the entire situation, and I was entirely willing to leave it in their hands." The statement that Foley asked her to sign went on to say that even though Commander Lansdowne disapproved of a "political flight" by the *Shenandoah*, he did agree to take the ship for military purposes, no matter what the weather conditions were.

Q. Was that statement false?
A. False.
Q. Who sent you this letter?
A. Captain Foley.

Reid then quoted for the court-martial record from Mrs. Lansdowne's testimony before the *Shenandoah* court of inquiry:

My husband was very much opposed to the flight and protested as vigorously as any officer is allowed to do to his superiors. Everyone knows that in the military or naval services, orders are given to be obeyed and no officer cares to earn the stigma of cowardice or insubordination. . . .

Q. Did you give that statement?
A. I did.

Sherman Moreland's cross-examination did not damage Mrs. Lansdowne's testimony. To the contrary, it did more to damage the Navy's case. In Mrs. Lansdowne's words,

Captain Foley sought to impress me with the importance of the court and told me that the court had all the powers of any federal court and that the solemnity of my appearance was very great and that I should be sure to tell the truth. . . . He then asked me what I was going to say and I answered him that I preferred to make my own statement to the court.
He asserted that he wanted to find out what I had on my

mind, and please to get it off, and said, "Let's rehearse the statement you are going to make to the court. Tell me the entire thing you are going to say." And I answered again that I did not want to make any statement.

He told me that I had no right to say that the flight was a political flight, as the taxpayers in the Middle West had a perfect right to see their property, to which I answered that in the case of a battleship you wouldn't take it out to the Great Lakes . . . to which he answered that it couldn't be done—and I said that it couldn't in the case of the *Shenandoah*, but they were so stupid it had to be proven to them.

Retired Admiral William S. Sims, a longtime advocate of air power, was an equally dramatic defense witness. The Navy, he said, had no policy with regard to the handling of aircraft. It went along "from day to day, more or less in a higgledy-piggledy way." He confirmed Mitchell's charge that some naval officers who favored air power were fearful of speaking out. He agreed with Mitchell that a powerful, well-organized, land-based air force could destroy any invading naval fleet. Finally, he said, in his opinion it was wrong to have sent the *Shenandoah* on a political trip to a fairground.

Mitchell did not need prodding to take the stand himself. Although he anticipated a withering cross-examination by Allen Gullion, he was still eager to testify. Reid first led him skillfully through a summary of his military career, his interest in and devotion to the cause of air power, and then to the recommendations he had made for creating and maintaining an independent first-rate air force. Mitchell's vision ranged years ahead and seemed to foresee some of the great air battles of the Second World War.

Mitchell's tendency to hyperbolize and his free-swinging exaggerations made an easy target for Major Gullion on cross-examination. At one point in his testimony regarding one of his writings, Mitchell had declared that Japanese submarines might carry guns of almost any size. When Gullion asked what size they might be, Mitchell replied that he did not know. Soon he was boxed into a corner.

Q. Then, if you don't know, why did you say in your statement . . . that they could carry any size?

A. I say that was my opinion.
Q. That is your opinion now?
A. Yes.
Q. Then, any statement—there is no statement of fact in your whole paper?
A. The paper is an expression of opinion.
Q. There is no statement of fact in your whole paper?
A. No.
Q. Any statement of fact in your whole paper?
A. No.

Whether or not Gullion's tactics and his sneering cross-examination of Mitchell were effective in helping the judges reach their decision is questionable. From what evidence is available, the judges had already made up their minds as they listened stonily to the testimony. In a military, as distinguished from a civilian, court the attorney for the defense cannot turn away from the judges and direct his appeal to a jury, unless it is to the jury of public opinion. But such a tactic had not much impact on the verdict of the nine army officers.

The prosecution was not required to prove the truth or falsity of what Mitchell had said, but only that his statements tended to disrupt discipline. He was a lawless person whose behavior, according to a letter from Secretary of War Weeks to President Coolidge, was "so contrary to the building up of any efficient organization, so lacking in responsible team work, so indicative of a personal desire for publicity at the expense of everyone with whom he is associated, that his actions render him unfit for a high administration position such as he now occupies."

The testimony of Rear Admiral William A. Moffett was telling. He denounced Mitchell as of "unsound mind and . . . suffering from delusions of grandeur. . . . The revolutionary methods of the communists have been invoked to overcome the opposition of loyal men who have sought to thwart the ambition of unscrupulous self-seekers." Then Moffett, pointing at Mitchell, boomed out in his southern accent, "Instead of an eagle soaring aloft with eyes for the country's defense, we have, instead, one who really played the part of a vulture swooping on its prey once it is down."

General Leroy Eltinge, onetime Assistant Chief of Staff for War

Plans, attempted to discredit Mitchell's notion of an independent air force: "The Army is organized primarily for and trained for duty on land, the Navy primarily for duty in the water. These two overlap at the shoreline. An additional service which overlapped both of them completely would make cooperation absolutely impossible." Geometrically neat, if somewhat simplistic.

When Captain Alfred Johnson, who had been Mitchell's leading adversary during the 1921 bomb test, was asked why the Navy Department's film, *Eyes of the Fleet*, showed only the misses among the bombs dropped on the battleships, he replied that he did not know. When he was asked about a penciled note on a document which read, "The object of this is to combat the effect of General Mitchell's testimony and to belittle the value of airplanes," he replied that he could not recall the note. Upon objection, however, Johnson's testimony was stricken.

Gullion offered half a dozen prosecution witnesses in an attempt to deny Mitchell's claims that the Navy had mishandled the *Shenandoah*. Reid's cross-examination of Admiral Edward Eberle, the Navy's senior officer, was successful in exposing the non-military purpose of the flight:

Q. Was the *Shenandoah*'s crew badly in need of training?
A. It was. They had been in the hangar for about four months.
Q. What was the matter with the *Shenandoah* that she had been in the hangar for four months?
A. There was no helium.
Q. Where was there helium?
A. In the *Los Angeles*.
Q. Do you mean you have got two rigid airships in this country and only one set of helium?
A. I regret to say that is the case.
Q. And they have to borrow helium from each other whenever you want to use one of these?
A. That is the situation now and has been for the last two years.

Eberle was asked to explain why the *Shenandoah* had been sent barnstorming over a state fair.

A. We always tried to pass over cities she had never visited before.

Q. What for?

A. Because millions of people have requested to see the ship that belonged to the government—to see an airship—requests from chambers of commerce, from governors, from members of Congress. . . .

Q. All right, do I understand you to state that this flight was taken to satisfy the curiosity of the American people, then?

A. No, I did not. I told you what the flight was undertaken for, and, incidentally, we like to fly over as many places as possible to let the people see it.

Q. What was the object of satisfying the curiosity of the people?

A. I suppose the people have an interest in their Navy as well as in the Army.

Q. Captain Lansdowne would be alive today if he hadn't gone on the trip, wouldn't he, under your direction?

A. I don't care to answer any such question.

Finally, after seven weeks, the drama came to an end. In summing up for the prosecution, Gullion called Mitchell a demagogue seeking self-aggrandizement, a megalomaniac, and a charlatan. He compared him to Aaron Burr, differing only in that Burr was superior "in poise and mental powers."

The defense counsel chose not to give a summation. Mitchell spoke for himself instead. He challenged the court for having broken its promise. It had refused to rule on whether Mitchell had proved that he had spoken the truth. He remained defiant.

My trial before this court-martial is the culmination of the efforts of the General Staff of the Army and the General Board of the Navy to depreciate the value of air power and keep it in an auxiliary position, which absolutely compromises the whole system of national defense.

The truth of every statement which I have made has been proved by good and sufficient evidence before this court, not by men who gained their knowledge of aviation by staying on the ground and having their statements prepared by numerous staffs to bolster up their predetermined ideas, but by actual flyers who have gained their knowledge first hand in war and in peace. This court has refrained from ruling whether the truth in this case constitutes an absolute defense or not.

In less than thirty minutes after beginning deliberations, the tribunal returned its verdict. Mitchell was found guilty as charged and sentenced to five years' suspension from active duty, without pay or allowances. This was without precedent in American military justice. President Coolidge, after reviewing the sentence, reduced it to five years' suspension with half pay. Stripped of his command and his rank, Mitchell chose to resign from the service.

Mitchell had been convicted on a split vote, but since the members of the tribunal were sworn to secrecy it was not known how General Douglas MacArthur voted. An enterprising newspaperman, looking through a wastebasket, found a crumpled ballot marked "Not Guilty," and determined from an examination of the handwriting that it was MacArthur's ballot. Two other bits of evidence make clear that MacArthur's was the single dissenting vote. In his own memoirs the general noted that "I did what I could in his behalf and I helped save him from dismissal." There is also a letter he wrote to Wisconsin Senator Alexander Wiley nine years after Mitchell's death. Without equivocation, MacArthur stated directly that he had cast the only vote against conviction.

Until his death in 1936, Billy Mitchell continued to develop new and broader arguments in magazine articles in behalf of air power. In the late 1940s, the 1950s, and the 1960s, he received belated recognition for the accuracy of his prophecies regarding the Japanese attack on Pearl Harbor, the war over England, the Luftwaffe, and the blitzkrieg. More recently his reputation has come down somewhat. Modern warfare, with its ICBMs and high-tech weaponry on the one hand and guerrilla and terrorist activity on the other, seems outside the sweep of Mitchell's thinking. His prophecies have been criticized because he underestimated the combat value of the aircraft carrier; he guessed wrong about the effectiveness and accuracy of future anti-aircraft guns; and though massive air raids in World War II killed hundreds of thousands, they could not destroy the war effort of a determined nation. The unchallenged supremacy, and strategic ineffectiveness, of American air power during the Vietnam War further brought Mitchell's premises into question.

The issue of military discipline—the focus of the court-martial—is fundamental. As the *New York Times* wrote editorially following the court's ruling, "An Army exists and functions by the enforcement of discipline. Colonel Mitchell broke the bonds of discipline defiantly. The effect upon the morale of the army would have been destroyed if he had not been convicted." Mitchell no doubt knew that military discipline cannot be flouted, that an army cannot exist if an officer goes unpunished after calling his superiors incompetent and treacherous. He also knew that someone had to defy discipline and question the military policy of the American military services. He did not seek martyrdom, but deliberately sacrificed his career for the sake of alerting his countrymen to the need for modern air power. He believed he would be vindicated; Mitchell was positive of victory. Years after his trial, he told military historian S.L.A. Marshall that he regretted his false estimate of his chances.

But the Billy Mitchell controversy still holds its place as part of a larger theme of the 1920s, as part of the political debate, in the Unted States and elsewhere, over disarmament and military budgets. Naval armaments were at the center of the debate because of the widely held idea that they were the foremost expression of modern militarism. The lengthy naval arms race that had preceded the outbreak of fighting in 1914 was seen as a major cause of the First World War. Air power, as Mitchell described it, promised to provide both effective and relatively inexpensive security.

The debate over preparedness, disarmament, and military budgets continues unabated. Efforts to control atomic and nuclear weapons have gone hand in hand with efforts to get a bigger bang for a buck by increasing the destructive power of each weapon. As the war in the Persian Gulf revealed, weapons become more accurate, more expensive, and more capable of imposing death and demolition, while attempts to achieve disarmament have struggled to keep up. The end of the Cold War presents both new opportunities and new dangers.

L'Envoi

Rather than a series of tidy resolutions and closed doors, the important trials of the 1920s present a myriad of causes, concerns and conflicts that are with us yet. Instead of dealing with issues that came to a head and blew away in a flurry of newsprint, America has still not resolved its internal tensions concerning xenophobia, gambling, Hollywood morés, organized crime, racial intolerance, local control of schools, criminal psychology and capital punishment, governmental corruption, high finance hanky-panky and non-traditional members of the military. We are still struggling to put these things to rest, or at least trying to fit them, and their implications, into our national psyche.

While emotional legal cases have punctuated history from the time of Socrates, in the 1920s these trials became part of the national fabric, a touchstone that linked a newly literate public with the larger issues of the day. How long did it take for news of the trial of Joan of Arc to reach southern Spain? When did people in London find out that there had been accusations and sanctioned blood-letting in Salem, Massachusetts in 1692? Weeks? Months? In the case of the trials of the Twenties, aggressive newspaper reporting (and in some cases, radio) put the average person "in the know" in a matter of hours. They could see the concerns of their neighborhood played out in the national arena, and witness the wisdom and folly of judges, lawyers, defendants and victims in something approaching today's "real time." And the mirror that these trials held up to the country displayed an unsettling erosion of cherished beliefs, and a disquieting view of the human heart in all its mystery.

In many ways these trials tell us more about how our present society relates to its 1920s predecessor than any other process of which we have a record. We like to think of the United States as a kind and welcoming nation—Emma Lazarus and the lady in New York harbor—yet the vitriol aimed against the "wrong kind" of immigrants in the 1920s does not differ from the hostility that greets many new arrivals today. At this writing, gambling has become a state-run enterprise in much of the country, yet the threat posed by a sports "fix," not clumsily done but with 21st century finesse, remains ever present. Hollywood has brought our dreams to life, lit up our fantasies and lightened our days—yet what do those entertainment people do in Lotus Land during their off hours? We suspect the worst.

Corruption in all its forms continues to fester in our society, and organized crime, crooked politics and Wall Street monkeyshines continue, often with a wink and a nod, in "business as usual." One tangible area of progress in America since the 1920s has been the eradication of official, institutional racism, with the concomitant exile of groups such as the KKK to the fringe of society. Yet does anyone believe that legislation alone can, or has, eliminated racial prejudice? Not according to the string of what are now called "hate crimes" that continue to be placed before the courts.

The relationship between our sense of justice, or fairness, and the implementation of the death penalty continues to be fiercely debated, as does the issue of criminal psychology. As scientists discover more factors, including genetic or chemical ones, that underlie incorrigibly violent personalities, the new question has become: should we "understand" evil behavior or simply adhere to our centuries-old moral code?

And what are we to do with members of the armed forces who speak their minds? During 1998 military officers were disciplined for making disrespectful remarks about their commander-in-chief, the president. Free speech? Article 88 of the Military Code of Justice prohibits them from disseminating their views.

And yet—to give our nation and legal system credit—lawyers and judges continue to wrestle with unsettling issues, and try to resolve them in the time-honored tradition we have inherited from

English Common Law: all sides get a hearing, a jury of peers decides, and a being whom we have agreed to call a "judge" sets forth a resolution to the issue, no matter how thorny, no matter the implications. We have tried to make "trial by rumor" and flagrant misuse of the legal system a thing of the past.

We can ameliorate some of the sting of today's tawdry trials (and the reporting thereof) by looking back to the 1920s, taking some comfort in the fact that in a free society under the rule of law every point of view can, and usually does, have its advocates. At times, in retrospect, the outcomes of our major trials may seem lamentable, but on the whole we have tried to do the right thing as a nation, and continue to try.

To paraphrase Winston Churchill on the subject of democracy, our legal system is the worst of all possible processes—except for the other choices. And the trials of the Twenties show us people much like ourselves, faced with much the same choices we have today, struggling to make sense of people's intentions and actions, and striving to discover the truth, in so far as it can be known. Just as cruelty, violence and corruption never seem to go out of style, likewise the quest for wisdom and justice tempered by compassion knows no season.

Select Bibliography

Allen, Frederick Lewis. *Only Yesterday*. New York: Harper & Row, 1931.

Asinof, Eliot. *Eight Men Out*. New York. Henry Holt & Co., 1963.

———. *1919: America's Loss of Innocence*. New York: Donald I. Fine, Inc. 1990.

Aymar, Brabant. *Laws and Trials that Created History*. New York: Crown Publications, 1974.

Braeman, John et al eds. *Change and Continuity in Twentieth Century America; The 1920s*. Columbus: The Ohio State University Press, 1968.

Busch, Francis X. *Enemies of the State*. London: Arco Publications, 1957.

———. *Guilty or Not Guilty*. London: Arco Publications, 1957.

———. *Prisoners at the Bar*. London: Arco Publications, 1957.

Coletta, Paolo E. *William Jennings Bryan (Vol. III): Political Puritan, 1915–25*. Lincoln: University of Nebraska Press, 1965.

Coughlan, Robert. "Konklave in Kokomo," in Isabel Leighton, ed. *The Aspirin Age, 1919–41*. New York: Simon and Schuster, 1949.

Davis, Burke. *The Billy Mitchell Affair*. New York: Random House, 1967.

Earle, Edward Mead, ed. *Makers of Modern Strategy*. New York: Atheneum, 1967.

Edmonds, Andy. *Frame-Up*. New York: William Morrow, 1991.

Frankfurter, Felix. *The Case of Sacco-Vanzetti*. New York: Grosset & Dunlap, 1967.

Furniss, Norman. *The Fundamentalist Controversy, 1918–1931*. Hamden, Conn.: Anchor Books, 1963.

diGrazia, Roger K., and Edward Newman. *Banned Films: Movie Censors and the First Amendment.* New York: R.R. Bowker Co., 1982.

Grebstein, Sheldon N., ed. *Monkey Trial.* Boston: Houghton Mifflin, 1960.

Higdon, Hal. *The Crime of the Century: The Leopold-Loeb Case.* New York: G.P. Putnam's Sons,1975.

Jackson, Kenneth. *The Ku Klux Klan in the City, 1915–1930.* New York: Oxford University Press, 1967.

Joughin, Lewis and Morgan, Edmund M. *The Legacy of Sacco and Vanzetti.* New York: Harcourt Brace, 1948.

Kobler, John. *Capone.* New York: G.P. Putnam's Sons, 1971.

Leuchtenburg, William E. *The Perils of Prosperity.* Chicago: University of Chicago Press, 1958.

Luhrs, Victor. *The Great Baseball Conspiracy.* New York: A.S. Barnes, 1965.

Murray, Robert K. *The Harding Era.* Minneapolis: University of Minnesota Press, 1969.

Nash, Roderick. *The Nervous Generation: American Thought 1917–1930.* Chicago: Rand McNally, 1970.

Noggle, Burl. *Teapot Dome: Oil and Politics in the 1920s.* New York: W.W. Norton, 1962.

Parrish, Michael E. *Anxious Decades: American in Prosperity and Depression, 1920–1941.* New York: W.W. Norton, 1992.

Perrett, Geoffrey. *America in the Twenties.* New York: Simon & Schuster, 1982.

Ramsey, Marion Livingston. *Pyramid of Power: The Story of Roosevelt, Insull and the Utility Wars.* Indianapolis: Bobbs-Merrill, 1937.

Russell, Francis. *The Shadow of the Blooming Grove: Warren G. Harding and His Times.* New York: McGraw-Hill, 1968.

Schoenberg, Robert J. *Mr. Capone.* New York: William Morrow, 1992.

Seymor, Harold. *Baseball: The Golden Age.* New York; Oxford University Press, 1971.

Sinclair, Andrew. *Prohibition: The Era of Excess.* Boston: Little Brown and Co., 1962.

Smith, Page. *Redeeming the Time.* New York: McGraw-Hill Book Co., 1987.

Sloat, Warren. *1929: America Before the Crash.* New York: Macmillan Publishing Co., 1979.

Stone, Irving. *Clarence Darrow for the Defense.* New York: Doubleday, 1941.

Tierney, Kevin. *Darrow: A Biography*. New York: Thomas Y. Crowell, 1979.

Wade, Wyn Craig. *The Fiery Cross: The Ku Klux Klan in America*. New York: Simon & Schuster, 1987.

Weeks, Robert P., ed. *Commonwealth vs. Sacco and Vanzetti*. New York: Prentice Hall, 1958.

Yallop, David A. *The Day the Laughter Stopped*. New York: St. Martin's Press, 1976.

Young, William and Kaiser, David E. *Post-Mortem: New Evidence in the Case of Sacco and Vanzetti*. Amherst: University of Massachusetts Press, 1985.

Index